THE ENDS OF PARADISE

THE ENDS OF PARADISE

Race, Extraction, and the Struggle
for Black Life in Honduras

Christopher A. Loperena

STANFORD UNIVERSITY PRESS
Stanford, California

Stanford University Press
Stanford, California

This book has been partially underwritten by the Stanford Authors Fund. We are grateful to the Fund for its support of scholarship by first-time authors. For more information, please see www.sup.org/authors/authorsfund

Printed in the United States of America on acid-free, archival-quality paper

Library of Congress Cataloging-in-Publication Data
Names: Loperena, Christopher, author.
Title: The ends of paradise : race, extraction, and the struggle for Black life in
    Honduras / Christopher Loperena.
Description: Stanford, California : Stanford University Press, [2022] | Includes
    bibliographical references and index.
Identifiers: LCCN 2022012211 (print) | LCCN 2022012212 (ebook) | ISBN
    9781503632950 (cloth) | ISBN 9781503634008 (paperback) | ISBN 9781503634015
    (ebook)
Subjects: LCSH: Garifuna (Caribbean people)—Land tenure—Honduras. |
    Garifuna (Caribbean people)—Honduras—Government relations. | Tourism—
    Government policy—Honduras. | Economic development—Honduras. | Land
    use, Rural—Honduras. | Black people—Honduras—Social conditions.
Classification: LCC F1505.2.C3 L66 2022 (print) | LCC F1505.2.C3 (ebook) | DDC
    305.80097283—dc23/eng/20220316
LC record available at https://lccn.loc.gov/2022012211
LC ebook record available at https://lccn.loc.gov/2022012212

Cover design: Angela Moody
Cover photo: Garifuna community at sunset. Photo by author.
Typeset by Elliott Beard in Minion 10.5/15

To my aunt, Lily Martinez. I am eternally grateful.

CONTENTS

ACKNOWLEDGMENTS

I MANY TIMES DOUBTED my ability to complete this book. But I felt an enormous responsibility to finish—to myself, my family, and most importantly, to the people and communities I worked alongside in Honduras. None of this would have been possible without the brilliant insights of my friends there, particularly Miriam Miranda—the visionary leader of the Black Fraternal Organization of Honduras (OFRANEH, by its Spanish acronym). Thank you for all you have taught me over the years. OFRANEH activists, including Carlos, Odilio, Gregoria, Arsenia, Selvin, Doña Amada, and others have provided me with protection, guidance, and analysis that continues to inform my thinking and writing.

I also want to acknowledge my friends in Triunfo de la Cruz, especially Tavo, Teresa, Chepe, Tomasa, Fanni, Angel, and Panchy. The time I spent living and working in Triunfo changed me. This book, an imperfect work, is a testament to the experiences we shared and to the profoundly transformative impact you had on my life. Thank you for your willingness to share your lives, aspirations, and struggles.

I finished writing this book during a period of tremendous loss and grief. My grandfather departed in May 2019. In one of his last lucid moments, he said to me, "Mijo, confía en tu trabajo." I have held these words close ever since. Just over a year later, my aunt, Lilybette, passed away after succumbing to COVID-19. She was a loving *tía*, a mentor, and a rigorous interlocutor. She believed in me and the importance of this work. Gracias querida Tía por tu luz. And my brother, Johan, who left this world tragically at the age of nineteen. Rest in peace.

My mother, Maritza, is and will continue to be a shining light on my path. Amid so much loss, you still found ways to hold me up. Your spirit and remarkable ability to see beauty, even in the darkest moments, animates much of my scholarly work. My older sister, Tania, has held me accountable, forcing me to face my fears as she has throughout her life. Last, I want to thank my father, Wilfred, and my stepmother, Anne, for their calls, prayers, notes of encouragement, and probing questions about the nature of my work.

My mentors at the University of Texas at Austin have supported this project in profound ways with their thinking and writing. Charles R. Hale, Kamala Visweswaran, João Costa Vargas, and Ted Gordon are not only accomplished scholars but deeply thoughtful and engaged researchers who continue to redefine the boundaries what anthropology can be.

Graduate school is a long journey, and I made many friendships along the way. Here I want to acknowledge a few key people with whom I share intellectual kinship and a commitment to confronting anthropology's colonial past and present—Mariana Mora, Courtney Morris, Barbara Abadía-Rexach, Amanda Irwin, Jennifer Geott, Lynn Selby, Alix Chapman, Naomi Reed, Amy Brown, Teresa Velásquez, Mubbashir Rizvi, Mohan Ambikaipaker, Pablo Gonzalez, and of course Mattie Harper, Ernest Gibson, and Claudia Anguiano, whom I befriended while on fellowship at Dartmouth. I was at Dartmouth when I met Lourdes Gutiérrez Nájera and Jim Igoe—two beautiful souls who, through their kindness and acts of radical vulnerability, have shown me how to be a better scholar.

Over the years, I have extended my network of scholar-activists, mentors, and allies: Shalanda Baker, Duana Fullwiley, Chris Zepeda-Millán, Megan Ybarra, Alejandra Aquino, Paul López Oro, and Christien Tompkins. I am inspired by your creativity and, perhaps most importantly, your unwillingness to settle for academic conventions. Thanks to Sharlene Mollett, Ana Leonor Lamas, Ellen Moodie, Jossianna Arroyo-Martínez, David Lobenstine, Ayelet Even-Nur, Dorothy Kidd, Susana Kaiser, Kathy Coll, Anne Bartlett, Elisabeth Friedman, the entire CELASA crew at the

University of San Francisco, and of course one of my oldest friends and academic interlocutors—Lucia Cantero, for your important contributions to my scholarly development and writing.

A special thank you is in order for Mónica Jiménez and Roger Reeves, who opened their home to me in the middle of the pandemic. Thank you for your boundless love, creative nourishment, and intellectual generosity. I'm so fortunate to have you in my life. Courtney Morris and Martin Perna are part of my chosen family too—genuine comrades in struggle. And my friend Jonathan Rosa who in addition to being my writing partner and a truth teller, is always down for a healthy dose of judgment-free indulgence.

Aaron Correa saw me through the final chapters of this project, providing me with his unbending partnership, love, and space for me to write even when that meant less time for us. He called on me to keep sight of the stakes of the work, not just for my professional commitments but for the people and communities at the center of this book.

My colleagues at the Graduate Center are extraordinary—Jeff Maskovsky, Bianca Williams, Katherine Verdery, Dána-Ain Davis, David Harvey, Gary Wilder, John Collins, Marc Edelman, Don Robotham, Ruth Wilson Gilmore, Kandice Chuh, Setha Low, Yarimar Bonilla, and Julie Skurski—I am truly humbled to be in your company. Marc Edelman, Don Robotham, and Mark Anderson all read and commented on a full draft of this manuscript; their insights and encouragement helped me reach the finish line. My editor at Stanford University Press, Dylan Kyung-lim White, provided careful feedback and enthusiastic support throughout the publication process. His sharp editorial suggestions have made this a better book.

Last, I want to recognize a very special group of people who I met during my college days at the University of Chicago, and with whom I first traveled to Honduras to work in collaboration with the Civic Council of Popular and Indigenous Organizations of Honduras—then under the leadership of Berta Cáceres. Rising Roots International was an audacious project, one rooted in a deep commitment to social change and solidarity. We were young, but our work together laid the foundations for my subsequent research in Honduras. Many thanks to Mateo, Tarik, Della, Crystal, Ricky, and Jill for always being down.

Research and writing support for this project was generously provided by the Inter-American Foundation, the Social Science Research Council, Andrew W. Mellon Foundation, the Caribbean and Central America Research Council, the University of Texas at Austin, the University of San Francisco, Dartmouth College, and the City University of New York (CUNY).

I have presented portions of this work before audiences at the CUNY Graduate Center, the University of California Berkeley Center for Race and Gender, Pennsylvania State University Mellon Sawyer Seminar on Racial Disposability, Stanford University Department of Anthropology, Dartmouth University Department of Anthropology, the University of Barcelona, the University of San Francisco, the University of Costa Rica, Columbia University, and the Centro de Investigaciones y Estudios Superiores en Antropología Social (Oaxaca and Mexico City campuses).

Sections of chapters 1 and 2 were previously published as "Radicalize Multiculturalism? Garifuna Resistance and the Double-Bind of Participation in Post-Coup Honduras," *Journal of Latin American and Caribbean Anthropology*, vol. 21, no. 3 (2016); "Conservation by Racialized Dispossession: The Making of an Eco-Destination on Honduras's North Coast," *Geoforum* 69 (2016); and "Honduras Is Open for Business: Extractivist Tourism as Sustainable Development in the Wake of Disaster?," *Journal of Sustainable Tourism* (2017), https://www.tandfonline.com/doi/full/10.1080/09669582.2016.1231808.

All errors are my own.

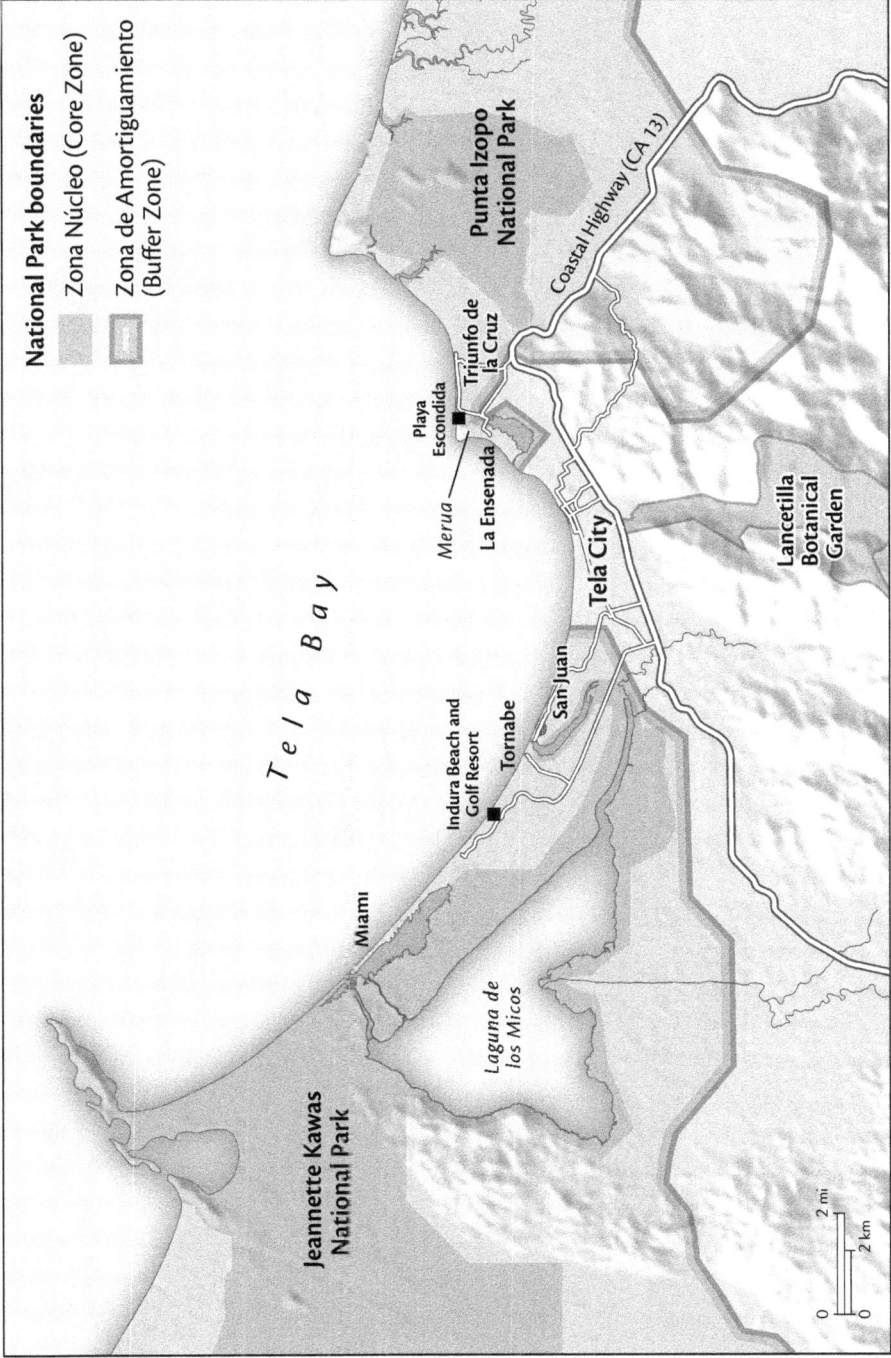

National Park boundaries

Zona Núcleo (Core Zone)

Zona de Amortiguamiento
(Buffer Zone)

Tela Bay

Jeannette Kawas
National Park

Miami

*Laguna de
los Micos*

Indura Beach and
Golf Resort

Tornabe

San Juan

Tela City

La Ensenada

Merua

Playa
Escondida

Triunfo de
la Cruz

Punta Izopo
National Park

Coastal Highway (CA 13)

Lancetilla
Botanical
Garden

0 2 mi
0 2 km

MAP OF TELA BAY

THE ENDS OF PARADISE

IMAGINING BLACK
INDIGENOUS FUTURES

*They want us to be gone. This is not an isolated event but part of a plan
to destroy Indigenous peoples. But we deserve another destiny. Honduras
deserves another destiny.*

MIRIAM MIRANDA, Black Fraternal Organization of Honduras[1]

THIS BOOK BEGAN WHILE WAITING for a bus. It was February 15, 2003,
just before 4 a.m. The air was frigid. The Civic Council of Popular and Indigenous Organizations of Honduras (known as COPINH in Spanish) had
summoned its members to a protest against the Iraq War in the Honduran
capital Tegucigalpa. We began gathering in the street adjacent to the *mer-
cado central* (central market) in La Esperanza, a small city in the country's
lush western highlands. I was struck by the sheer energy of the Indigenous
campesinos who had traveled—some on foot—from dozens of tiny rural
Lenca communities nestled into the mountainous slopes of Intibucá, one
of the poorest regions (or "departments") in Honduras.[2] These were subsistence farmers, standing in the freezing cold, eager to participate in this
act of global antiwar solidarity.[3] Why were they so committed? What did
Indigenous farmers in southwestern Honduras have to do with US foreign
policy in the Middle East?

Eventually, a yellow school bus arrived. The decrepit kind that are an ubiquitous feature of regional transportation throughout Central America. Crowded onto the small vinyl seats, I asked the *compas* (comrades) sitting next to me why they had chosen to participate in the rally. Their matter-of-fact responses made it clear that they had answered this question many times. Their answers were world-weary, as if the question itself were absurd. The Iraq War, US foreign policy, and the global ascent of neoliberal economic policies were inextricably linked; these policies, they explained, have been particularly heavy-handed in Honduras, and a source of extraordinary social and political precarity in their home communities. Lenca campesinos spoke frequently about *yanqui* imperialism and the rapacious expansion of neoliberalism, which in their assessment was by and large a political and economic campaign to destroy Indigenous ways of being. They were adamant that US economic policy in the region, including the proposed Free Trade Agreement of the Americas, was a formidable threat to their livelihoods, not only for its duplicitous pledge to end tariffs on foreign goods and services but also for the introduction of genetically modified seeds and other technologies deemed necessary to increase productivity. This formula for growth, they argued, would endanger the larger notion of a collective commons and ultimately their very survival.[4]

The perilous living conditions of Indigenous and Black Hondurans were inseparable from the expansion of global capitalism, the industrialization of agriculture, and the unsustainable exploitation of the country's abundant land, water, forest, and mineral resources—all in the name of "development." Although I did not know it then, in that predawn bus ride, sitting next to those painfully astute strangers, I had stumbled onto the crux of what I would study for the next fifteen years: how we can imagine a future to save us from an untenable present. This is not what I was expecting to see. And yet the more I immersed myself into this world, the more it was clear that protest movements required more than just protesting; they required a radical imagination. What I saw that day, and again and again in the following years in Honduras, was that the daily struggle to survive, struggles against crushing odds, were made possible by alternative imaginings of the future and hope for "another world" in which Indigenous and Black peoples thrive.[5]

Months later, back in Chicago, I realized that I had to return, but with the tools of ethnography to gather data on the lived experience of broader economic transformations. I was drawn to the Caribbean coast, 250 kilometers to the north, where Garifuna—the descendants of runaway African slaves, Arawak, and Carib Indians—had been fighting for over a decade to defend their ancestral lands from the grips of tourism developers and the rapid expansion of African palm plantations. There, too, future imaginaries were inextricable from nonnormative desires to live freely,[6] and a deep commitment to just development, autonomy, and sustainability. Each of these goals was under immediate threat in the wake of the 2009 coup d'état against then president Manuel Zelaya. The coup, and the forms of privation it authorized, was the catalyst for a bold power grab that has been conceptualized as extractivist in form and purpose. Extractivism, as it plays out in Honduras, is a government-sanctioned effort, nearly always aided by multinational capital, to take whatever resources it can both from a place and its people.

The history of extractivism has long been relatively simple: foreign companies—often multinationals, and typically in the mining or agricultural sectors—set up shop in a poor country, garner enormous profit, and offer very little benefit to the countries in which they operate. As such, extractivism has a clear spatial narrative, in which external forces, mostly from the developed North act upon more vulnerable geographies in the Global South that are dependent on foreign capital and technologies. The exploitation of local resources is always the result. This dichotomy— between the external and the internal, between the foreign invader and the local victim—distracts us from seeing the ways in which national elites are complicit in the expansion of extractive capitalism in their own countries, and also how extractivist agendas are carried out under the guise of development.[7] What we have seen in the past two decades is a more complex version of extractivism, one conjoined with the tenets of development and the advancement of social well-being (Gudynas 2009; Acosta 2013).[8] Yet for peasants and other historically marginalized populations in Honduras, the extractivism of today feels all too familiar—unsettlingly similar to the pain and inequity that were the hallmarks of US-controlled banana enclaves in the early twentieth century. Moreover, enduring patterns of natural resource exploitation are responsible for extraordinary environmental destruction and loss of livelihoods.

The enclave is an apt spatial metaphor to query the *longue durée* of extractivism on the Caribbean coast, which has, in its most recent iteration, pivoted to resort tourism.[9] It is easy to downplay the problems of tourism; indeed, the Honduran government is determined to do just that. It refers to the tourism industry as the *industria sin chimeneas* (industry without smokestacks), a rhetorical ruse intended to position tourism as an environmentally sustainable alternative to heavy industries, such as mining. But it is only by conceptualizing tourism as a form of extractivism that we can truly understand the myriad and seemingly contradictory ways that tourism upends life for the Garifuna and other Indigenous groups, and for Honduras more generally. Enclosure, dispossession, and environmental degradation are intrinsic to the politics of destination making in Honduras, bringing into sharp relief the convergence of varied but fundamentally similar visions of development, via mining, agribusiness, and tourism. Moreover, explicitly linking these economic strategies in the same conceptual framework facilitates a deeper understanding of how Garifuna experience tourism as a form of exploitation analogous to traditional extractive industries (see Loperena 2017a).[10]

Partnerships between the state and private enterprise have supported the most robust projects.[11] This mode of development, fashioned from the neoliberal policy recommendations of the World Bank and the Inter-American Development Bank, is designed to generate investment opportunities for domestic capital just as much as foreign capital. Of course, there is another "domestic" group that is involved—the Garifuna themselves. Both their lands and their culture are key to the success of tourism in Honduras, and yet the benefit of such extractivism for them is far less clear.

This book is largely an effort to grasp the projected futurity to which Garifuna aspire and the ways that political struggles for territorial autonomy respond to and reshape the extractivist mandate of the Honduran state and multinational capital on the Caribbean coast. By demanding to be accounted for on their own terms, as both Black and Indigenous, Garifuna demystify the workings of extractive capitalism and its tendency to differentiate and objectify racialized populations and their territories for the purposes accumulation. I will not limit my discussion to conventionally defined extractive industries, such as mining and energy developments that are prevalent throughout Honduras, including on the Caribbean coast (ERIC 2016), and that have garnered much interest from scholars of the region (Bebbington et al. 2018). Rather, I want to address the extractivist logics of progress, and the mechanisms through which the country's Black and Indigenous peoples are simultaneously rendered as obstacles to, and at times beneficiaries of, national development.[12] I argue that this possibility is promoted by the state and multilateral institutions through development policies that hinge on an autonomous Indigenous subject with the capacity to harness market opportunities for self-improvement and progress.[13]

Black Indigeneity

The Garifuna are fundamentally confusing to everyone but themselves. As we have seen, they identify as a Black Indigenous people, a category that for many academics and government bureaucrats and even fellow Hondurans, doesn't seem to exist; this negation, as I explain later, has deep political and material consequences for Garifuna.

Garifuna trace their ancestry to the year 1635, when two Spanish vessels carrying enslaved Africans shipwrecked off the coast of Yurumei (St. Vincent) in the Lesser Antilles (Suazo 1997). The shipwrecked Africans, likely from many different ethnic groups, took refuge on the island, which was inhabited by the Island Carib. There they intermarried with the Caribs, adopting their language and many of their cultural practices. This fusion, combined with the addition of runaway slaves from nearby islands, led to the formation of a new ethnicity that came to be known as the Garifuna, or as the English referred to them, the Black Caribs.

British and French settlers vied for power and control over the island of St. Vincent until the signing of the Treaty of Paris in 1763, when the French conceded the territory to the English. However, conflicts between the British and the Garifuna continued to escalate; in 1797, the roughly five thousand Garifuna living on St. Vincent were deported to the island of Roatán, off the Caribbean coast of present-day Honduras. According to the anthropologist Nancy González (1988, 48), the permanent settlement of Roatán would have yielded only "desultory subsistence agriculture." Consequently, many Garifuna left for the shores of mainland Honduras, eventually establishing forty-six communities, as well as several additional communities along the Atlantic coast in what is today Guatemala, Belize, and Nicaragua.

In spite of the historical presence of Black peoples, Central America is a geographic space that has until relatively recently remained peripheral to anthropological explorations of Blackness and the Black diaspora.[14] The sparse scholarly attention to issues pertaining to Black peoples in general, and anti-Black racism in particular, is a testament to the popular perception that Central America is place in which peoples of African descent are either nonexistent or merely recent arrivals.[15] The pioneering research of Edmund T. Gordon (1998) and subsequent anthropological studies have helped to fill this gap in the literature, drawing attention to Black political struggles in Central America, as well as exploring the place of Blackness in relation to both the state and the complexities of Indigeneity in the region.[16]

I hope to take the next steps on the path that Gordon and others have begun. Through his granular ethnographic account of Garifuna activism, Anderson (2009, 8) demonstrates why we should understand Blackness and Indigeneity as overlapping as opposed to mutually exclusive categories of identification. Blackness, he contends, can take on symbolic meanings that are akin to those we associate with Indigenous peoples, and which are necessary to access collective rights (Anderson 2007). These insights are important precisely because of how they facilitate a rethinking of the conceptual boundaries that separate Blackness and Indigeneity.

As noted by Tiffany Lethabo King (2019), Black studies has long meditated on the ocean and water as key metaphors for interrogating the Black diaspora experience. In contrast, my research has mostly revolved around land and questions of autonomy, two concepts that are theorized centrally in the Indigenous and Native studies literature. Despite their apparent distance from issues of Blackness, I hope to show that they are essential to making sense of Garifuna political claims in Honduras. This is because Garifuna identify as Black and Indigenous, a union that defies the presumed analytical and political borders that structure academic debates around racial categorization in the Americas.[17] Indeed, when we analyze

Indigeneity and Blackness as separate phenomena, we misunderstand the ways these two historically constituted racial groups are coarticulated.

I refuse the analytic temptation to reduce the complexity of Black Indigeneity to either-or logics (see also López-Oro 2021). I believe that such differentiations, aside from being inaccurate, also are counterproductive to the essential political projects of our era: seeking to undo our fealty toward Western humanism and Eurocentric conceptualizations of Man (Wynter 2003). But instead of framing Garifuna political subjectivity as Indigenous-like,[18] I seek to emphasize the ways Blackness and Indigeneity are mutually constituted as categories of difference in relation to, and exclusive of, whiteness. Thus, I argue for a more expansive conceptualization of Blackness, one in which Black peoples in the Americas can be understood as Indigenous—that is to say, historically, spiritually, and culturally connected to place. This is not to erase the long history of Garifuna seafarers or the networks of migration and trade around which Garifuna figure as a diasporic people (González 1988). Rather, I seek to overturn (or at least complicate) the notion that Black peoples are somehow placeless—or, to use Catherine McKittrick's (2006, 26) term, *ungeographic*. What are the theoretical and political stakes of situating Blackness in relation to place and geography?

The Latin American project of building a nation-state with a homogeneous national community, predicated on racial mixture, or *mestizaje*, was violent, entailing processes of forced assimilation and cultural genocide (Paschel 2016, 5–7), and one in which Blackness and Indigeneity were effectively eliminated or subsumed into the national body politic (Castellanos 2017; Loperena 2017). Therefore, we might understand the process of state formation in Latin America as embedded within settler colonial logics of elimination, similar to those that have been widely theorized in the United States and Australia (Wolfe 1999).

Settler colonialism is a historical and contemporary process contingent on the elimination of Indigenous peoples and their territories. It is also an ideological project that reifies settler grammars of sovereignty and law under the guise of liberal freedoms, and thus it remains, as Speed (2017) suggests, the fundamental underlying structure of the contemporary Latin American state.[19] With this conceptual framework in place, we can better understand how settler law undergirds the emergence of the mestizo nation. This is because *mestizaje* entailed state policies and social practices that, in the name of racial egalitarianism and anti-imperialism (Hooker 2017), reinscribed essentialist notions of Indigenous and Black inferiority. According to Juliet Hooker (2017, 171), "it was the new mestizo race, not whites, that occupied the highest rung" of José Vasconselos's racial schema, but the "existence of racial hierarchy in which blacks and Indians were at the bottom remained constant."

Mestizaje is a racial ideology that, under the façade of racial mixture and cultural hybridity, sought to shed the yoke of European colonialism. It is a practice made visible in policies that encouraged racial miscegenation between European and Native peoples (and sometimes Black peoples) and a uniquely Latin American nationalist ideology. It is thus fundamentally anti-Black and anti-Indigenous because it prioritizes the moral and racial superiority of whiteness as a means of obtaining human progress or improvement. Scholars of Latin America have referred to it as a whitening ideology (Wade 2010), but for my purposes, *mestizaje* is simultaneously a settler colonial logic that seeks to dilute Indigenous peoples within the mestizo (read: white) category while erasing Blackness from the spatial and temporal boundaries of the nation.

Black Indigeneity, in contrast, powerfully reformulates the moral underpinnings and racial hierarchy of *mestizaje*. This is because it is not oriented toward the moral superiority of whiteness or a pseudowhite mixed population; rather, in the intentional elision of whiteness, Black Indigenous being creates a paradigm to interrogate Blackness and Indigeneity on the same conceptual plane—and, in the process, disrupts our foundational assumptions about the presumed racial distinction between the two.[20]

Black Indigeneity is also fundamentally problematic for the state, evidenced by the repeated attempts of Honduran state officials to define Garifuna as strictly Afro-descendant in order to differentiate them from the category of Indigenous and to deny them land rights that Indigenous people are entitled to under international law. Although Garifuna arrived in Honduras prior to Central American independence from Spain, Garifuna claims to land, especially lands in and around the highly coveted Tela Bay, are deemed illegitimate. On account of their Blackness, as we will see, Garifuna are excised from the category Indigenous and thus deemed unrightful heirs to national territory. It is for this reason that many of the Garifuna activists I worked with refused to be identified as Afro-Honduran (but did not refuse to be identified as Black); by rejecting the label *Afro*, they sought to tether Blackness to Indigeneity and thus situate it firmly within the territorial boundaries of the nation (see chapter 5).

In pursuing state recognition of their territorial rights, Garifuna not only find it necessary to prove that they are from Honduras, but also, more importantly, they must situate their claims not just geographically but also temporally. As Rosa (2019, 14) argues, "Place of birth is of little relevance when one's racially overdetermined body, primordially anchored in an imagined foreign elsewhere, demands to be accounted for." Extending this line of thinking, it is important to account for the ways in which historically constituted communities of color are relegated to an illusory *otherwhere*, outside the space and time of the present. In Honduras, questions of when and where you are from are applied almost exclusively to Black and Indigenous peoples, who must continuously legitimate their presence on the land, even though their historical settlement predate the creation of the modern nation-state.[21]

The Setting

Triunfo de la Cruz is a Garifuna community on the northern coast of Honduras. It sits along a bay of exquisite natural beauty, framed by lush tropical forests and lined with coconut palms, pine trees, and colorful dugout fishing canoes. An uninterrupted stretch of pristine sandy beach connects the eastern end of the community to its westernmost tip, where a densely forested cliff, known locally as Merua, descends dramatically into the sea. On calm days, the water laps at the sand gently, revealing a trail of glistening gemlike stones—green, red, yellow, purple, and black—each time it recedes. This bay, approximately thirty-eight kilometers wide, is called Tela Bay, and it is one of the most desirable stretches of land in the whole country (see p. xiii).

Triunfo—as it is commonly referred to—straddles the buffer zone of the Punto Izopo National Park, a designated protected area that was once a community preserve and that has since the 1970s been used to market Tela

Bay as an ecotourism destination.[22] Together with the Lancetilla Botanical Garden, the Jeannette Kawas National Park, and the Cuero y Salado Wildlife Reserve, Tela promises visitors a rich assortment of nature and wildlife experiences.

This idyllic and carefully produced landscape has garnered significant attention from developers who are eager to exploit Tela's touristic potential, which has fueled violent land grabs within neighboring Garifuna communities (fig. I.1). Indeed, Triunfo is already home to two residential resorts on each end of the community. The elaborate vacation homes in Marbella and Playa Escondida are owned by some of Honduras's most powerful families and stand in stark contrast to the modest one-story homes owned by Garifuna.

A surge in tourism development in and around Triunfo has impelled entrepreneurship among local Garifuna residents, many of whom have been lured by the promise of formal employment opportunities. Development initiatives backed by a constellation of state, private investors, and multilateral institutions, such as the World Bank, have encouraged local participation in the tourism economy through the branding of the coast as a distinct ecological and cultural destination. The politics of destination making has increased the visibility of Garifuna music, food, and dance globally. At the same time, Garifuna territorial rights have been violently constricted as they face increasing pressure to forfeit communally held lands to incoming developers.

As a result of tourism speculation, all five Garifuna communities in Tela Bay—Río Tinto, Miami, Tornabé, La Ensenada, and Triunfo de la Cruz—are ensnared in conflicts over land. The most ambitious development is the Indura Beach and Golf Resort, opened in 2014. The project includes a luxury boutique hotel, an eighteen-hole golf course, and private residences on lands claimed by neighboring Garifuna communities. This resort is projected to pave the path for tourism developments along the country's 700-kilometer-long Caribbean coastline. Anticipation for the promised benefits of tourism has deepened existing communal divisions in Triunfo, where during my fieldwork, two parallel governing factions vied for power over the community's fate. One group, commonly referred to as the *empresarios* (businessmen), worked alongside municipal authori-

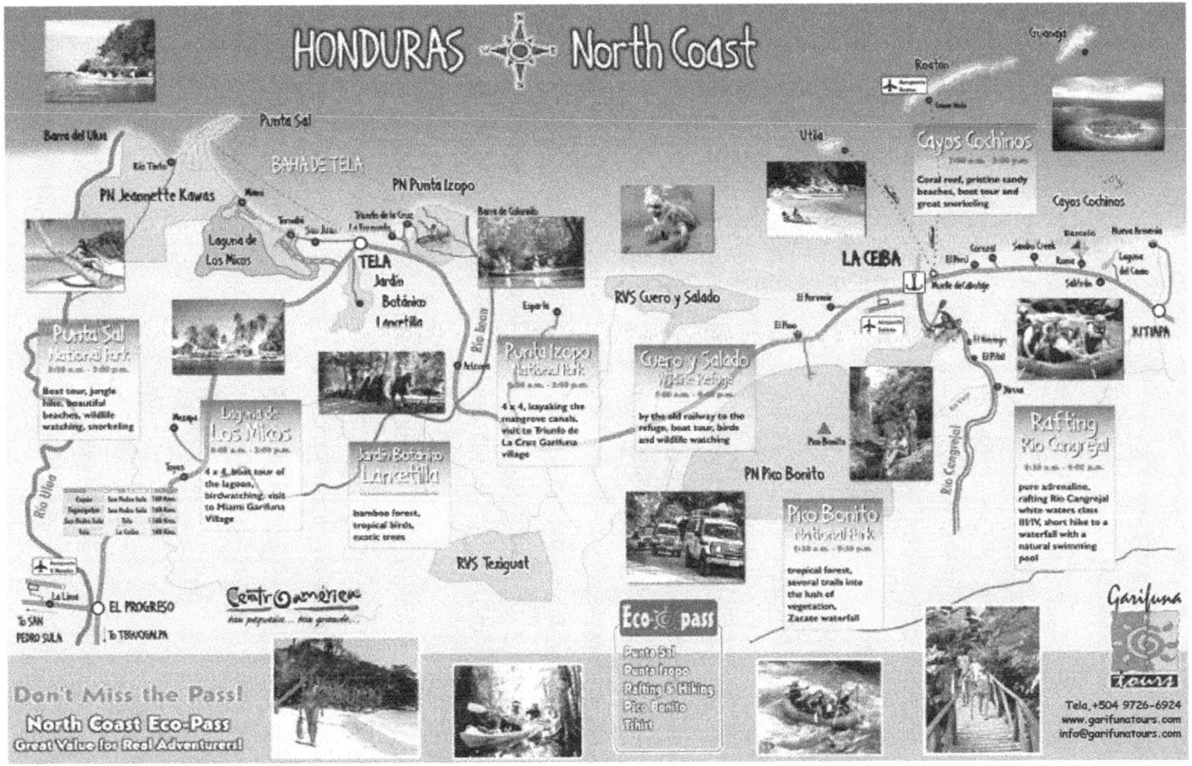

FIGURE I-1: Tela Bay Tourism Map, created by Garifuna Tours.

ties in Tela to advance the state's development agenda in Triunfo. The other group, the self-proclaimed *defensores de la tierra* (land defenders), sought to protect the community's autonomy and collective land rights from further incursions by outsiders.

Tourism in Honduras is a territorial project that is crucially bound up with processes of state modernization (Mollet 2014) and nationalist desires for progress. It is contingent on settler colonial expansion into rural communities of color, the alienation of land, and racialized modes of extraction. As I explain in this book, extractivism entails spatial, geographic, and racial boundary making; it is through the differentiation of these categories that allows for profound forms of value to be created.[23]

Racialized Extraction

To understand how value is created, we need to go back to Marx. A thing, he explains, can have utility prior to and independent of human intervention. Its use-value to others is created through exchange (Marx [1867] 1990, 131). Thus, while use-value is inherent in certain natural resources such as water that are necessary to sustain life, value undergoes alchemic distortions through the exploitation of labor (Harvey 2018) and nature for capitalist accumulation (Coronil 2000).[24] These distortions have long served as fodder for the ethnographic imagination, as anthropologists have endeavored to theorize the transition from precapitalist forms of social organization to one dominated by capitalist modes of commodity exchange. Taussig ([1980] 2010, 25) asserts that modern capitalism "engenders a marketing mentality in which people tend to be seen as commodities and commodities tend to be seen as animated entities that can dominate persons." This of course has generated significant opposition from peasant groups and other peoples that have figured in the anthropological imagination as "traditional."

Today, the Garifuna people are at a similar crossroads. Garifuna culture, in combination with spectacular Caribbean beaches, has elevated Honduras's status as an international tourism destination. However, a surge in land conflicts indicates that the state's vision for future economic prosperity is far less idyllic than sandy shorelines and intriguing culture— precisely because of the ways in which land and culture are being transformed into extractable commodities. These conflicts have exacerbated racial tensions between Garifuna communities and the mestizo elite, who harness the legal and military power of the state to manifest a vision of economic and social progress that is predicated on Black and Indigenous dispossession.[25]

For land defenders, resistance to the state is not just a strategy to demand rights but also an effort to diagnose the role of government institutions, legislation, and state security forces in generating the conditions necessary for resource dispossession to flourish. The tourism agenda, in particular, is tethered to racialized development imaginaries in which Black territories figure as frontiers of progress for the mestizo majority. I frame the legal and spatial politics of dispossession as assertions of anti-Blackness.

In *Black Marxism*, Cedric Robinson (2000, 26) explains, "The tendency of European civilization through capitalism was not to homogenize but to differentiate—to exaggerate regional, subcultural, and dialectical differences into 'racial' ones." Racialism, as defined by Robinson, is a regime of social organization that makes the (ultimately small) differences among people seem fixed and natural, and then organizes those differences into hierarchies of value. Differential human value (and devaluation) is thus a crucial component of capitalist modes of production, consumption, and accumulation (Melamed 2015, 77). This book builds on those insights by highlighting how racialization—the process by which historically constituted communities of color are rendered simultaneously disposable and desirable—facilitates modes of material and nonmaterial extraction within the tourism economy. How, I ask, is wealth generated vis-à-vis regimes that graft value onto differently raced bodies and geographies?

What I term *racialized extraction* is a conceptual framework that is attentive to both value creation and to the mechanisms by which culture and the body are naturalized as part of the landscape and then extracted to fuel the accumulation of wealth for the mestizo elite. What constitutes land, a person, or a commodity is a dynamic racializing process that folds Black and Indigenous peoples and their territories into capitalism's overarching, and perpetual, profit-making aims.

Extractivism, thus, is a particularly tangled web of capitalist exploitation that emerges from and continues to be tethered to histories of racial conquest and colonial plunder.[26] The Black body is prized not just for what it can do—grow cotton, mine for diamonds, serve tapas at a ritzy resort—but also for what it represents: an intriguing and authentic and sellable experience. The cultural alterity of Black peoples, their image, and the very fungibility of their bodies are thus crucial for the production of surplus value, particularly within the Caribbean tourism industry (Alexander 2005; Williams 2013).[27] These are not new patterns, but legacies of colonial spatial grammars that, according to Katherine Yusoff (2018, 70), are tied to the social reproduction of whiteness: "What is apparent is that the slave and the mineral are recognized as regimes of value, but only so much as they await extraction (where Whiteness is the arbiter and owner of value)."

Through a critical engagement with the social relations of extraction, I query the conceptual groundings of property, rights, and autonomy. The meaning of these terms seems self-evident. And yet what seem like commonsense meanings are in fact far more complex, and problematic, than we want to believe. To establish the rightfulness of claims to property, for example, one must enter into an epistemic and ontological relationship with the law, one that reinforces the law's power to render an individual or community as a subject deserving of rights—or not (Povinelli 2002; Simpson 2014; Loperena 2020). Moreover, the law is continuously deployed to criminalize, to dispossess, and to buttress the sovereign interests of mestizo property owners over the collective claims of Black and Indigenous peoples.[28]

Black Autonomy

In October 2015, the Inter-American Court of Human Rights (IACHR) issued a judgment against Honduras for the violation of Garifuna territorial rights in Triunfo. The IACHR condemned state development policies on the Caribbean coast that led to the dispossession of Garifuna lands and recurring conflicts between investors and community land rights defenders. Although Triunfo's court victory was widely anticipated, the legal decision provides no clear solutions about how to safeguard the abundant land, water, and forest resources concentrated within Indigenous and Black territories. Contests over these resources have increased dramatically since the 2009 coup against Manuel Zelaya, resulting in the murders and disappearances of several high-profile Indigenous and Black land defenders, including COPINH founder and Goldman Environmental Prize recipient Berta Cáceres, who was brutally murdered in March 2016. According to the international human rights organization Global Witness, in 2019, Honduras had the world's highest rate of murders per capita of land and environmental activists.[29] The dramatic increase in violence and targeted criminalization of land defenders has fueled a nearly permanent state of crisis within affected communities.

Living through crisis, what Cross (2010) has referred to as the "everyday precariousness" of life, generates a different political sensibility, a different epistemology of the future that challenges the very spatial and temporal assumptions upon which capitalist notions of progress are predicated. In Honduras, Garifuna land defenders situate their struggles over territorial resources as struggles over the future. *Rescate territorial*, or territorial rescue, is synonymous with rescuing the future. Land rescue missions are not an attempt to achieve future prosperity through forms of predatory propriety, as in those sanctioned by the Honduran government. Rather, a different notion of futurity is at play, one that is not tied to hegemonic temporalities of progress, as represented by profitable infrastructures and normative understandings of a good life yet to come.

Through the assertion of autonomy, Garifuna land defenders aspire for a world that posits collectivist living and the commons as ethical alternatives to the individualizing logics of the market, in which living well is not tethered to value making for others but by valuing norms and ways of being that disrupt this profit-making ethos.[30] For the land defenders, this was essentially embodied by practices of living *with* as opposed to living off the land. In this way, the struggle to defend communally held lands was at once a refusal (Simpson 2014) of the extractivist logics of multinational capital and a sociospatial strategy to imagine a collective future in the face of a life-annihilating economic system premised on resource extraction. Honduran social movement activists have begun to refer to this system, steeped in over five hundred years of anti-Black and anti-Indigenous racism, as the *sistema de la muerte* (death system). The value of the land lies in its ability to sustain communal life and to provide for a collective future in which Garifuna continue to exist as a people. It also stands in opposition to the mechanisms by which Black peoples are alienated from their lands; by claiming collective rights to their territory, Garifuna seek to safeguard the future possibility of a commons that can sustain human and more-than-human life on this planet (Estes 2019).

Resistance to extractivism, therefore, is a form of ethical practice (Dave 2012) that both contests and reconfigures these hegemonic development imaginaries. The future imagined by coastal Garifuna communities is an ethical future, rooted in notions of racial equality, community, autonomy for Black and Indigenous Hondurans, as well as ecological well-being. Tourism is the backdrop for the political processes and territorial struggles I analyze and that constitute the core story. I am equally concerned with the ethico-political dimensions of Garifuna notions of collective belonging and narratives of placeness, and how those narratives get deployed in the struggle to defend territorial resources, which have historically been held in common.

A focus on autonomy, then, is generative for its ability to frustrate ordinary notions of freedom premised on sovereign rights and liberal equalities, forcing us to think about other values that may not align with these liberal conventions.[31] For instance, the work of mothering, or caring for children and for the community, aligns with gender ideologies that are deeply critiqued among feminists and perhaps even contrary to liberal notions of gender equality, and yet the praxis of Black mothering in Triunfo is fundamental to struggles for collective autonomy within Garifuna communities. This book brings debates on emancipatory ethics and space together to frame an analysis of Garifuna land defense strategies in which everyday practices of autonomy are crucially bound up with the community and collective forms of living.

Methodological Musings

Is anthropology an extractivist endeavor? This is the question I faced more than fifteen years ago, when I first talked with a group of activists working at the Black Fraternal Organization of Honduras (OFRANEH, by its Spanish acronym) in the coastal city of La Ceiba. My colleagues at OFRANEH asked me to account not only for the aims and methods of anthropological research; they also insisted I explain how my approach would differ from those of other anthropologists. For the previous several years, they had endured a stream of academics who had come to study Garifuna culture, society, and politics, and then left without producing tangible returns to the communities, from published research to direct collaboration on organizational initiatives.

César, a brilliant but cantankerous member of the team, spoke to me of anthropology's imbrications with the military-industrial complex, implying that I, too, as a researcher from the United States, was entangled in those webs of power. His questions were sharp and relentless: about my funders, my institutional ties, the very foundations of my training. At first I thought he was being overly dramatic. Then I realized that his questions were devastatingly accurate. I mumbled a few responses, quickly grasped their inadequacy, and finally admitted that I could not offer sufficient answers. Since then I have tried, in my academic and political work, to think deeply about anthropology's historical complicity with colonial and imperial projects of domination.[32] I have tried to bring these critiques into my research design.[33] I hope that my work will convince César and others that not all anthropologists are what he called *antropófagos*—knowledge cannibals in disguise as researchers.[34]

My commitment to politically engaged research methods has been deepened in dialogue with people like César, who have reminded me—again and again—that methodological debates were not merely of interest to anthropologists, but of fundamental importance to people in "the field."[35] The individuals who are the foundation of this book have given me huge amounts of their time and knowledge. And I hope that I, too, have given them something in return.

This book is the result of over two years of continuous ethnographic research, from 2008 to 2010, in Triunfo de la Cruz. In the five years after, between 2010 and 2015, I conducted several shorter research trips to Honduras, totaling approximately six months. During this seven-year period, my work in Honduras included the collection of data and ongoing political collaborations with the communities my work engages.

My work with OFRANEH began during an earlier period of field research. In 2005, I served as the lead ethnographer for a multicommunal study on Garifuna land use practices and conflicts in the departments of

Iriona and Gracias a Dios. The final publication, published by the Caribbean and Central America Research Council, wove together collaboratively produced research that OFRANEH then used to advocate for state recognition of Garifuna territorial rights before national courts and the Inter-American Commission on Human Rights. In 2014, OFRANEH invited me to serve as an expert witness for the Inter-American Court in the *Case of the Garifuna Community Punta Piedra and Its Members v. Honduras*. This work provided an opportunity for me to respond to calls to decolonize anthropology (Harrison 1991; Smith 2012; Allen and Jobson 2016; Mora 2017), not just through the use of collaborative methodologies but also by producing a concrete *devolución* (a return) premised on my field research (Loperena 2016b).[36]

Serving as an expert also enabled me to see how ethnographic insights can and do coarticulate with the exacting legal logics used to determine the rights-worthiness of Indigenous and Black peoples (Loperena 2020). It pushed me to reflect more deeply on the labor of witnessing itself and how that work can operate in ways that may in fact be contrary to the emancipatory projects with which I have sought to align myself and that have informed my identity within the discipline of anthropology.

Deborah Thomas (2019, 2) points out that some forms of witnessing, for example, eyewitnessing, are "limited in and through their relationships to the categories through which they are mobilized, such as human rights and reconciliation." This form of witnessing stands in contrast to what she terms "witnessing 2.0," a mode of anthropological engagement that produces the ability "to be response-able, to ourselves and others" (Thomas 2019, 3). I follow in this tradition, seeking to bear witness to the violence of racial capitalism but also to critically reflect on my own complicity in these systems, and of course my responsibility to work toward their undoing.

A crucial component of this endeavor to rethink the practice of anthropology in the wake of liberalism is to "care more than we can know, to extend our analyses past the ruins of the world (and the discipline) as we know it" (Shange 2019, 10). This implies a refusal to acquiesce to positivist research norms and at times explicit political alignments in the pursuit of shared political goals (Hale 2006; Speed 2006; Loperena 2016b; Kirsch 2018). It also necessitates practices of ethnographic humility and at times subterfuge. By this, I refer to the practices of using our institutional networks, recognized expertise, and the tools of ethnography to advance projects that shake the foundations of the institutions and structures from which we derive our professional legitimacy. This mode of intellectual engagement requires that we recognize the expertise of those with whom we work and their status as coproducers of the knowledge over which we claim authority and for which we garner recognition as experts.[37]

Chapter Overview

The Ends of Paradise is divided into two parts. Part 1 analyzes the extractivist logics of progress on a national scale; part 2 immerses us into the Garifuna communities to demonstrate how those logics affect daily life and are in turn contested by a people who seek to defend their autonomy. From this clash of progress and daily life we can glimpse the fight for a collective future.

Chapter 1 establishes a historical genealogy of extractivism in Honduras. From the creation of banana enclaves in the early national period to the contemporary bid to establish semiautonomous charter cities in purportedly unpopulated areas of the country, the state has tried to enact various visions of progress—but all these visions are intimately tethered to extractivism and in particular to racial extractivism.

Chapter 2 analyzes how the tourism economy in particular facilitates racialized extraction. The advent of multicultural rights unfolded alongside state programs designed to transform Garifuna into subjects of development. But the inclusion of Black and Indigenous communities seems inseparable from the commodification of those communities; the government's policies all seem to render Garifuna lands and culture as tourism products. These policies are presented as a win-win for everyone, equally beneficial to Garifuna and working class non-Indigenous Hondurans who remain stymied by poverty and the legacy of "underdevelopment." The only clear winner is neither of these groups, but rather the mestizo elite. Garifuna resistance to these policies, as we'll see, exposes the inner workings of supposedly inclusionary politics and how those efforts ultimately advance not inclusion but rather racial and spatial expulsion.

Part 2 explores the results of these larger processes, which manifested most consequentially in conflicts over land and belonging in Triunfo de la Cruz. In chapter 3, I examine how statist development objectives seep into the everyday lives of Triunfeños. Neoliberal economic paradigms emerged in the 1990s in tandem with morally saturated development discourses that tout poverty reduction, inclusion, and sustainability, and that imagine Garifuna as stakeholders with the capacity to benefit from and contribute productively to Honduras's burgeoning tourism economy. Policies that promote participation in the tourism economy are entangled with local contests over land and belonging. Conflicts over the fate of the community figure prominently in daily life, as community members—for and against government-sponsored development—reckon with the dispossession that seems inevitably to come with development and debate how to negotiate with and when to protest against these vast forces. Garifuna land defense strategies are articulated through the practice of Black autonomy: an ethico-political proposal that refuses dominant narratives of progress and that instead asserts a notion of autonomy as collective action and social good.

Chapter 4 theorizes the spatial and temporal dimensions of Garifuna political subjectivity through an analysis of the movement to recuperate or "rescue" communal lands from privatization. I examine how Garifuna women lead the *lucha* (the struggle) in defense of their territory with their bodies, and how that defense is bound up with gendered narratives of ancestrality and the praxis of territorial mothering. To live ancestrally is a way of being in relation with the land, which is crucial to Garifuna autonomy and a key feature of the struggle to contest the destination-making strategies of multinational capital on the Caribbean coast.

Chapter 5 examines how court testimony, as a form of storytelling about the collective self, bridges legal and affective discourses in the making of Garifuna autonomy. In April 2014, the case of the *Garifuna Community of Triunfo de la Cruz and Its Members v. Honduras* advanced to the IACHR, located in San José, Costa Rica. During the court proceedings, Honduras's deputy attorney general argued that Garifuna should not be considered an "original people" (indigenous to Honduras) and thus could not make legitimate claims to national territory. State officials not only undermined the possibility of Black Indigeneity but also, I contend, exalted the rights of officially recognized Indigenous peoples to defend, circuitously, mestizo property rights in the zone. This politics of (mis)recognition tethers Indigenous subjectivity to the mestizo nation-building project and ideologies of whitening. It also reinforces the popular perception that Black people are foreigners in Honduras. The court's judgment in favor of the community established an important legal precedent for the recognition of Black territorial rights but also served to buttress state sovereignty over natural resources deemed to be of "public use."

The conclusion to this book begins with the violent murder of the Indigenous activist Berta Cáceres. At the time of her death, she was leading a daring community uprising against the development of a large hydroelectric project that was slated to be built on the Gualcarque River in the Lenca community of Río Blanco. Her death marked the beginning of a new wave of repression against Indigenous and Black activists that reached its apex on July 18, 2020, with the kidnapping of four community leaders in Triunfo. This worrisome pattern—what Juliet Hooker in the 2020 volume *Black and Indigenous Resistance in the Americas* refers to as "racial retrenchment"—demonstrates a deep seated racial animus against Black and Indigenous peoples and the rights they fought so hard to obtain during the preceding decades.

Throughout these pages, my aim is to immerse us into this world to show how extractivism affects individual lives in this one small corner of the world, and in turn to reflect on what that means for the rest of us.

PART ONE

1 THE EXTRACTIVIST LOGICS
OF PROGRESS

ON JUNE 28, 2009, just before dawn, dozens of Honduran soldiers descended on the residence of President Manuel Zelaya Rosales in Tegucigalpa. They moved swiftly and with brute force, breaking into Zelaya's bedroom, detaining him, and then escorting him to the Soto Cano Air Base, where the US military has maintained a semipermanent presence since 1983.[1] There, he was forced onto a military jet bound for Costa Rica. News of his ouster spread quickly, as Zelaya—still in his pajamas—told airport officials in San José that he had been the victim of a military-backed coup d'état.

The Congress, controlled by National and Liberal party deputies, acted quickly. First, it declared that Zelaya's forced removal was constitutionally mandated; then, in a special session held that same day, it named Nationalist party official Roberto Micheletti as the country's interim president. These actions, while extraordinary, were preceded by a period of sharpening political tensions between Zelaya and his political adversaries, who viewed him and his left-leaning policies as a direct threat to their control over the country's economy and abundant natural resources. For decades, Honduras's infamous oligarchy had unfettered access to the country's land, water, and mineral resources, and used them for astonishing personal economic gain, resulting in one of the most unequal societies in the Western

Hemisphere.[2] Zelaya, who assumed office in January 2006, represented a formidable threat given his budding alliance with president Hugo Chávez of Venezuela and his increasingly public denunciations of neoliberal economic policy prescriptions.

In the weeks and months following the coup, legislators scrambled to secure a series of reforms that were designed, first, to roll back the seemingly progressive policies instated by Zelaya and, second, to open the country to massive foreign investment. The new government sought investors across every sector of the Honduran economy, but particularly in mining, energy, agribusiness, and tourism. In other words, postcoup Honduras is a case study in extractivism: not only in how that concept is utilized to describe the renewed valorization of raw materials and untapped natural resources (Svampa 2015) but also in how it is made central to the functioning of government.

Extractivism, long a mode of economic production in Honduras, resurfaced as an explicit logic for growth in the postcoup conjuncture. Aided by the suspension of democratic norms, investors and government officials flouted the legal protections folded into previous iterations of neoliberal development policies, such as Indigenous rights to consultation, environmental protections, and so on, to generate quick and rapacious profit. This state of siege produced particularly dire consequences for the country's forty-six Garifuna communities on the Atlantic coast. I will detail how tourism has become a leading sector of the national economy, which Garifuna understand and experience as an extractivist enterprise. Tourism entails enclosure via the privatization of communally held lands, the environmentally destructive commodification of nature, and the promise of modern infrastructures; it is therefore resonant with the spatial practices that undergirded elite aspirations for advancement in the early national period.

In this chapter, I provide a historical genealogy of extractivism, charting Honduras's transformation from a banana republic to an ecotourism destination and a haven for neoliberal economic experimentation.[3] Through examining and recounting the history of the enclave and subsequent efforts to promote a private property market, I hope to demonstrate how these seemingly disparate development proposals fit together under a larger extractivist mandate that, in the name of progress, has furthered the racist and disproportionate concentration of wealth into the hands of the political and economic elite. Over the course of the twentieth century, Garifuna lands and customary land use practices emerged as problems for the state's economic agenda, not only because of their increasing import to national development goals but also because Garifuna collective land-holdings were rendered as obstacles to progress. I then analyze Garifuna activism in the anticoup resistance movement that arose in response to Zelaya's ousting. How, I ask, do struggles for land and territorial autonomy on the coast articulate with the national movement in defense of popular sovereignty? In the final section, I turn to Honduras's proposal to establish semisovereign "charter cities" in purportedly unpopulated areas of the country, which I understand as the most recent instantiation of the extractivist logics shaping the postcoup development agenda.

The Enclave

Honduras was the site of intensive experiments in extractivism throughout the nineteenth and twentieth centuries, first in mining and logging, and then in commercial agriculture. In 1821, Spain's provinces in the region—Honduras, Nicaragua, El Salvador, Costa Rica, and Guatemala—all gained their independence, and in 1823 formed the Central American Federation.[4] This early attempt at regional governance gave way to the formation of sovereign nation-states in 1838. The ensuing political-economic systems controlled by the *criollo* and mestizo elite, though fiercely anticlerical, furthered the extractivist mandate of colonial authorities (Barahona 1991; Perez-Brignoli 2000), for whom the land was that from which things should be extracted and sold.[5]

Echoing political and economic practices in neighboring countries, Honduran independence from Spain was followed by concerted efforts to spur national development through liberal reforms. During this period, ideas of progress were tied to land privatization and specifically to the creation of agro-export economies (Díaz 2007, 60). To stimulate the growth of the agricultural sector, namely coffee and bananas, the governments of Guatemala and El Salvador pivoted from national landholdings and collective land tenure systems to the expansion of private property; in so doing, they increased the pool of landless peasants who could then labor on the farms of the landowning elite (Edelman and León 2013). In southern Mexico, laws created to spur agrarian development opened lands surrounding Indigenous communities, defined as "excess lands," or *terrenos baldíos* (empty lands), for privatization and development (Stephen 2002, 219–224). Liberal reforms unfolded alongside the secularization of life and politics within the Mexican polity and the correspondent acculturation of Indigenous peoples into the nationalist agenda (Saldaña-Portillo 2016, 122).

Similar reforms were pursued by Honduran legislators but ultimately fell short due to a notable absence of infrastructure for the transportation of goods across its mountainous terrain and a shortage of exploitable labor (León 2015). Sequential waves of liberal reforms, beginning in 1876 under Marco Aurelio Soto and his secretary-general Ramón Rosas, failed to produce the anticipated economic boom. Legislation to expand agricultural production, for instance, had the paradoxical effect of strengthening national and communal landholdings in Honduras (Sieder 1995, 104).

The newly consolidated nation also had to contend with the purported "Indian problem"—the presence of Indigenous (and by extension, Black) peoples who, according to the government, represented a potential barrier to progress (Díaz 2007). To realize its vision of progress, Honduras would turn to foreign laborers, mostly of European stock, to spur an immigrant-led agricultural frontier in areas that were deemed to be lacking in development.[6] Racial attitudes about the moral deficiencies of the country's Black and Indigenous population, including their alleged indolence, undergirded pro-European and North American immigration policies, tethering ideas of progress to race and to the whitening of its population (Barahona 1998; Mollett 2010) and echoing official policies of *blanqueamiento* (whitening) in other parts of Latin America (Wade 2010; Helg 2004). But the projected economic gains again failed to materialize.

In the absence of a viable agricultural sector, Honduras became increasingly reliant on foreign capital, primarily from North America, which deepened the dependency of national politicians on foreign investors and set the stage for the emergence of enclave economies (Meza 2010).[7] The *bananeras*, as they were known locally, attracted migrant laborers from throughout the British West Indies, neighboring Central American countries, and from a cross section of Honduran society, including mestizo peasants and day laborers from nearby Garifuna villages.

Following their arrival in Honduras, more than a century earlier, in 1797, Garifuna had established dozens of small communities along the Caribbean coast, from the Bahía de Omoa near the border with Belize (British Honduras) to the community of Plaplaya in the Moskitia.[8] Garifuna laid collective claim to vast expanses of arable lands, including portions of the present-day Cuero y Salado Reserve in the Department of Atlántida, which comprises thousands of hectares of wetlands and an extensive natural canal system. In the late nineteenth century, the fertile lands of Cuero y Salado emerged as an important site for banana production, which eventually garnered the attention of fruit companies in the United States eager to gain a foothold in the growing banana trade.

The Italian American Vaccaro brothers and their associate Salvador D'Antoni, founders of the Standard Fruit Company, arrived in La Ceiba in 1899. Their aim was not just to buy land to grow more bananas; they also had a much more ambitious plan to control transportation routes for the export of bananas and other goods to North American markets. With over seventy kilometers of natural canals, the acquisition of Cuero y Salado was deemed necessary for their expansion plans. The Honduran historian Antonio Canelas Díaz (2001, 163) documents how Salvatore D'Antoni convinced the Garifuna to cede control of the canals to the Vaccaro Brothers Company and then proceeded to implement an arbitrary transportation tax on all boats.

Eager to legalize their hold over the banana trade, the Vaccaro brothers entered into negotiations with President Manuel Bonilla, who in 1903 issued a twenty-five-year concession to the company to create canals at the river mouths at Salado and Porvenir (Canelas Díaz 2001, 180). Decree No. 20 (May 23, 1903) ensured the company's monopoly of the growing banana export business in and around the city of La Ceiba. The following year, the National Congress approved a second concession to the Vaccaro Brothers Company, which extended its rights over large tracts of nationally owned lands for the construction of a railroad and effectively sidelined Garifuna dominion over Cuero y Salado. This act of racialized expropriation demonstrated the government's disregard for the historical presence of Garifuna in Honduras, as well as the willingness of national legislators in Tegucigalpa to act as clients of the *bananeras* for personal gain.

Patron-client relations between US fruit company executives and Honduran state officials persisted throughout the first decades of the twentieth century. In return for money, arms, and transportation infrastructure, the government lavished US companies with legal concessions to national lands (as well as generous tax exemptions). In addition, the concessionaires received rights to timber, water, and mineral resources (Soluri 2005, 43).[9] The multinational fruit companies' monopoly of the banana trade was contingent on both the systematic extraction of natural resources to sustain enclave economies along the North Coast and the exploitation of labor.

The arrival of the Cuyamel Fruit Company—predecessor to the United Fruit Company—and the Standard Fruit Company in the early 1900s firmly entrenched US corporate power in Honduras, giving rise to a distinctly xenophobic nationalist fervor, which targeted not only the profit-making schemes of US investors but also the West Indian laborers of African descent brought to work on the banana plantations (Chambers 2010). Black laborers, including Garifuna, were deemed a threat to the Indo-Hispanic nation (Euraque 1998, 2003).[10] Ultimately, labor union activism within the *zonas bananeras*, in particular the general strike of 1954, spawned a powerful alliance between banana workers and peasant groups (Soluri 2005), whose demands for land redistribution led the administration of Ramón Villeda Morales to pass the Agrarian Reform Law of 1962 (Posas 2019, 263–64).[11]

The new law intended to incorporate the rural peasantry, primarily landless mestizos, into the Honduran political system through the substitution of the large and smallholder land system with a "fair system of ownership, tenure and exploitation of land" (Article 1). Under the guise of creating a more just property system, the government sought to quell growing social unrest among peasants and, at the same time, safeguard the political system from the perceived communist threat (Thorpe 1992). Article 9 stipulated: "The existence and maintenance of idle uncultivated land is contrary to the principles of the social function of property and incompatible with national well-being as well as the economic development of the country."[12] The social function of property was, from this perspective, to advance the economy through the productive use of the land. Idle lands, including those claimed by US owned banana companies (and eventually the country's Indigenous and Black populations), were potential targets for expropriation and redistribution among landless peasants.

The new legislation threatened to upset the economic stranglehold of US fruit companies over Honduras, which the mestizo elite feared would lead to wider acts of expropriation, similar to those that were spearheaded under the presidency of Jacobo Árbenz in Guatemala.[13] In 1963, a US-backed coup deposed Villeda Morales, bringing the land reform project to a dramatic halt. However, conflicts between the landless peasant movement and landowning elites remained a problem for subsequent administrations, requiring successive iterations of land reform legislation.

Land to Property

Experiments in extractivism during the early national period tethered state modernization schemes to the unbridled exploitation of land and labor on the banana plantation, fueling campesino demands for land redistribution. However, the utopian aims of organized peasant movements were rooted in the same logics of resource possession and exploitation and were therefore in tension with the territorial claims of Garifuna who interpreted these attempts to render land into property as a concerted strategy of expulsion. The right to appropriate land was increasingly tied to nationalist visions of progress and race.[14]

Katherine Verdery (2003: 4) defines private property as a symbol, "a schema only loosely related to how it actually works, even in market economies themselves." She argues that property making does not unfold naturally but is the result of historical and political processes. I follow Verdery's lead here in attempting to trace the transformation of national and communal landholdings into property in Honduras, which emerged as a key criterion for state modernization goals in the final decades of the twentieth century. Beginning with the Agrarian Reform Law of 1974 and culminating with the highly controversial 2004 Property Law, state authorities sought to replace collective land tenure with individual property rights. This push for privatization, backed with funding and technical support from multilateral development institutions, slowly penetrated every corner of the country, including Indigenous and Black territories.

The National Agrarian Reform Plan, drafted in 1972, again placed a significant emphasis on the incorporation of landless peasants into the productive process.[15] This time, however, the government sought to stimulate the agricultural sector via the redistribution of national and *ejido* lands to peasant cooperatives.[16] Each cooperative was in turn granted rights of "possession, ownership, and exploitation" to the lands its members labored, which could not be sold or rented. In an apparent victory for peasant movements, the program established a new precedent for state-backed collective land tenure regimes. From 1973 to 1977, over 120,000 hectares of land were redistributed to peasant farmers (FoodFirst Information and Action Network 2000).[17]

While the Agrarian Reform Law of 1974 focused on the conferral of land rights to peasant cooperatives, the Small Farmer Titling Project (PTT, by its Spanish acronym), a pilot titling program backed by the Suazo Córdova administration, placed a heavy emphasis on the titling of individual land parcels (Jansen and Roquas 1998). Launched in 1982, the titling program was partially funded by the United States Agency for International Development and signaled the state's commitment to further maximize agricultural productivity by giving full property title—*dominio pleno*—to individual peasant families (Nelson 2003, 13). This turn in national land tenure policies marked the beginning stage of an aggressive push for individual property rights (Nelson 2003) that would ultimately threaten the collective landholdings of Indigenous and Black Hondurans and lay the groundwork for extractivist developments along the North Coast, this time under the aegis of national elites.

While Garifuna lands are collectively owned and managed, community residents lay claim to individual plots of land where they build their homes and agricultural plots for the cultivation of staple foods. In accordance with customary practice, Garifuna can sell their individual plots to other Garifuna, but the sale of land to non-Garifuna is strictly prohibited. These norms have been weakened considerably by state-led agrarian reform and the concomitant expansion of the mestizo colonization frontier.

In 1992, the government of Rafael Callejas ratified the Law for the Modernization and Development of the Agricultural Sector (LMDSA, by its Spanish acronym), solidifying the privatization of publicly held lands and the retreat of the reformist state. The sociologist William Robinson (2003, 131) provides a succinct description of the law: "Drafted by USAID and the World Bank, the law eliminated all state intervention in agriculture (including any further state expropriations), strengthened property guarantees, called for the acceleration of land titling and the conversion of all titled land into marketable property (including the 'right' to use property as collateral against loans), the conversion of cooperative lands into individual tradable shareholdings, stipulated the privatization of state support infrastructure, such as grain storage facilities, and the privatization of the National Agriculture Development Bank (BANDESA), and promoted new foreign and domestic investment in export agriculture." Under the new law, the key to economic prosperity was the production of cash crops for export (e.g., bananas, coffee, palm oil), which was to be achieved through the consolidation of a property market. Accordingly, the country's 2,800 agricultural cooperatives were granted the right to individually parcel and sell their collectively owned lands (Jeffrey 2002, 40). The Lower Aguán River Valley along the North Coast in the departments of Yoro and Colón became the principal site for the implementation of these reforms, resulting in a massive transfer of land from peasant cooperatives to the landowning elite. Between 1990 and 1994, more than 70 percent of the land distributed to peasant cooperatives during the agrarian reform was sold, although peasant families often sold under conditions of duress (Edelman and León 2013, 1710).

Commensurate with the state's embrace of neoliberal economic doctrine, the agrarian counterreform buttressed the economic interests of large landowners, including Miguel Facussé, who presided over a rapidly expanding agricultural empire on the North Coast, closely linked to his manufacturing businesses that spanned food, home, and personal care products.[18] His chief investment was African palm, a tree with long thick fronds that could be farmed for oil palm. Officials in Tegucigalpa aided Facussé, not only via legislation such as the LMDSA but also through investments in transportation infrastructure, hoping to position Honduras as a regional leader in the production of biofuels, a potentially lucrative export-oriented industry (León 2015; Solís 2018). By 2011, over 130,000 hectares of land were dedicated to oil palm cultivation (Gomez 2012), positioning Honduras as one of the top exporters in Latin America.[19]

Peasants from the Lower Aguán, newly dispossessed, were invited to move eastward to the Sico-Paulaya Valley, and from there they eventually began to settle lands within nearby Indigenous and Black communities (Mollett 2006). The lands they settled were ostensibly unoccupied and underutilized and thus apt for expropriation, in accordance with the LDM-SA's provision on "idle" lands (Article 51). Garifuna immediately sounded the alarm, arguing that mestizo settlers were infringing on their territorial rights by failing to recognize or respect their customary land use practices. Historically, Garifuna communities practiced a system of shifting agricultural production known as *barbecho*. This mode of production entails the collective clearing and cultivation of lands within a designated area for two to five years, followed by five to fifteen years of no activity. This practice of letting lands lay fallow after a relatively short period of cultivation was intended to ensure the fertility of the land for future use, but this was often misinterpreted as "idle" by incoming settlers.

Doroteo, a Garifuna land activist from the community of Punta Piedra in Colón, summed up the conflict as follows: "The *ladinos* [mestizos] use arms to take our lands. They are robbing us of our patrimony and threaten the community with guns. More importantly, they have another way of using the land. They kill the land, leave it sterile. They say we are lazy, but they don't understand our culture" (interview, June 26, 2005). He went on to explain how the arrival of settlers from other parts of the country had impelled shifts in customary land use practices among Garifuna, such as shifting agricultural production. In short, lands that were occupied in low-impact ways, or only seasonably, were perceived to be *terrenos baldíos* (empty land), placing greater pressure on Garifuna to adopt more permanent farming techniques readily recognizable to outsiders as productive use. "The Garifuna are destroying their own territory to save it," he lamented.

The modernization of the agricultural sector was indispensable to long-term development goals, but it also echoed earlier logics of Indigenous dispossession: across the Americas, starting in the colonial period and into the first decades post-independence, waves of settlers sought to render native land claims null on the basis of their presumed inability to use the land productively. This practice has carried forth into the present as illustrated by the juridical bases for appropriation (Mollett 2011; Loperena 2020). Lands that were idle or remained uncultivated for more than eighteen consecutive months were deemed to be out of synch with the "social function" of property and thus subject to expropriation (Article 51, LMDSA).

The impulse for newly landless peasants to grab "unused" land is perhaps not surprising, and yet the effectiveness of this land grab is surprising.[20] The strain of agrarian reform policies from decades earlier had not died with the overthrow of Ramón Villeda Morales in 1963, even though they had been overshadowed by the rush to privatize. Indeed, there were laws created to prevent just this sort of thing from happening. In 1994, Honduras signed onto International Labour Organization Convention No. 169 on Indigenous and Tribal Peoples, which was designed to protect Indigenous collective landholdings and rights to use the resources within their territories in accordance with customary practices. But instead of producing greater land tenure security for the communities, government authorities proceeded with plans to further the expansion of the private property market.

The PATH to Progress

Increasingly, Garifuna lands became potential targets for expropriation. This was the result of a two-pronged economic strategy. One, state authorities sought to establish a dynamic land market and real property registry. Two, the strengthening of property rights and land titling within Indigenous and Black territories would be used to further land transactions deemed fundamental to the expansion of key industrial sectors of the economy, namely agribusiness, mining, and tourism, primarily located in rural areas. This strategy posed immediate threats to Garifuna coastal communities, whose lands remained largely untitled.

After approving the Agricultural Modernization Law, the government conferred full property titles to all forty-six coastal Garifuna communities, but these collective titles only encompassed a small portion of their ancestral land claims.[21] Under the guise of securing Garifuna property rights, government officials in Tegucigalpa staked out a new strategy, one that would satisfy Garifuna demands for the *ampliación* (extension) of existing titles while also safeguarding the rights of mestizo settlers within their territories and still providing a path to privatization.

The World Bank played a formative role in this process by way of its structural adjustment lending program and, more immediately, its market-led agrarian reform program. Firmly anchored in the neoliberal economic thinking of the era, the World Bank sought to strengthen property rights to ensure economic transactions (Trubek and Santos 2006). Material and economic progress was contingent on using the latent potential of land to generate wealth, achievable through the transfer of ownership from one individual to another or through the use of property as collateral for loans. But this possibility, according to the "law and development" school of thought favored by the World Bank, was not viable without the formalization of property rights. The leading Peruvian economist Hernando de Soto (2000, 47), who became an amplifier for World Bank policies, concluded at the start of the twenty-first century that property law "is the place where capital is born." For de Soto, the formalization of property rights via titling would not only lead to a reduction in terrorist activities, as he argued in *The Other Path* (2002), but, and perhaps more importantly, the ensuing boom in capital could be used to reduce poverty. The push to formalize property rights thus was positioned as an inherently moral argument, a means by which to cast off economic stagnancy and to generate a more prosperous and peaceful society.

What de Soto ignores is, of course, of equal significance, even though it may be harder to quantify. Informal property arrangements and collective land tenure regimes, which as we know are common in Indigenous and Black territories, have long provided a foundation for collectivist politics and ways of living. Thus, while the formalization of property rights via individual land titles may in fact facilitate access to capital, it also threatens entire ways of being by creating the necessary conditions for the alienation of land once the individual title is obtained. As Lund (2011, 886) argues, proponents of land reforms "tend to focus on the elements of granting

rights and securing people's possessions, not on the elements of dispossession embedded within them."

The World Bank's Land Administration Project of Honduras (PATH,
by its Spanish acronym) was approved on February 17, 2004, on grounds
that Honduras would pursue "long-term and far-reaching legal, institutional, and technological reform to formalize property rights for the vast
majority of Hondurans, facilitate access to land by the poor, reduce trans-
action costs, and encourage the emergence of dynamic land based asset
markets" (World Bank, Project Information Document No. AB457, 2003).
PATH was proposed as a measure that would benefit not only the Honduran state by establishing a viable land market to attract foreign investments
(and in turn increase government revenues from property taxes) but also
poor Hondurans, by reducing the prevalence of informal land rights arrangements, and through the titling of squatters' landholdings. According
to World Bank officials: "Only about 30 percent of the estimated 2.6 million land parcels in [Honduras] are registered in the property registry. A
recent study estimated the total value of these extralegal assets amounts
to US$12 billion. Failure to use even a fraction of these assets to mobilize
credit is a key source of stagnation and inequality" (World Bank, Project Information Document No. AB457, 2003). "Poverty reduction" quickly
emerged as a guiding ethos and moral justification for land-titling programs, including collective titling within Black and Indigenous territories.
However, as Anderson (2009, 155) notes, "Overall, the state has sought to
delimit small areas of highly valued land on the North Coast to a communal land regime and secure the surrounding areas for capital investment and protected areas while at the same time upholding the legitimacy
of 'third-party' property titles." The industrial development of the North
Coast, which took off in the 1990s in tandem with the expansion of export-
processing zones, tourism, and oil palm production, was looming in the
background of these seemingly progressive land-titling programs.

In preparation for PATH's implementation, World Bank officials completed a "social assessment" within the Garifuna communities.[22] The authors of the report highlighted two factors as causes for Garifuna land
tenure insecurity: the inadequacy of the national land registry system and
conflicting viewpoints among the Garifuna regarding individual versus

collective land tenure.²³ The social assessment acknowledged the problem of illegal land sales within these communities but attributed the growth of an informal land market to ongoing political discord between representative organizations and individuals within the communities, largely ignoring the detrimental impacts of state-backed agrarian development policies and legislation.²⁴

The PATH was pitched as a project that would not only further land tenure formalization within Indigenous and Black territories but also create a property rights regime wherein individuals would have the right to "choose" their own path. In effect, PATH was intended to further the moral imperatives of the market and the triumph of liberal freedoms in the pursuit of material progress. So why did so many Garifuna oppose the project?

The Garifuna organization OFRANEH (the Black Fraternal Organization of Honduras) alleged that the program, buoyed by the 2004 Property Law, would result in the dissolution of Garifuna collective landholdings, akin to what had happened to agricultural cooperatives following the Law for the Modernization of the Agricultural Sector. While Chapter III of the Property Law acknowledges the inalienability of Indigenous communal property, which cannot be transferred from its present ownership, its Article 100 states: "The same communities can put an end to these communal regimes." This provision would give individual communities the right to choose whether they would like to continue with communal land tenure or relegate it to the past.

In January 2006 OFRANEH submitted a "Request for Inspection" to the World Bank, citing flaws and violations in the consultation procedures mandated by the World Bank's Operational Directive 4.20 on Indigenous People, among other concerns about the design and implementation of the bank-funded PATH project. In an interview with Olegario López, director of community participation and Indigenous affairs for the PATH, he expressed frustration with OFRANEH and defended the PATH's efforts to engage the communities in a just consultation process:

When the project started, the PATH coordinators wanted to collaborate with OFRANEH and ODECO [Organization for Ethnic Community

Development],[25] so that they could be the counterparts or the interlocutors for the project in the zone, but they never came to an agreement. So the project decided to coordinate a Mesa Regional Garifuna, which was a structure composed by *patronatos, clubes de danza*, churches—all of the local organizations. (interview, Olegario López, February 3, 2010).

López, a Garifuna land activist turned World Bank employee, claimed that the Mesa Regional Garifuna would allow for participation among a broad spectrum of stakeholders. OFRANEH activists disagreed, alleging the consultation protocol was designed to circumvent their authority and opposition to the project and that it had the potential to legitimate the rights of mestizo settlers.[26] In 2007, the Inspection Panel, in its Report No. 39933-HN, offered its tacit agreement; it concluded that the World Bank was in violation of its own policy provisions on consultation with Indigenous peoples, leading the bank to suspend PATH implementation within the Garifuna communities. While OFRANEH celebrated the World Bank's decision, López noted that coastal Garifuna communities would now be excluded from the "benefits of participation."[27]

The PATH was framed in terms of solving land tenure "insecurity" within Indigenous and Black territories and as a means to reduce the high incidence of poverty, but the legislative framework—the 2004 Property Law—also had the potential to further exactly what was causing the initial problem: the parcelization and alienation of collective landholdings within Black and Indigenous territories.[28] Ybarra (2018) suggests that the divide between individual and collective property rights marks important ontological distinctions between Indigenous peoples and *ladinos*. In this sense, the grafting of individual property rights onto collectively held lands constitutes an act of epistemic violence against Indigenous communities that functions as a tool of dispossession (Ybarra 2018, 16).

At this critical juncture one can begin to distinguish the tensions that have manifested as a result of claims and counterclaims grounded in the same conceptual framework—the protection of Indigenous land rights. The cumulative effects of these measures have contributed to shifts in how Garifuna on the coast think about territory and land ownership, spurring deep internal divisions between those who are committed to defending the communities' collective landholdings and those who would be willing to adopt an individual property rights regime. These tensions, which I analyze at length in chapters 3 and 4, have grown in tandem with the rise of tourism as a development strategy.

Development as Ruse for Extractivism

A few years before the dalliance with the World Bank, before PATH became an ever-discussed acronym, Honduras was transformed virtually overnight. On October 29, 1998, Hurricane Mitch swept through the North Coast. The catastrophic storm resulted in billions of dollars of infrastructural damage and was responsible for the deaths of over twelve thousand people in Honduras alone. It had devastating effects throughout Central America, but particularly grave ones in Honduras: "An estimated 70% of Honduras's physical infrastructure was seriously damaged including 169 major bridges, all major highways, and most secondary roads" (Stonich 2008, 4).

The destruction wrought by Mitch created the ideal conditions for the unhindered expansion of neoliberal capital in Honduras (Klein 2005) and opened the door to vigorous investments in tourism (Stonich 2008). This cornerstone of neoliberal development was necessitated by the urgency of economic recovery in the wake of widespread destruction and legitimated the sudden implementation of extraordinary juridical measures, such as the proposed reform of Article 107 of the National Constitution, which had since 1982 prohibited the sale of lands within forty kilometers of the coastline to foreigners.[29] Additionally, Article 5 of the Tourism Incentive Law (1999) granted new tourism establishments a nonextendible fifteen-year income tax exemption and onetime exemption from taxes and any other duties on imports of new goods and equipment required for project construction and start-up operations.[30]

Paradoxically, these reforms were advanced in a climate of increased governmental concern about the environment, and about the ecological damage caused by the storm, but also made possible by a long history of lax environmental protections in the country.[31] A few months after Mitch, the government released the *Master Plan for National Reconstruction and Transformation* (PMRTN, by its Spanish acronym), which laid out a clear vision for development, based on an explicit acknowledgment that the unsustainable use of natural resources had made Honduras more vulnerable to natural disasters: "The existence of such factors as outmoded technological and scientific management of natural resources, the prevalence of an extraction mentality and the limited application of the *General Environmental Law*, along with the deficient institutional development of environmental management and its low priority among decision makers, has favored the accelerated deterioration of natural resources and the environment, thus increasing the country's vulnerability to its natural environments" (PMRTN 1999, 98). The vision outlined in the PMRTN included the following environmental objectives:

(1) Protect the environment in order to develop, conserve, and utilize it for the benefit of present and future generations;

(2) Develop the country's ecotourism potential and conserve national biological patrimony;

(3) Make effective the participation of different civil society sectors in the making of decisions. (PMRTN 1999, 99)

Hurricane Mitch set the country on an innovative path to economic recovery, one that would purportedly include greater participation from civil society and local governments, as well as increased sensitivity for the preservation and conservation of the environment to mitigate the potential risks posed by natural disasters. Ecotourism emerged as a key development strategy within this framework, which, according to the PMRTN, represented an alternative to the "extraction mentality." This was complimented by a series of environmental protection ordinances, as well as increased collaboration between the public sector and private environmental nongovernmental organizations (NGOs) to achieve environmental conservation goals alongside a robust tourism agenda (Brondo 2013; Loperena 2016).[32] The seemingly sincere efforts to develop ecotourism post-Mitch were happening at exactly the same time that the World Bank was backing policies designed to further its extractivist development mandate in Honduras.

Following Mitch, tourism, the so-called *industria sin chimeneas* (industry without smokestacks), became the third-largest source of foreign exchange earnings, after *maquilas* (offshore manufacturing) and remittances. From 1998 to 2001 the sector grew about 18 percent, demonstrating the effectiveness of new legislation designed to incentivize tourism investments (Canales 2009). Significantly, tourism's rise did not correlate to a decline in traditional extractive activities; rather, these grew in tandem, as corresponding modes of development in the post-Mitch recovery period. This was illustrated by the Mining Law of 1999, approved by the National Congress a few months after Mitch, which provided foreign mining corporations with increased access to the country's bountiful land, water, and mineral resources, in particular precious metals.

The 1999 Mining Law, like the tourism legislation outlined earlier, was extremely unpopular with social movement activists, who accused the government of corruption, of selling the national territory to foreigners, and ultimately of undermining Honduran sovereignty. Post-Mitch recovery efforts demonstrated the state's willingness to exploit the disaster to advance the decades-old aim of increasing exports as a way to facilitate quick and rapacious profit seeking. Indeed, the National Congress passed the reform of Article 107 of the Constitution, permitting the sale of coastal lands to foreigners, just two days after Hurricane Mitch devastated Honduras.

Social movement activists, opposed to the reform of Article 107, convened a protest in Tegucigalpa on October 12, 1999. The Front for the Defense of National Sovereignty, which police forces violently repressed, led to the deaths of two protesters, injuring several others. Following this manifestation of state violence, the National Congress agreed to shelve the planned reform (Anderson 2000, 131–33).[33] Popular opposition to the reform of Article 107 points to a tension between the aims of development and sovereignty, as well as individual and collective will, which has surfaced repeatedly throughout Honduran history, spiking tensions over access to and possession of land, water, and forests. The sale of coastal lands to foreigners would most certainly yield advancements in tourism, but those investments would be tethered to Garifuna dispossession and would be unlikely to yield significant benefits for poorer sectors of Honduran society, either in the form of dignified employment opportunities or through the expansion of needed infrastructure. Popular sentiment was increasingly critical of the government for its misuse of national resources and its utter failure the meet the basic needs of its citizens.

In 2006, just a few years later, Manuel Zelaya assumed the presidency; he was a standard Liberal Party politician, but he slowly shifted to the left, embracing populist policies that produced small gains for the country's poor.[34] In Executive Decree PCM-09-2006, he raised the minimum wage from $150 to $230 per month and, in a surprising reversal of previous policy, he instated a mining moratorium on all new concessions of natural resources to foreign and national corporations. The mining moratorium followed on the heels of several high-profile negotiations between Zelaya and activists affiliated with the Alianza Cívica Democrática.[35]

Zelaya's policy shifts signaled his willingness to entertain the demands of social movement activists, including those of Black and Indigenous organizations, further bolstering his standing among the left.[36] In August 2008, Zelaya made what was perhaps his boldest move and brought Honduras into Hugo Chávez's Bolivarian Alliance for the Peoples of Our America (ALBA), a trade bloc of South American countries that was championed as an alternative to the US-backed Free Trade Agreement of the Americas. Zelaya's actions not only threatened the country's political and economic elite; it was also a significant blow to the long-standing geopolitical alliance between Honduras and the United States, thereby undermining the influence and power of US foreign policy in the region.[37] He was led out of the presidential palace in his pajamas ten months later. Zelaya's ouster sparked a massive wave of social protest that brought together a cross section of Honduran society into a unified movement to restore democratic order, dubbed *la resistencia*. Garifuna were among the first to join the protests.

At the time of Zelaya's ousting, Garifuna activists aligned with OF-RANEH were embroiled in a bitter struggle over lands targeted for tourism development by state officials and private investors. Conflicts over the control and ownership of lands claimed by coastal Garifuna communities were exacerbated by the interventionist policies of government authorities in places like Tela, where the municipal land registry had legitimated the sale and transfer of property rights within Garifuna territories. Although these conflicts predated Zelaya's removal from power, many land defenders believed the subsequent suspension of democratic norms would undermine their ability to defend the legality of their collective property claims.

Additionally, many of my friends who chose to participate in *la re-sistencia* viewed this historical conjuncture as an opening not only to clamor for the rights of Garifuna but also to ensure that their political aspirations would not be left out of the institutions and juridical norms that they hoped would emerge from this process. Participants, Garifuna and non-Garifuna alike, believed that constitutional reforms—which had been backed by Zelaya and ultimately contributed to his overthrow—were necessary to alleviate some of the systemic exclusions that have plagued Honduras's fragile democracy and to provide new avenues for the redistribution of economic and political power.

During a passionate speech on November 27, 2009, at a regional meeting of the National Front of Popular Resistance (known as the *frente*) in Gracias, Lempira, the Indigenous activist Berta Cáceres, declared, "We only have one option . . . to *refundar* [refound] this country to one that is more just, more human and more equal, with a constitution of and for the people." Her discourse highlighted the importance of popular self-determination and the reconfiguration of politics "from below" vis-à-vis "a Popular Democratic, Plenipotentiary, Inclusive and Original National Constituent Assembly." This call to *refundar* Honduras created an opportunity for Black and Indigenous peoples to articulate their demands for rights in solidarity with other groups that had been victimized by the state, including landless peasants, the LGBTI community, feminists, and labor union organizers. All were in support of a new constitution because it would create new avenues for political participation and for the exercise of popular sovereignty. Paradoxically, the *frente* endorsed this position by abstaining from participating in the 2010 elections.

In figure 1.1, the elections and the new constitution are presented as mutually exclusive channels for participation. To participate in the elections amounted to accepting a political system that was co-opted by the National and Liberal parties and that foreclosed the more radical political aspirations of *la resistencia*. In contrast, *refundación* is depicted as something to be obtained through popular participation in the drafting of a new constitution; what was desired was a truly democratic process wherein the people of Honduras could have voice and vote. This was a potentially

FIGURE 1.1: Political cartoon from the *Manifiesto Espacio Refundacional*, National Front of Popular Resistance (FNRP, by its Spanish acronym).

¿Cuál es el objetivo del FNRP?

REFUNDACION   ?   ELECCIONES

NUEVA CONSTITUCION

HDH

Que no nos confundan

Source: FNRP.

transformative agenda, which placed social movements supporting the anticoup resistance in a direct head-on confrontation with Honduran legislators and the country's powerful oligarchy.

Immediately following the coup, Honduras was suspended from the Organization of American States. OFRANEH's leadership feared Honduras's suspension would jeopardize their cases before the Inter-American Commission on Human Rights, in which the Garifuna communities of Triunfo de la Cruz and Punta Piedra had accused the state of violating Garifuna collective property rights. Triunfo first submitted its petition to the Commission in October 2003. It would be nearly a decade before the hearing at the Inter-American Court of Human Rights, but readmission into the organization was imperative.

Reflecting on the local significance of the coup, Carla, president of Triunfo's communal governing council, argued on July 7, 2009:

We have to support this struggle [*la resistencia*], or Triunfo and the Garifuna communities will lose. There are no rights now. We have signed

many agreements with the government and we need these to be resolved,
which is why we must support. We have to support in order to *reclamar
después* [make demands later].

The indeterminacy facing community land claims gave force to Carla's
statements, as many worried privately that investors would feel emboldened by the suspension of democratic norms, potentially giving way to
further land grabs within the community.

Leticia, a single mother in her thirties and a native Triunfeña, con-
curred. She clearly identified the *golpistas* (coup-mongers) as the primary
actors behind efforts to dispossess Garifuna of their lands:

The powerful groups, the elite—as they say—don't support [the constitutional assembly], because they consider themselves to be the owners
of this country. They are the ones that have large companies, profitable
businesses, and they consider themselves the owners of our Garifuna
communities.

Through their involvement in this movement, Garifuna activists—
historically excluded from national politics—became visible as active
agents of transformation, and, in turn, they worked to combat rampant
anti-Black and anti-Indigenous racism.[38] Garifuna activists brilliantly
linked the fight for popular sovereignty and against extractivism with the
fight for autonomy on the coast. In this way, Garifuna articulated their
political desires with the desires of other dispossessed social groups, even
those with whom they had quarreled in the past, to confront the supremacy of the political and economic elite.

Ultimately, the *frente* failed in its efforts to delegitimize the elections
called for by the de facto regime of Roberto Micheletti. In January 2010,
following a contested election and amid wide popular opposition, Porfirio
Lobo took office as president of Honduras. His mandate, first and fore-
most, was to revive the country's ailing economy.[39]

Extractivism after the Coup

Lobo was eager to demonstrate that Honduras was not only an attractive place for investment but also a safe place for investment. He did this by approving probusiness legislation aimed at increasing Honduras's industrial productivity and competitiveness.[40] In May 2011, he championed his economic mandate at an international conference, which was beseechingly called Honduras Is Open for Business.

Organized by the Ministry of Foreign Affairs, Honduras Is Open for Business provided a stage for the postcoup regime and its allies in the business community to showcase the immense opportunities awaiting international investors. The event drew over 1,300 attendees, including the former Colombian president Álvaro Uribe, the Mexican telecommunications magnate Carlos Slim, president of the Arab Bank Nasri Victor Malhame, and the US secretary of commerce Francisco J. Sánchez, who sought to deepen trade relations between Honduras and the United States.[41]

During the conference, tourism was one of six investment areas promoted by the Lobo administration.[42] *Oportunidades de Inversión en Turismo* (Tourism Investment Guide), a slick brochure handed out by the Honduran government during the conference, stated, "According to the World Tourism Organization (UNWTO), during 2000–2008, the arrival of tourists to Central America has shown a positive trend, standing out as the fastest growing sub region in the Americas." And, in 2009, Honduras captured 11 percent of total tourist arrivals to the region. Honduras's ability to sustain positive growth and to continue developing into a global travel destination was nearly guaranteed, according to the authors of the report, and further investment in the tourism industry would be a profitable way to help Honduras emerge from the economic downturn ignited by "the crisis."[43] Following the event, Lobo pushed ahead with reforms in multiple sectors, including mining, but perhaps the most striking feature of Lobo's postcoup development agenda was his promotion of charter cities (Plan de Gobierno 2010–2014, 62).

The charter city initiative was based on the ideas of Nobel Prize–winning economist Paul Romer, who proposed the creation of semiautonomous "start-up" cities, without the weight of government bureaucracies and with the potential to generate enormous social and economic opportunities for locals and foreigners alike.[44] In a TEDGlobal talk from 2009, Romer emphasized two pillars of the charter city proposal: the necessity of creating rules that preserve choices for peoples and firms, and the availability of "uninhabited lands" for the creation of new cities.[45] Lobo embraced Romer's vision and began campaigning to create the legislative infrastructure needed to bring that vision into reality. He did this first through the creation of the Special Development Regions (RED, by their Spanish acronym), through Decree 283-2010.

Charter cities were intended to have their own public administration system as well as a judicial presence for representation at the national level. Lobo's legislation was approved by the National Congress and signed into law in 2012. Months later, the Supreme Court declared the legislation unconstitutional. The judges argued "the foreign investment expected to be received by the state of Honduras implies transferring national territory, which is expressly prohibited in the constitution."[46] This judicial rationale was startingly simple: charter cities could function, the judges recognized, only via massive amounts of money from foreign companies, and such extreme transfers of wealth would mean that, in all practicality—even if not explicitly stated—these companies "owned" the charter cities. The Lobo administration responded by ousting four of the five Supreme Court judges and then reintroduced a slightly different version of the legislation, Special Employment and Economic Development Zones (ZEDE, by its Spanish acronym), via Decree 120-2013. A report by the Center for International Environmental Law explains: "While free trade zones exist elsewhere in Latin America, the ZEDE law envisions a more radical model, one that gives broad powers to a small group of unelected offcials who run the zones with little public oversight or mechanisms for accountability" (Alford-Jones 2017, 1).

Although the ZEDE proposal is not explicitly tied to tourism, it lays bare the extractivist aims of the Honduran government. By dividing the nation's territory into zones of concentrated economic production, with special legislative and financial protections, the state paves the way for extractive activities to flourish. OFRANEH contends these special development zones will encompass more than twenty of the forty-six Garifuna communities in Honduras (OFRANEH communiqué, June 24, 2016).

According to the government, charter cities were to be established in purportedly unpopulated areas of the country, but the prospective sites for the ZEDE proposal indicate otherwise. As in the past, economic progress is being made possible through the selective elision of Indigenous and Black presence. This is plainly visible in the first planned charter city to receive approval, Próspera, which has begun construction on the north shore of Roatán, one of Honduras's coveted Bay Islands. Próspera will be built in multiple phases and is projected to include a fifty-eight-acre village featuring "sustainably sourced" eco-residences by Zaha Hadid Architects (fig. 1.2). The project represents an imagined future that would not only situate Honduras among the leading economies in Latin America but also establish a precedent for similar ventures in other areas of the country and the world, at least that is what Lobo and his successor Juan Orlando Hernández touted to would-be investors. This initiative has already attracted investment commitments from high-profile venture capitalists, including Pronomos Capital, which is backed by tech billionaire and PayPal founder Peter Thiel.

The ultramodern city points toward a potentially dazzling future, but

FIGURE 1.2: Concept drawings for residential component, Zaha Hadid Architecture.

one that is contingent on the substitution of economic libertarianism in place of democratic norms and on a government that prioritizes the rights and autonomy of capital over those of the local population. If successful, the charter city proposal will have particularly menacing consequences for Black and Indigenous Hondurans who have long fought to defend their territories from extractivist enterprises. ZEDEs will entail the systematic expropriation of Black and Indigenous peoples' lands, as well as their erasure, ultimately, from the ultramodern and prosperous future that these audacious proposals will purportedly generate.[47]

Conclusion

Spatial enclosure through the creation of enclave economies in the early national period generated the conditions of possibility for extractivism to flourish along the Caribbean coast. Tracing these continuities creates an opportunity to underscore the *longue durée* of extractivism while also highlighting the centrality of race to the state's development agenda today. Black and Indigenous territories now, as in the period immediately following independence, figure as frontiers of progress for the mestizo majority (Loperena 2017b).

This is visible not only in the actions of the mestizo elite who have profited handsomely from their investments in tourism, mining, and agribusiness but also in the government's concerted efforts to render land into its commodity form, property, which brings the social relations of extraction into sharp relief. The dissolution of collective property regimes, including national and *ejido* landholdings, has further imperiled Garifuna territorial rights. Under the pretext of formalizing property rights for poor Hondurans, the government, with the backing of multilateral development institutions, has opened Black and Indigenous territories to further pillage. For coastal Garifuna communities, tourism is the primary culprit. Thus, we must come to understand how tourism articulates with the extractivist logics undergirding the state's bid for prosperity in the postcoup period.

As I argue throughout this book, Garifuna experience tourism in ways that echo the forms of exploitation and violence underpinning extractivist developments in other parts of the country, particularly those resulting from the enclosure and overexploitation of land, water, and forests and through the violent repression of opposition to these projects. Garifuna resistance to state-backed tourism developments on the Caribbean coast serves to contest the rhetorical strategies used by the state to position tourism as a sustainable alternative to extractivism, powerfully elucidating the analogous sociospatial practices inherent to these ostensibly oppositional development logics.

2 THE GARIFUNA COAST™

The Inclusionary Politics of Expulsion

THE SWEET SMELL OF FRESHLY sawed wood was faint but noticeable in the thick June heat. Claudio was seated at one end of the workshop with a chisel and a mallet, slowly shaping the rounded base of a *tambor* (a wooden drum). "He crafts most of the *artesanías* from wood, and I make the dolls," said Ana, as she looked proudly onto one of her most recent designs, drawing my attention to the doll's plaid dress, hair wrap, and long black braids. She said that people come from Tegucigalpa, Copán, Tela, and La Ceiba to buy their products—miniature *cayucos* (dugout canoes), slingshots, *tambores*, and other "traditional" Garifuna handicrafts. After a short tour of the shop, Ana invited me to sit. We had met previously, but this was my first encounter with Claudio, whom I knew only through the stories of land activists I had befriended in the community.

"What brought you our way, Cristian?" she asked. I explained that I was on my way back from taking pictures of the *hipoteca* (a tract of land acquired by a wealthy mestizo landowner from Tela). "Since I was near, I decided to pay you a visit."

Ana grimaced. "That land was sold by Professor Abel. Now that it has been cleared, it will be *lotificado*," or parcelized. "Actually," interjected Claudio, without looking up from his work, "the land was taken from him by the bank for an unpaid loan." Neither Claudio nor his wife was eager to discuss the topic, apparent from Claudio's unwavering dedication to the *tambor*. "But I thought it was illegal to sell the land in individual plots," I prodded.

Ana was hesitant to respond. "I don't know, Cristian. I think they are going to divide the area into individual lots and sell the land, but Garifuna will also be able to buy there."

"I think he's referring to the collective land title," Claudio interjected. She was quiet.

"Isn't that what happened here in Barrio Delicias too—isn't this re-cuperated land?" I asked. "Yes," she sighed, "and Claudio was one of the people at the head of that effort." He looked up from the *tambor*: "I was incarcerated for one week as a result of my role in the land recuperation." After he secured his plot of land, he retired as head of the movement, be-cause the persecution that he and his family suffered was unbearable.

Claudio abruptly stopped his work and went into the house. When he returned, he planted his seat in front of me. He glared directly into my eyes. "The *negritos* are the ones that create the problems, because they go against those of us who are trying to defend the rights of the community. They are the ones that put me in jail."[1] Claudio used the epithet *negrito* to denigrate Garifuna who are complicit in the sale of communal lands to non-Garifuna, which is prohibited by customary land tenure practices. Eventually a lawyer from the Confederation of Autochthonous Peoples of Honduras (CONPAH, by its Spanish acronym) helped to free him, he ex-plained. He then showed me a copy of his release certificate: "I am saving this to show to my children, so they can know the history and the role that I played in the recuperation of Delicias."

"There is no more land in Delicias," he continued. "Look how densely populated this neighborhood is—there is no land left for new homes, for the future generations." Claudio indicated that people have sold land in Delicias, too, but only to other Garifuna. "That is allowed?" I asked. "Yes," he said, "but lands cannot be sold to outsiders." I told him I understood this to be the case, but that others in the community had told me the rule is racist. Claudio furrowed his brow: "It is not racist to defend the rights of our people! Look, the situation here is very complex. I am not opposed to tourism, but the community should manage it and the benefits should come directly to us as the owners of the land."

As artisans of handmade goods, Claudio and Ana relied on visiting tourists for their living, and yet every sale was tempered by their insistence upon Garifuna territorial rights, which Claudio had been instrumental in defending. This tension stems from the economic necessity of participating in state-backed tourism development initiatives and the lived experience of racialized dispossession that has seemed the inevitable companion of such development. In this chapter, I explore the mechanisms by which the multicultural policies of the state—ostensibly designed to redress centuries of Indigenous and Black exclusion—in fact serve to further the extractivist aims of multinational capital and elite investors.

Through official channels of multicultural recognition and the attendant commodification of Garifuna difference, state institutions have sought to stir the latent touristic potential of the Caribbean coast while at the same time furthering a spatial regime that relegates Garifuna to an imagined *otherwhere*—not of Honduras. Tourism propaganda preys cannibalistically on Garifuna difference to further the destination-making politics of the state while also hardening notions of Garifuna folkloric Blackness, which ultimately serves the profiteering aims of developers. Importantly, this double play of expulsion through inclusion nullifies Garifuna claims to national territory.

State multiculturalism is executed through two distinct but interconnected processes: Garifuna are recognized as a racially and culturally distinct minority population through the provision of special rights, and Garifuna cultural difference is transformed into a marketable commodity for tourist consumption.[2] In this vein, multicultural inclusion has been harnessed to superimpose economic value onto Black bodies and geographies—national resources yet to be exploited by the growing tourism industry.[3] Garifuna, like the lands they inhabit, are primed for extraction.

I begin here with a short history of the Honduran ecotourism agenda, which leads into an analysis of state multiculturalism and how it has been used to further the destination-making politics of the state, developers, and international financial institutions. I then analyze the specific ways in which Garifuna figure in emerging tourism development imaginaries as objects of consumption. I detail the mechanisms by which surplus value is rendered from folklorization to fold Garifuna people, culture, and geographies into the overarching tourism product. This was perhaps most explicit in the planning and buildout of the Indura Beach and Golf Resort, a major ecotourism development in Tela Bay. The viability of the Honduran tourism industry is therefore contingent on Garifuna symbolic presence, yet Garifuna Blackness is also used to deny Garifuna Indigeneity and, by extension, their rights to coastal lands. I follow this with a discussion of Garifuna efforts to supplant empty folkloric representations with a counterhegemonic assertion of Black Indigenous being and political expression. In what ways do they leverage their newfound cultural value to contest the anti-Black racism that undergirds the state's development agenda on the Caribbean coast?

The Making of an Eco-Destination

In July 1965, the Central American Bank for Economic Integration published the report *A Regional Study of Tourist Development in Central America*. The report traced tourist development in Central America from 1959 to 1963 and established guidelines for the growth and development of new tourism markets. These guidelines were designed to attract a specific demographic, namely North American tourists from upper-income brackets:[4] "The evidence would suggest concentration on mature, upper-income prospects who have not only an interest in international tourism but also the financial ability to do so. It would not be inconsistent simultaneously to endeavor to attract the smaller segments of the market such as retirees or students who may have a special interest in the unique attractions of Central America" (Ritchie et al. 1965, 56). The authors hypothesized tourist arrivals from the United States would significantly outpace arrivals from Europe and other Latin American countries: "Its proportion of the total [number of tourist arrivals] will move from the established 52–56 percent in the direction of the 89 percent seen in Mexico" (Ritchie et al. 1965, 6). The Central America region, it was recommended, should develop strategies to target this demographic and to position the region as an up-and-coming tourist destination.

The report cited Honduras as a particularly promising site for tourism. At the time of publication, Honduras was the least affected by tourism in the region, but given its numerous attractions—including the Mayan ruins of Copán and the idyllic Bay Islands—and planned public investments in transportation infrastructure, Honduras's North Coast was expected to experience a tourism boom. Tela Bay was particularly attractive for its "excellent white sand beaches," proximity to the then soon-to-open international airport in San Pedro Sula and natural features, such as the United Fruit Company's experimental botanical garden La Lancetilla, and other areas of interest for "adventure seekers." In sum, the Atlantic coast of Honduras was constructed as a place of dreamy beach landscapes and experiences with exotic nature.

The making of Honduras as a tourism destination simultaneously constructed the tourist and the geographic space designated for tourism development. In this vein, Tela was marketed as a place for adventure seekers, beachgoers, and, eventually, authentic cultural experiences. The findings of the Central American Bank for Economic Integration's report would, by the 1990s, become standard practice for travel agencies, hotel publicity teams, and, shortly thereafter, internet search engines. Costa Rica's widely celebrated reputation as a nature lover's paradise and the sterling reputation it enjoys among international environmental NGOs has produced ripples throughout the region, fueling interest in ecotourism as a strategy for economic development and as a promising solution for the high incidence of poverty and unemployment.

In 2004, the Secretariat of Tourism drafted the National Sustainable Tourism Program (PNTS, by its Spanish acronym), which again emphasized Honduras's distinct natural beauty as a resource for development.[5] The PNTS defines sustainable tourism as "development that is equitable, socially and environmentally responsible and oriented toward the betterment of local livelihoods."[6] As we will see, the government's intransigent commitment to this model of development has instead fueled the destruction of local ecologies and widespread land speculation on the coast, resulting in greater pressures on Garifuna to sell their land to outsiders.

From 2005 to 2009 tourism maintained its position as the third-largest source of foreign exchange earnings (table 2.1), and this sector of the economy continues to be one of the strongest performing national industries. The promise of coastal tourism was self-evident, according to its advocates, but increasingly hinged on the ability of Honduras to develop a unique product, one that would distinguish it from more seasoned Caribbean destinations. It was at this juncture that Garifuna racial and cultural difference emerged as the face of the Caribbean tourism brand, which coincided with the rise of state multiculturalism.

Multicultural Extractions

Honduran multicultural reforms began in 1994, when the government of Carlos Roberto Reina officially recognized the pluricultural and multiethnic makeup of Honduras via Executive Order No. 0719, establishing a policy of "intercultural bilingual education" for the country's Indigenous populations.[7] The following year, Honduras ratified International Labour Organization Convention No. 169 Concerning Indigenous and Tribal Peoples, which protects the collective rights of Indigenous peoples.[8] The government went on to create a post for a public prosecutor assigned specifically to investigate crimes against Honduras's ethnic peoples, known in Spanish as the *la fiscalía de las etnias*. These official concessions signaled the ascent of state multiculturalism—a marked shift from the historical

TABLE 2.1: Main sources of foreign exchange, 2005–2009.

	2005	2006	2007	2008	2009 p	2009/2008 relative variation
Remittances	1,775.8	2,328.6	2,580.7	2,807.5	2,475.7	−11.8%
Maquila	1,074.1	1,083.4	1,060.7	1,277.1	974.4	−23.7%
Tourism	465.8	516.0	546.2	620.4	616.0	−0.7%
Coffee	366.3	425.8	518.3	620.2	531.5	−14.3%
Bananas	260.3	241.4	289.3	383.8	327.1	−14.8%
Palm oil	56.3	74.8	121.2	465.8	125.4	−39.0%
Farmed shrimp	124.5	156.4	120.3	99.0	112.9	14.0%
Soaps and detergents	42.5	45.9	43.9	52.4	4	−7.6%
Woodwork	40.8	32.1	40.0	29.8	23.5	−21.0%

Source: Honduran Institute of Tourism, prepared by Central Bank of Honduras.

practice of manufacturing political consent through coercive policies of assimilation to the recognition and accommodation of cultural diversity (Van Cott 2000). It was also a testament to the vigor of Indigenous and Black social movement activism (Yashar 1999; Hale 2002; Anderson 2007, 2009; Brondo 2010; Paschel 2010). However, as Indigenous and Black Hondurans transitioned into ethnic citizens, the multicultural state and the market subjugated these peoples in new constellations of liberal hegemony.

Hale's (2002, 2004) analysis of "neoliberal multiculturalism" illustrates how, in the context of neoliberal economic reforms, the state endorses Indigenous rights to culture to circumvent more radical political demands and opposition to neoliberal capitalism. It is my contention that multiculturalism is also crucially bound with extractivism. That is, the conferral of rights premised on racial and cultural difference is a prerequisite for the forms of predatory inclusion that are endemic to capitalism (Taylor 2019). This form of inclusion hinges upon repackaging coastal culture as uniquely Caribbean, Black, and exotic.

I suggest the escalating value of Garifuna cultural difference was realized through a neoliberal appropriation of the racial geography I outlined in the previous chapter and a growing consensus that Garifuna Blackness could be harnessed to realize coastal tourism development objectives. This process of racialization reconstitutes the coast as a space of geographic and cultural alterity, positioning Blackness as a central component of national development schemes while ensuring that Black people remain on the fringes of economic and political life.

Although scholars have documented the increasing valorization of Blackness in relation to cultural heritage in countries such as Brazil, the Honduran case is distinct in at least one crucial way: Garifuna culture is valorized by the tourism industry as a *cultura viva* (a living culture) as opposed to a culture that is deemed to have historical significance for Honduran national identity. [9] As I demonstrate, Garifuna have been included in Honduran development schemes as objects of tourist consumption while they are routinely and systemically rendered as foreigners or recent *arrivants*.

On December 12, 2008, I visited the Municipal Tourism Unit in Tela. The assistant director, René, whom I had met previously, greeted me warmly and eagerly oriented me to the resources available at the unit. He handed me a stack of tourism maps and pointed me in the direction of its library—a small wooden bookcase with three partially filled shelves—that included copies of research reports, policies, and laws created to facilitate the growth of tourism in the region. The office was awash with representations of Garifuna culture: two miniature *tambores* dangled from an interior window, and the brightly painted walls were adorned with two large hanging banners featuring photographs of Garifuna village life. One of the banners depicted a young Black woman balancing a woven basket on her head as she walked along a deserted white sand beach. Her dark skin was dramatically juxtaposed to her flowing white skirt and white blouse, fluttering against her exposed stomach.

Within a matter of minutes René brought me samples of other handicrafts made locally, including jewelry carved out of coconut shells, an assortment of "traditional" Garifuna dolls with braided hair and plaid skirts—strikingly similar to the ones I watched Ana craft—and an intricately textured and multicolor costume typically worn by men during the performance of the *yancanu* dance. All these cultural artifacts are critical components of the destination-making politics of the municipal government. During my meeting with René, he spoke enthusiastically about how Garifuna villages contribute to regional tourism, but he also expressed concern: "They are in danger of losing their authenticity." According to him, the community of Miami, a Garifuna fishing outpost situated on a narrow strip of land between the Caribbean Sea and the Los Micos Lagoon, was still "authentic," but others along the bay had become too modern (fig. 2.1). He contrasted the quaint thatched-roof huts in Miami with the "modern" cement-block homes of Triunfo de la Cruz, which he lamented are less appealing to incoming tourists.

My understanding of these dynamics was furthered in a subsequent interview with David Zaccaro, then mayor of Tela, who elaborated on the typology of tourism services and products offered to visitors, ranging from sun and beach tourism to nature tourism to cultural tourism. He said he wanted Tela to become the principal tourism destination in the country, and he was adamant about the role to be played by Garifuna in the development of the region. "It is a *cultura viva* and it will be our main point of

FIGURE 2.1: Garifuna house featuring typical construction materials, Casa de la Niñez, Triunfo de la Cruz.

Photo: Christopher Loperena.

leverage, our main attraction, our principal added component to be able to compete with other global tourism destinations" (interview, April 9, 2009). The mayor went on to explain how specific cultural goods would be used to market the region: "Here we dance *punta* and where does *punta* originate? In *our* Garifuna communities of course . . . [Garifuna culture] is a unique attraction that we have, and, well, Cancún does not. They give us an added edge." *Punta* is a traditional Garifuna music and dance. In recent years *punta* musicians such as Aurelio Martínez have attracted a large national and international following.

In his comments, the mayor conveyed a sense of propriety over Garifuna culture and lands, both of which are critical for the expansion of tourism in Tela. His statements echoed folkloric representations of Garifuna racial and ethnic difference within tourism propaganda. However, unlike other Indigenous groups, Garifuna were rendered nonnative inhabitants, notable for their "African" origins and cultural expressions. For example, the investment guide circulated at the Honduras Is Open for Business conference in May 2011 stated: "Eighty percent of the Garifuna community is scattered in dozens of villages on the Caribbean coast. Their unique language, percussion drums, the voices of their songs, and exotic dances such as *punta* revive the ancient traditions that originated in Africa." Other promotional materials highlighted the mixture of African and Indigenous cultural ancestry possessed by Garifuna in Honduras. The key to these formulations of Garifuna difference—African and Afro-Indigenous—is the uniqueness of their culture, which cannot be found in other locations but is overdetermined by their Blackness.

Sherwood Bonilla, a hotel owner and president of the Tela Tourism Board, also pointed to the significance of Garifuna culture for the sake of place branding:

> They have very special dances that have certainly influenced Latin American dance culture more broadly . . . and the coastal food is a very nice attraction, right? The [tourists] view this culinary style favorably. We receive many guests that ask us for this style of food—seafood soup, food from the sea and cooked with coconut. It has a very particular taste . . . it would seem that it is from another place [not Central America].

Thus, place making, and more specifically the rebranding of the coast as distinctly Black, is very much dependent on Garifuna displacement from the nation. The otherness of Garifuna bodies, coastal culture, and landscapes coalesce in the production of Caribbean paradise, which is amply reproduced and disseminated in tourism marketing materials.

In her analysis of Black women's oppression in the United States, Hill Collins (2000) demonstrates the extent to which stereotypical representations, or "controlling images," serve to normalize racism, sexism, and other forms of social inequality. Her concept of "controlling images" helps us to think through the ways in which the Honduran state and international financial institutions manipulate representations of Garifuna cultural and racial difference to advance development imperatives, particularly within the coastal tourism industry. These representations bind Black Hondurans to soccer, *punta* music, and entertainment, thus providing the basis for the objectification of the Black body, widely consumed and redeployed for commercial purposes.

Figures 2.2 and 2.3 represent two poles of Black subjectivity in Honduras, as defined and consumed by the mestizo nation-state. In the first image, Garifuna are represented within the cultural script of international Black politics (fig. 2.2). The demand for 10 percent of public offices is a reference to affirmative action–like policies in the United States and elsewhere in Latin America, in which Afro-descendant peoples have sought and obtained greater representation within government structures, including public universities (Paschel 2016).[10] Moreover, Blackness is aggressive and gendered as male but devoid of any explicit cultural otherness. The caricature is racially demarcated by the Afro hairdo, which also serves to tie Garifuna to radical Black politics in the United States. The Afro, however, stands in tension with the business suit, which demonstrates class and educational privilege, and the potential to accept and accommodate the norms of the modern Honduran citizen-subject. This form of political subjectivity is tolerated and accommodated by the multicultural state—as illuminated by Hale's (2004) discussion of the *indio permitido*—since demands for recognition and representation can be met through the bequeathal of rights and reforms within existing institutional practices.[11]

In the other image, the faceless Garifuna woman, in contrast, is wearing a traditional dress with a red hair wrap—a common feature of coastal dress—and positioned alongside a set of *tambores* (fig. 2.3). Her arms are spread wide in a welcoming gesture, and she appears to be dancing. Her large hoop earrings and the shawl around her waist are important signifiers of diasporic Blackness. Her attire is a reference to the private sphere, the space of the community, where the female subject is said to dominate. Whereas the male subject is tied to the public sphere, the business suit suggestive of his status as negotiator with the outside world and the state, the Garifuna woman is the warm and friendly representative of the Honduran Caribbean. The image is a brand elaborated by the Tela Tourism Board in collaboration with international financial institutions. This form of multicultural inclusion is nonthreatening to state sovereignty and the privileging of whiteness in state discourses on national identity.

FIGURE 2.2: "We demand 10 percent of public offices!" Political cartoon published in *El Tiempo* on April 8, 2006.

NO SOLO LA PUNTA Y EL FUTBOL...

¡EXIGIMOS EL DIEZ PORCIENTO DE LOS CARGOS PUBLICOS!

AFRO-HONDUREÑOS

FIGURE 2.3: Tela Garífuna Coast: To the beat of the Honduran Caribbean.

Tela Costa Garifuna

Al calor del Caribe hondureño.

Blackness is rendered valuable to the state vis-à-vis its commercial appeal, and thus Garifuna cultural difference is brought into public view through tourism propaganda and tourism development initiatives. State institutions, including the Honduran Institute of Tourism, play a vital role in the mediation of Garifuna visibility and subsequent incorporation into the national imaginary.[12] However, as I explain, the folkloric representations sanctioned by the state through tourism development flatten the political subjectivity of Black peoples and at the same time reinforce the dominant narrative that tourism is good for all. The celebration of ethnic and cultural diversity could be profitable for the state. But the notion that Garifuna lands and culture are for sale has generated contentious debates within Garifuna communities, where many oppose the profit-driven appropriation of Garifuna culture by the state and private investors (Kirtsoglou and Theodossopoulos 2004).

In figure 2.4, three Garifuna women donning colorful head wraps and three shirtless Garifuna men are pictured alongside a young white couple. The white woman—presumably a North American or European tourist—is also wearing a head wrap, which is a sign of both her affinity with Garifuna culture and her ability to embody these signifiers of ethnic and racial difference. The close proximity between her and the Garifuna drummer hints at an element of sexual and racial desire, because tourism entails more than the commodification of culture; it also commodifies bodies. In this rendering, the body is objectified and eerily fungible. As Hartman (1997, 21) notes, "The fungibility of the commodity made the captive body an abstract and empty vessel vulnerable to the projection of others' feelings, ideas, desires, and values." Similarly, the racial desires propagated by the national tourism industry in Honduras serve to strip the Black body of subjectivity and agency. The body becomes a vessel for the fulfillment of state desires, as well as the desires of visiting tourists.[13]

Returning to my conversation with Sherwood Bonilla, I was struck by his candor when addressing the sexualized desires of foreign tourists. "There is also an attraction for the body, the corporeal structure of the Garifuna," he said. "Why?" I nudged. "I don't know. I have noticed that white women are very attracted to Garifuna men. I don't know if it is because of their skin color or their physical structure. It gives the impres-

FIGURE 2.4: Tela Tourism Board (CANATURH Tela) home page.

Source: Honduras Tips tourism guide, https://www.hondurastips.hn/negocio/camara-de-turismo-de-tela/.

sion of strength. And in the case of the women, it is their bumps—their breasts and their butts too." Thus, Garifuna bodies are also potentially part of the services offered to foreign tourists. No one at the Tela Tourism Board explicitly advocated for sex tourism, but they are all relying on this tacit element of sexuality and desire to keep the tourists coming. The above analysis brings desire and development together in a distinctly racialized configuration, wherein desire is expressed as exotic racial longings to consume the Black body (hooks 1992; Sheller 2003) and as an anticipatory desire for the luxury Caribbean resort landscape investors seek to develop. The role to be played by Garifuna is as object of desire or deliverer of authentic Caribbean culture or marginal service worker.

For Honduras to fully realize its touristic potential, Garifuna needed to maintain the façade of authenticity and of its "African" village life. And yet when it comes to questions of territory, Garifuna who insist on defending communal property rights are repeatedly chastised for being "stuck in the past." In my interview with Isabel Pérez, country coordinator for the World Tourism Organization, I asked whether tourism development officials had policies in place to abate the high incidence of land privatization in the communities they promote as tourism destinations. She furrowed her eyebrows. "That is difficult," she said, "because the sale of land is seen by the state as a component of economic development. . . . You cannot demand that they [the Garifuna] continue their culture as they did 200 years ago" (interview, March 11, 2010).

Authenticity, it turns out, is appealing only when it fulfills development objectives. To obtain rights predicated on cultural difference, Garifuna must perform and preserve traditional ways of being, but failure to bend to the whims of state development desires was grounds for expulsion, not only from the promised benefits of progress but also potentially from the nation. In sum, Blackness is rendered into a commodity, detached from political struggle and from territory.

Rightful Heirs of the Land?

Garifuna presence, while crucial for the touristic valorization of coastal lands, also represents a threat to the government's development goals in agribusiness and tourism. These goals are often contingent on the expropriation of Indigenous and Black lands in areas of the country that are deemed critical for Honduras's economic advancement. Because of their presumed foreignness, Garifuna are popularly portrayed as usurpers of national lands; their territorial claims imperil the state's economic agenda and the rights of mestizo, or *ladino*, peasants.[14]

Growing anxieties about Indigenous and Black territorial claims, including lands that they do not currently hold title to, and the menace they pose to the Honduran state's extractivist designs have fueled widespread conflicts over land and resources. These tensions were vividly brought to light following a court order to remove *ladino* settlers from the Garifuna community Cristales y Río Negro, in Trujillo—a natural bay 250 kilometers east of Tela. Several peasant families, reportedly from Copán and Santa Bárbara, established a small settlement on lands titled to the community. Garifuna filed a formal complaint with the National Agrarian Institute, and on April 5, 2006, the Preventive Police and Directorate General of Criminal Investigation executed the peaceful eviction of the settlers.

The next day the Honduran newspaper, *El Tiempo*—owned by the business tycoon Jaime Rosenthal Oliva—published an article under the incendiary headline: "Garifunas Remove Ladinos from Their Lands." The article presented the landless peasants as hapless victims of Garifuna territorial claims: "Elvira Mejía, a young peasant woman who dreamed of settling in Trujillo, saw her dreams frustrated when the presiding judge told her that she would have to vacate her house, which was built of earth walls and a thatched palm roof, which housed her husband and her little one-month-old son, who was sleeping peacefully in his mother's arms." This overtly sympathetic portrayal led Garifuna activists to accuse Rosenthal, who is also a key player in the Honduran tourism industry, of attempting to drum up racial animus and even provoke violence against community land defenders.

The accompanying photo depicts an older mestiza woman who resided within the encampment. She is being comforted by a police officer who has been tasked with carrying out the eviction. In an act of kindness, the officer holds the woman, who clasps her hands together as she tearfully laments the loss of her home. In the article, the author maintains the peasants moved to the Aguán in search of better living conditions. The Aguán Valley, as we have seen, is home to the country's thriving African palm plantations; it abuts several Garifuna communities, which have faced significant pressures from newly arrived peasants in search of lands to settle.

As in Tela, Garifuna are understood as potential threats to the overarching extractivist development agenda, which imagines these lands and surrounding ecosystems as fundamental to national progress. Significantly, the image also gestured toward a nationalistic sentiment which upholds the inalienable quality of mestizo land claims over the rights of Garifuna coastal inhabitants. This is so in spite of Honduras's ratification of the ILO Convention No. 169. In this sense, the photo powerfully inverts the actual extraction that is happening in Honduras, in which Garifuna coastal inhabitants face a barrage of pressure from investors, developers, and state authorities intent on taking their lands in the name of development. It also engenders empathy and racial affinity among mestizo Hondurans while at the same time buttressing the false notion that Garifuna are illegitimate heirs to national territory.

In a sharply worded retort, the Garifuna community leaders affiliated with OFRANEH stated:

El Tiempo newspaper has been creating a disinformation campaign and now it seems that they are instigating hatred against our people. . . . We warn all Hondurans not to be fooled by [El Tiempo owner Jaime Rosenthal Oliva] who for decades has plundered Honduras through his economic monopolies and is currently at the highest echelons of power, trying more than ever to milk the country.

The feudalism that exists in this country is the mother of poverty and injustice. The best lands are in the hands of few families and that is the true cause of the national peasantry's misfortune. We Garifuna are not the creators of the agrarian crisis, as the newspaper *El Tiempo* maliciously and underhandedly intends to incline public opinion.[15]

The plight of landless and land-poor peasants in rural areas of the country is not due to the rights claims of Indigenous and Black peoples; rather, it is a structural condition that is in fact contingent on the monopolization of natural resource wealth by the tiny yet powerful Honduran oligarchy. The plunder of Garifuna lands by the Honduran political and economic elite has been aided by the prevalence of anti-Black racism, which permeates nearly all sectors of Honduran society and upholds the erroneous notion that Garifuna, by virtue of their Blackness, are not entitled to the lands they claim.

Extractivist Tourism as Sustainable Development?

Tourism officials understood the value of Garifuna cultural difference for the region's brand, but they were also keenly aware of Tela's deficiencies relative to more established tourism destinations, specifically the lack of infrastructure—potable water, paved roadways, and hotels with modern amenities. They pinned their hopes on the success of the Indura Beach and Golf Resort. First conceived in the 1970s under the name Tornasal, the Indura project did not materialize into a viable development until receiving the backing of the Inter-American Development Bank, which in 2005 approved a government loan for US$14.5 million to complete the basic public works infrastructure for the tourism complex.[16]

Inaugurated in 2014, Indura is located within the buffer zone of the Jeannette Kawas National Park between the communities of Miami and

Tornabé on lands that Garifuna claim as their ancestral territory.[17] It includes an eighteen-hole golf course, sixty luxury suites nestled among the palm trees, a convention center, a fitness center and spa, and five restaurants that draw on the culinary traditions of neighboring Garifuna communities. Hotel rooms at the resort start at US$209 per night, and guests can partake in a number of nature-inspired activities, including hikes through the surrounding Jeannette Kawas National Park, a trip to the Lancetilla Botanical Garden, and fishing excursions.

The resort ostensibly encompasses many of the principles set forth in the National Sustainable Tourism Plan—tourism that is both environmentally and socially responsible, and that is oriented toward the betterment of local livelihoods. In reality, the so-called eco-resort has generated extensive damage to the surrounding ecosystem and severe conflicts over land that have accelerated territorial dispossession and constricted access to key resources for neighboring Garifuna communities. In May 2016, the Indura resort was added to Hilton Curio, a small collection of luxury hotels that "meet independent-minded travelers' needs for local discovery and authentic experiences."

Importantly, the luxury amenities available at Indura are inaccessible to local Garifuna communities, and the community has not experienced noticeable economic benefits, not in terms of employment or spillover from visiting guests. Freitag (1994) argues that all-inclusive resorts follow an enclave model of development with very little "trickle-down" economic impact into secondary industries. Similarly, Mbaiwa (2003, 159) demonstrates the ways enclave tourism development in the Okavango Delta in Botswana not only failed to consider the needs and wishes of surrounding communities but also hastened environmental degradation. He also acknowledges a point that is painfully obvious to anyone who has ever lived near a resort: most of the goods and services available at these facilities surpass the financial means of local communities.

Building on this work, I contend that the ecotourism model pursued in Honduras operates in ways analogous to other extractive industries, which contribute to "territorial fragmentation," and increase economic (and by extension, social) vulnerabilities for local economies (Acosta 2013, 66–73). Indura relies on the privatization of collectively owned coastal lands and the sale of prime coastal real estate to foreign and national investors, and it capitalizes on natural and cultural resources for the benefit of private enterprise, all under the veneer of sustainable development. Moreover, resort tourism is an export-oriented industry; the products (e.g., hotel stays, package tours, air and ground transportation) are primarily marketed to and consumed by foreigners and national elites (Honey 2008).

The Indura project also lays bare the close alliance between the public and private arms of the economy, or what David Harvey (2009) has referred to as the "state-finance nexus." Indeed, the project was funded through a public-private partnership between the Honduran Institute of Tourism, which owns 51 percent of shares, and the Tela Bay Touristic Development Society (DTBT, by its Spanish acronym), which holds 49 percent of shares.[18] Camilo Atala, a Honduran business magnate, is on the board of the DTBT as well as president of the Grupo Financiero FICOHSA—one of the largest financial institutions in Central America. The Atala family is also associated with Desarrollos Energéticos, the energy company behind the infamous Agua Zarca hydroelectric dam project that was slated to be built on the Gualcarque River in the Indigenous Lenca territory.[19] Parallels between the financing for tourism resorts on the Caribbean coast and energy developments in southwestern Honduras make clear the extractivist aims of the state and business elite, despite claims to the contrary. A hydroelectric dam and a sumptuous seaside resort look completely different on the surface, and yet for the communities of color nearby, their impact is startlingly similar.

The idea that tourism development will benefit local livelihoods has been widely touted by investors, but the "development for all" mantra has proved false, as the benefits to local populations, in this case Garifuna communities surrounding the project site, have been marginal in comparison to the heavy ecological destruction caused by the project. For example, the eighteen-hole golf course required the dredging and filling of protected wetlands within the buffer zone of the Jeannette Kawas National Park. Garifuna living adjacent to the resort told me that Tornabé now faces more frequent flooding during the rainy season and a greater incidence of mosquito-borne illnesses.

At the time of the project's conception, the community of Tornabé was not in possession of a land title, but the testimonies of community members I consulted demonstrate that the lands where the project was constructed are indeed vital to the livelihoods of the local population. One resident who asked to remain anonymous because of the tensions that exist in the region as a result of the development and local opposition to it asserted: "These lands have always belonged to the community. The only thing is that back then our community did not have a title demonstrating ownership, but they have always belonged to the community." He explained that the lands were used for agricultural purposes and for hunting crabs, turtles, and other animals, activities that have been nearly eliminated since the opening of the resort.

The Honduran Institute of Tourism promised the local Garifuna population participatory and sustainable development, and through various means—including the potential for employment at the resort—convinced some community members that the Indura project (then known as Los Micos) would produce tangible benefits for the communities. A small group of community representatives from Tornabé eventually yielded to the pressure coming from the state, and in 1993 an "agreement" was reached wherein the community ceded control of 512 hectares to the Honduran Institute of Tourism (IHT, by its Spanish acronym). In his study *Tornabé ante el proyecto turístico*, the Garifuna intellectual Virgilio López (2006, 73) explains: "In 1993 the government took the lands from the Garifuna community of Tornabé, and conferred the rights over them to the IHT, destroying the community's crops and forcing them to sell their livestock." The results have been devastating.

Local understandings of territoriality and belonging are contingent on the fluid and sustainable use of resources within the area Garifuna conceive as their "functional habitat," but the construction of the resort has violently disrupted the relationship between Garifuna and the lands they occupy. Garifuna from Tornabé who previously traveled to and from Miami to fish in the Los Micos Lagoon are no longer able to do so, thus limiting resource access and foreclosing the viability of historical subsistence practices. In this way, the Indura resort is an example of what Rodgers and

O'Neill (2012, 405) describe as "infrastructural violence," that is violence that "flows through material and structural forms."

To ensure the success of the Indura project and the destination-making politics of the state, the IHT has developed plans to preserve and revitalize Miami's "traditional" housing constructions (fig. 2.5). The architectural plans include a tourism center, boat docks, and informational kiosks built using local construction materials and aesthetic styles. Community residences, currently dispersed in a nonlinear layout, will be reorganized along a neatly organized grid. Miami will be refashioned into a "traditional Garifuna village" where visitors can have "authentic" experiences with Garifuna.

The resort grounds and landscaping are designed to reflect the cultural and ecological particularities of the surrounding region (Loper-

FIGURE 2.5: Miami Architectural Guidelines, Courtesy of the Instituto Hondureño de Turismo.

ena 2016a). The landscape architecture and design firm EDSA maintains that "the nearby Garifuna community of Miami is the only one that to this day is still completely built of thatched huts. Indura replicates this building style along with the addition of stilts to its buildings allowing for zero disturbance in natural animal migration patterns as well as assisting with irrigation, drainage and air flow."[20] EDSA's aesthetic commitment to traditional building styles that draw on the architectural heritage of surrounding Garifuna communities also helps mask the environmentally and socially destructive components of the resort, including the eighteen-hole golf course, and the enclosure of communally held lands. These distinctive architectural features give the impression of local participation in the project, a hallmark of ecotourism development (Brockington, Duffy, and Igoe 2008).

Until recently the Indura resort was not responsible for the direct displacement of Garifuna. Rather, massive infrastructural investments, in addition to land speculation throughout the region have eroded the rights of Garifuna residents. With limited access to lands for agricultural production and renewed restrictions on fishing, many have abandoned the community for other areas of the country, or migrated to the United States. This insidious but persistent process of displacement also stands to jeopardize the state development agenda; as Mollett (2014, 4) argues, Garifuna labor is "central to the spatial imaginary of tourism development." Garifuna residents contributed to the initial phase of the project in construction, and some have found a foothold as lower-level employees, but mostly they have been excluded from participation. Thus, in spite of their symbolic inclusion within the creation of the resort, Garifuna have received minimal direct benefits. Moreover, their territorial claims directly conflict with the long-term vision for Indura. This was most apparent in the 2014 eviction of Barra Vieja, a mixed Garifuna and *ladino* community adjacent to the resort grounds.

Barra Vieja is located alongside the ancestral road linking the communities of Tornabé and Miami in an area the Garifuna designated for the cultivation of staple crops, such as rice and yuca (cassava), for the collection of coconut, and for fishing. My conversations with residents in 2010 revealed a deep fear that the Indura project would eventually expand into the community, forcing them to leave indefinitely:

> They want to come in as if the people here had no value. They want to construct a road through the center of our community, but we wouldn't let them. They also want to run the electricity and water lines through here, but when we asked if they were going to provide access to the community, they said no, so for that reason we didn't let them in.

Due to their opposition to the project, Garifuna residents of Barra Vieja have since been subjected to repeated threats and persecution at the hands of state security forces.

The state's first attempt to evict residents occurred in August 2014, but residents refused to leave, insisting on their ancestral rights to the land. On September 30, dozens of military and police officers made a second attempt to forcibly evict residents, and subsequently the IHT and the National Port Authority pressed charges against the entire community of Barra Vieja, alleging that residents had illegally usurped private property. Significantly, officials also denied the Indigenous status of the community:

> The doctrine promoted by the Attorney General's office in relation to the matter of considering the Garifuna people as foreigners in Honduras, thusly denying our territorial rights, is heavily impregnated with racism. A good part of the national elite is of foreign origin and has been here [in Honduras] for less than a century, without anyone questioning at any point their "hondureñidad." (OFRANEH communiqué, June 5, 2015)

In the subsequent trial, the attorney general presented evidence that the state had transferred rights to the disputed lands to the National Port Authority in 1975. This transfer of property rights conflicted with official documentation presented by the defense, which proved that Barra Vieja was registered with the Municipal Corporation in 1950. The Court of Tela ruled in favor of the community on June 5, 2015, but pressure to evict the community continues.

This analysis of recent land conflicts in the community of Barra Vieja demystifies the role of the state in these new configurations of public-private partnership, wherein public resources—security forces, courts—are used to protect the rights and assets of private investors to the detriment of the original inhabitants. In her analysis of Black women's land struggles in Salvador de Bahia, Brazil, Perry (2013, 50) asserts, "Places where black people once lived have become commercial sites for the consumption of black experiences and cultures, but without the people who have produced that culture." This parallels ecotourism development in Tela Bay, where Garifuna inhabitants of Miami and Barra Vieja remain only as visual representatives of the place they once called home—this is the inclusionary politics of expulsion.

"Tired of Failed Promises"

In spite of their growing visibility within tourism marketing campaigns, Garifuna demands for full participation in the development and management of tourism within their territories has been largely ignored by state agencies and investors. Their opposition to projects, such as Indura, has led to high-stakes confrontations between land activists and the state. On March 11, 2009, shortly after developers broke ground on the Indura resort, hundreds of Garifuna paralyzed traffic on the main highway connecting the coastal towns of Tela and La Ceiba. The protesters rolled tires across the highway and then doused them with gasoline and set them ablaze. The tires strewn across the two-lane highway obstructed the passage of vehicles, creating a platform for activists to express a politics of visibility that powerfully refused the folklorization of Blackness.

The protest took place at the entrance of Triunfo de la Cruz. However, the protesters hailed from all five Garifuna communities along Tela Bay and from as far as Iriona, Colón, some three hundred kilometers to the east. OFRANEH was responsible for organizing the protest, which was the first road blockade in the history of the organization. One of the protesters held a sign that read, "We are tired of failed promises!" The signs and protest chants echoed the sentiment of Garifuna who faulted municipal authorities and the central government for promoting development policies that hastened land loss within their territories.

The police tried in vain to convince the protesters that this was not the way to express their complaints. "All you want is for us to play the *tambor* and to shake our asses," the leader of OFRANEH, Miriam Miranda, protested, to affirmative shouts from the crowd. "Well, here we are playing the *tambores* of resistance! We also have the right to struggle." By this point, several news agencies had arrived at the scene of the protest. She exploited the media presence to discuss the development that would become Indura: "Here they talk about a famous project [Indura] that they say will bring us development, but they [the tourists] are going to go directly from the airport to the hotel and close themselves off behind a fence. They are not going to leave anything for our people."

"If we don't let the tourists come into our community, they—the government and private investors—would lose, because the dollars go to them!" Her statements astutely called attention to the immense wealth extracted from Garifuna communities via the commodification of their lands and culture by the government and private investors, who through investments in tourism further processes of territorial dispossession. Miriam continued, "We don't want to damage the economy of this country, but we made this decision [to take over the main coastal highway] so you will listen to us." She was keenly aware of how Garifuna assertions of territorial autonomy threaten the robust tourism economy officials hope to materialize on the coast and that is contingent on Garifuna racial and cultural difference. A road takeover during the height of Holy Week—the busiest travel season of the year—was fundamentally about competing sovereign claims between Garifuna and the state government over the use and exploitation of coastal lands and culture.

Such acts of resistance serve to demystify the aims of inclusionary politics promoted by the state, which have been used to subvert opposition and camouflage the embedded exploitation of tourism. The protest highlighted the ways the extractivist model of development negatively affected the communities, producing profits for investors and for the state, but with very little advantages at the community level. Further, the ideology of development has been used to dispossess Garifuna of their lands and to generate acquiescence to these initiatives, which has created internal communal divisions and hastened land sales to outsiders.

Conclusion

The tourism model pursued by the Honduran state, and which congealed in the late 1990s, is one premised on extractivist activities but one that professes to be a sustainable alternative to extractivism with the potential to generate extensive social benefits, including employment and poverty reduction. What these claims elide is the prevalence of conflict surrounding these proposals and the ways resistance to tourism on the Caribbean coast echoes resistance to mining and agribusinesses that has been a hallmark of Honduran social movement activism since the 1970s.

Indeed, Garifuna resistance to extractivist tourism developments, such as the Indura Beach and Golf Resort, is both a rejection of normative ideologies of progress and a refusal of the terms of inclusion established through state multiculturalism. By staking a claim to place, Garifuna also stake a claim to self-determination and control over the resources within their territories.

Folkloric constructions of Garifuna ethnic and racial difference have been used to add value to the coastal tourism product while simultaneously relegating Garifuna to a space outside the sovereign boundaries of the nation, to an imagined otherwhere. This, of course, hastens processes of accumulation by dispossession. And yet as Claudio cautioned in the chapter's opening vignette, some Garifuna are complicit in selling lands to investors. His critique of the *negritos* raises important questions regarding the politics of land as they unfold within the space of the community.

This story is not just about the government bulldozing Garifuna into submission, but about how development and attendant ideologies of individual free choice and liberal inclusion via the conferral of rights slowly create conditions and ethical orientations that imperil Black autonomy on the coast. Miriam Miranda (2011, 33) argues: "The participation and insertion of marginal populations in politics [multicultural inclusion] are contingent on the submission to strategies of displacement . . . of indige-nous peoples from their ancestral territories." Her statement demonstrates an acute awareness of the potential menace lying below state concessions to Black and Indigenous Hondurans and the profound limitations of na-scent cultural rights regimes that cannot be divorced from the politics of extraction.

PART TWO

3 TENSIONS OF AUTONOMOUS BLACKNESS

In the past things were very different. No one cared about Triunfo. It was almost a homogenous space and the ancestors had firm control over the community and who was allowed to come in. A lot of the men of the community did find work in Tela, with the Tela [Railroad] Co., but there was a sense of autonomy in the community, because there was no tourism. It was very tranquil here. We lived in peace. We need to have unity, because even though there are divisions now, the enemy is really an outsider.

MIGUEL, land defender (2010)

ON AN UNUSUALLY COOL OCTOBER morning, I traveled to Tela to buy produce at the local farmer's market. After completing my shopping, I hurried over to the corner of the market, across from the brightly painted Farmacia Delfín. This was where taxi drivers from Triunfo de la Cruz lined up to offer *colectivo* service back to the community. Since there were already two passengers waiting, we all boarded and headed in the direction of Triunfo. A well-dressed Garifuna man by the name of Ricardo was seated to my right, and Nancy, a Garifuna woman with short cornrows, sat in the front passenger seat of the small four-door sedan.

Eager to make acquaintances, I introduced myself as a volunteer English teacher at the recently opened Escuela Trilingüe and a North American researcher of Puerto Rican descent. Ricardo asked what I was planning to study. "I am interested in studying tourism development," I said earnestly. The taxi driver, who was also a native Triunfeño, responded with a chuckle, "What tourism development? *¡No existe el desarrollo en Triunfo!*" (development does not exist in Triunfo). His protest caught me off guard. Did he mean there was no development, as in state-financed development of infrastructure? Was he making a reference specifically to mass tourism development, as in large resorts, golf courses, and shopping districts? Or, was his protest more a metacritique of development and its failed promise?

Unsure of how to proceed, I tried clarifying my research goals: "I would like to analyze the efforts of community members to promote development initiatives—small and locally managed projects that are currently existing or in gestation." Both Nancy and Ricardo perked up. "We are business owners," said Ricardo with a beaming smile. He owned a small restaurant named Rico's Place and Nancy owned a hotel and restaurant just behind the local billiard hall in Barrio Centro. Incidentally, Nancy and Ricardo were returning from a workshop on the culinary arts coordinated by the Tela Municipal Tourism Office.

Ricardo remarked, "The development we need is rooted in education, such as the education you are providing to our children—*English language education*," he stressed. This, he assured me, would enable the community to generate employment opportunities within the tourism industry. Nancy agreed with Ricardo, but the *taxista*, who was significantly younger, adamantly disagreed. The problem, he stated, is that, "The Honduran worker is exploited." According to him, the average working adult earned $150 per month, which was even less than the legally mandated minimum wage. "People who have university degrees work as taxi drivers and in low-skill jobs," he added. He highlighted other economic disparities plaguing the country: "Honduran factory workers perform the same labor as their counterparts in the United States but make a substantially reduced salary and in poor conditions, which by most standards, is not dignified employment." Tourism, he argued, would not change these structural conditions. The taxi driver's critical assessment of development's promise diverged significantly from the optimistic tone of Nancy and Ricardo, who were both in their forties and scraping out a living from the incipient tourism market.

This taxicab conversation illustrates an array of perspectives on development and visions of the future. Ricardo was eager to tout their autonomous efforts to establish successful tourism businesses. But he also actively accommodated to prevailing moral discourses of progress (Pandian 2008) and believed in the untapped potential of tourism to generate economic advancement, as opposed to the *taxista*, who seemed unwilling to entertain the hype around tourism. For him, the systemic forms of economic exploitation and social marginalization that plagued Garifuna—and Hondurans more generally—would not be overcome simply through the creation of hotels and other tourism related infrastructure; rather, these initiatives would likely expand the economic dominance of elite groups and, in turn, hasten land dispossession within the community.

The taxi driver's sharp retort speaks to the complex relationship between policies designed to abet the growth of the coastal tourism industry—an increasingly important source of livelihood within the Garifuna communities—and the loss of territory. Whereas in the previous chapters our focus was on how the tourism economy creates the conditions of possibility for racialized modes of extraction to flourish, here we begin our immersion in the granular details of the divisions tourism development has provoked within Triunfo, a Garifuna community situated just a few kilometers east of the city of Tela.

As we have seen, the arrival of tourist dollars has created deep political fissures in Garifuna communities in Honduras, and especially along Tela Bay. In Triunfo, this divide was most vividly illustrated by the existence of two communal governing councils, or *patronatos*.[1] Carla, a celebrated activist in the land struggle, led one *patronato*—the self-proclaimed *defensores de la tierra* (land defenders). The other *patronato*—commonly mocked as the *patronato paralelo*—was presided over by Ricardo and comprised by a handful of *empresarios* (small-business owners) who criticized Carla for lacking the "preparedness" needed to lead the community to a prosperous future.[2]

Nevertheless, the enduring hope that the tourism economy would make everything better was widespread. This feeling, what Lauren Berlant (2011) would call "optimistic attachments," came up more often than not in the casual conversations I struck up with people on the streets. This optimism was fueled by the state in conjunction with multilateral development institutions, private investors, and Triunfeños who sought to become tourism entrepreneurs. Anticipation and hope for the good that the tourism economy might bring also epitomized a changing ethos around land ownership as well as a deepening rift across generations about the community's aspirations for the future. Would Triunfo remain a small fishing community at the margins of the state, or would it become a glistening tourism destination capable of meeting the employment needs of young Triunfeños, many of whom pursued degrees in hotel management, tourism, and English as courses of study? And what would this imagined future mean for Garifuna territorial rights and autonomy? Nearly all these tangled questions, and the knotted conflicts that ensued, came down to one very simple dilemma: should the will of the individual take precedence over the autonomy of the collective?[3]

I start with a discussion of Garifuna debates over the meaning of development and contested notions of prosperity. I then provide a brief historical account of how the contemporary land defense movement came to be, which I trace back to a violent dispute over a now defunct development called Marbella. Then, I analyze how through the promotion of entrepreneurial conduct and "productive projects," or small-business ownership, international financial institutions and state development agencies have engendered divergent ethical dispositions around land and land ownership within the community. Progress and concomitant discourses of improvement get deployed in ways that expand hope for the yet to materialize tourism economy while still profoundly restructuring communal life. For the *empresarios* Garifuna culture and customary land tenure practices represented a barrier to progress. Whereas individual titles to land can facilitate access to credit for the creation of businesses and other infrastructural improvements, they also often lead to people alienating their land—this, for the land defenders, was the greatest threat to Triunfo's collective survival.

Aquí hay vida, Here There Is Life

There are only a handful of job opportunities in Triunfo: as a *taxista*, in small convenience stores, at Garifuna-owned hotels, at the *centro básico* (grade school), at the community health center, and in local restaurants. Nevertheless, Garifuna have established many channels for informal employment, or *chamba*. Men often work as day laborers on local construction projects—usually houses being built by Triunfeños living abroad—and women sell *pan de coco* and other traditional sweets to get by. During the height of the tourism season, many people set up makeshift dining rooms in their homes, sell prepared foods on the beach, or offer other services—cornrows are popular among female tourists.

Remittances are probably the most important source of income for families residing in the community, contributing to the widely held belief that migration is a ticket to a better life, at least among younger generations. While older Triunfeños tended to wax poetic about the past and their nostalgia for a foregone time when Triunfo abounded with food, land, and opportunity, youth were in search of a future that was not obtainable locally. Leticia, a thirty-year-old single mother, told me, "Chris, I have to leave, to look for a future, to construct my house and to give my son access to a good education."

The impetus to leave was strongest among young adults, ages eighteen to forty. Many sought work outside the community: in La Ceiba, Tegucigalpa, and San Pedro Sula, or they migrated to the United States. Some young men opted to "ship out," trying their luck as seamen in the growing international cruise-ship industry. Regardless of the work pursued, it was generally understood that to *buscar un futuro*—obtain a future—one must leave the community. Youth I spoke with often complained about the economic stagnation they experienced on a daily basis. Job opportunities within the community were sparse and low paying. Therefore, leaving the community was the only means of acquiring the capital needed to build a durable home and to secure family well-being. But this perspective was tempered by the hardships Garifuna face when living and working in other areas of the country or in the United States.

Leticia's resolve to leave the community was echoed by Selvin and Wilson, students in my English class, who desired to find work as seamen. Wilson had experience working as a cook, and I assumed he would pursue that line of employment on the cruise ship, but instead he had applied for a lower-level position as a busboy. "Chris, I don't want to enslave myself—*¡la cocina es para matar!*" (kitchen work is brutal!). He saw the job as a means to an end, but he was not enthusiastic about the prospect of leaving Triunfo and was apprehensive about the sacrifices his work on the ship would entail.

Wilson extolled the privilege of living by the sea, the quality of the food, and the natural beauty of the beach—all things that would be denied on a cruise ship. Selvin agreed. Staring into the distance, he stated, "*Aquí hay vida* and we don't know how to value it. Without a doubt, life here is more comfortable and accessible than in the city." *Aquí hay vida* (here there is life) was a common refrain; this was not merely a reference to the privilege of living by the sea but also a declaration of the freedom lost when Garifuna go to work outside the community. Life in the city, or on the cruise ship for that matter, was rough.[4]

Selvin's comments about having a more comfortable life in Triunfo reveals a key element of prosperity frequently mentioned by Garifuna I spoke with—much of what is good in life, I was told over and over, has nothing to do with wealth. Instead, everyday experiences of racism and precarity generate a different orientation to the future that challenges the capitalist assumptions upon which normative ideas of progress are predicated. Thus, although it was important to have things such as a *casa de bloque* (cement-block home), fresh kicks, and a good education, the need for a space where "we rule ourselves" was also of crucial significance to community youth.[5] Both Wilson and Selvin decried the cost of living in the city—namely the high rents, taxes, and transportation expenses—but these frustrations were irrelevant, they conceded, since "there is no work here," and thus one feels obligated to leave. But even in the city, they observed, "dignified employment was difficult to find," a reality that was especially stark for Garifuna given the prevalence of employment discrimination against Black people.

Cristina, a recent high school graduate in tourism management, opined on this issue while articulating a particularly poignant vision of Garifuna autonomy:

> The Garifuna has always been autonomous and she doesn't liked to be bossed around by others. . . . For this reason there are many young people that leave and come back, leave and come back again. Why? Because we don't like to be ordered around. So, if we are going to be employed, we will not take shit from others! I will return to my community, because in my community I will eat. even if it is only *tapo con pescado* [fish with vegetable roots in coconut milk]. The Garifuna has always been this way and when she loses her autonomy, she will lose everything. (interview, November 19, 2009)

For Cristina and others in her peer group, Triunfo is conceived of as a space where one has the ability to live autonomously; that is, to live as a free Black person. Garifuna may be poor, but Triunfeños share an awareness about the value of their territory—not something that can have a dollar amount assigned to it. In many ways, then, Cristina's statement speaks to notions of Black autonomy as an alternative value system rooted in a collectivist ethos and history of struggle that is intimately tethered to a future to which they already have access and which they must defend.[6] While young adults may find it necessary to migrate in order to satisfy material desires, they do so aware of the risks and with full confidence that, in moments of distress, they can return to the community.

In contrast to the prevailing ideas of what constitutes development, community members often alluded to the good life already accessible in Triunfo, which was inextricable from the land and sea, and which was at risk of being usurped by wealthy mestizo investors and their allies in the National Congress. There is a palpable sense of pride among Triunfeños, a notion that "we have this and they want it," which muddles the temporal logics of progress. Nonetheless, some Triunfeños were willing to exchange communal resources for "development" and in particular for access to credit—as several of the *empresarios* had done to launch their businesses.

By recognizing the variety of perspectives on tourism and the contradictions that permeated everyday conversations on development, I was able to glean two opposing notions of a good life. One version was propagated by investors, state officials, multilateral institutions and local business owners who desired—with varying degrees of fervor—to transform the Bahía de Tela into the next Cancún. The other version was informed by the experiences of Triunfeños who had spent time living and working outside the community and the realization that in Triunfo *hay vida*.

Doña Lily, an Garifuna elder who was well known for her baked goods and, my favorite, *calabu* (a warm, sweet and hearty porridge made from coconut milk, hominy, sugar, and spices), told me, "Tourism will be development for *them*, not for us." By this, she meant to distinguish the beneficiaries of tourism development from the community. She lamented the trajectory of the community and the "individualistic vision" of younger Triunfeños who she assumed to be wrapped up in the promises of a future untold. These youth were, according to Doña Lily, too committed to materialism that would eventually lead to the demise of Garifuna culture, but as I have shown, their resolve to *buscar un futuro* was neither a wholehearted embrace of "progress" nor a complete rejection of the "ancestral."

Dispossession and Resistance in Triunfo

The Government of Honduras began titling Garifuna landholdings in 1887 under the *ejidal* system, in which public or national lands were conferred on Indigenous and Black communities.[7] Just about a century later, starting in the 1990s, Garifuna activists and organizations, including the Black Fraternal Organization of Honduras (OFRANEH) and the Organization for Ethnic Communitarian Development (ODECO, by its Spanish acronym), lobbied the government for the expansion of these titles, resulting in additional land concessions to the communities. The most notable was that, under the Law for the Modernization and Development of the Agricultural Sector, many of Honduras's coastal Garifuna communities received deeds of full ownership (*dominio pleno*) for the lands that they already occupied—thousands of acres that had been passed from one generation to the next, often without any formal acknowledgment of ownership from the government. Triunfo received title for 380 hectares of land; this was in addition to a previously conferred deed guaranteeing occupancy for 126.40 hectares. These collective titles, while a remarkable achievement, were mostly limited to the *casco urbano*—the area where community members constructed their homes.[8] Lands critical to Garifuna spiritual, economic, and cultural life remained untitled or with liminal legal status and protections. The state and private investors have repeatedly exploited gaps in existing titles to dispossess Garifuna of their lands.

Although community lands are collectively owned and managed, Garifuna also recognize individual rights to land for residential use and for farming.[9] Historically, as we have seen, Garifuna could sell their individual plots to other Garifuna but not to non-Garifuna. All sales were to be validated by the *patronato*, and a percentage of each sale went into the communal coffers, which were subsequently designated for projects of benefit to the entire community. Some Garifuna opposed to the existence of collective land tenure regimes have pointed to the discrepancy in who can buy and sell lands as a form of reverse racism, arguing that "whites" are intentionally barred from land ownership on racial grounds.[10] But those who are committed to land defense see the sale of lands to non-Garifuna as the beginning of the end. They argue that such a practice will ensure the disintegration of territorial resources and radically transform the cultural practices that have sustained these resources for generations. This position is maintained by the land defenders and OFRANEH.

As mentioned previously, the Honduran state has recognized the inalienability of collective land titles held by Indigenous and Black peoples. However, official recognition has been undermined at different levels of government. In the case of Triunfo, the municipality of Tela authorized land sales between Garifuna and non-Garifuna in a practice that accelerated in tandem with the emergence of tourism as a key development objective. Legal loopholes, such as those sanctioned by the Tela Property Registry, in combination with deepening community divisions around the issue of individual versus collective land ownership, has fueled a surge in speculative land grabs within Triunfo's territorial boundaries. Other forms of dispossession result from economic entanglements between individuals in the community and the financial system.[11] The use of lands as collateral for bank loans, for example, has resulted in several instances of land loss. Community members who are unable to repay their loans end up forfeiting communal lands. Another common tactic used by mestizos (often called *indio* or *blanco* by Garifuna) is to ask a Garifuna to buy a plot of land on their behalf; rights of ownership are then transferred to a third party in direct violation of customary land tenure rules.

Garifuna land defenders have met significant opposition, not only from agents of the state and private investors but also from within the community, particularly from the *empresarios* who looked favorably upon state-backed tourism development plans. The first major land conflict in Triunfo emerged following a proposal to build an eco-resort and residential community on eighty hectares of beachfront land in an area historically used by Garifuna for farming. First conceived in 1993, plans for "Club Marbella" included a Mediterranean style hotel comprised of twelve three-story buildings, each containing twenty-two rooms, a gym, a marina and dock, and 200–250 private homes. Luxury residences on the resort would range in size from 2,150 to 4,300 square feet.

Marbella was a dream project for the government, with the potential to spur investments in many more luxury real estate developments along the coast. The project, however, also generated fierce resistance from Triunfeños, who were furious about its impact on Garifuna land rights and the surrounding ecosystem. The investment firm backing the project, IDETRISA, claimed to have purchased the lands legally and in accordance with Honduran laws and provisions regarding the private acquisition of coastal lands for tourism development. Yet the firm's account contrasted dramatically with the stories I gathered from Garifuna who alleged that they were duped—or in some cases coerced—into selling the lands. Designed to abut the Río Plátano, in the buffer zone of the Punta Izopo National Park, Marbella also had the potential to generate significant ecological damage to the adjacent wetlands.[12]

Carla, leader of the land defenders, explained that the privatization of communal lands in Triunfo accelerated in 1993—just a few months before the Marbella project came to light—when the municipality of Tela expanded its urban jurisdiction to include the Garifuna communities of Triunfo, San Juan, Tornabé, Miami and La Ensenada. This corresponded with the promulgation of Decree 90/90, which was used to modify the constitutional prohibition against the sale of coastal lands to foreigners (Article 107 of the Constitution). Decree 90/90 allowed for the acquisition of coastal property by individuals and business societies, provided the land was located in urban jurisdictions and earmarked for tourism development. The regulatory framework stipulates that property acquisition by persons of foreign birth, or via business associations that include non-Hondurans, must request approval from the Honduran Institute of Tourism.[13] The implementation of this decree generated a significant shift in authority over lands within Garifuna communities. The Honduran Institute of Tourism (IHT) could now enter into direct alliance with municipal authorities and even environmental NGOs to facilitate tourism development objectives in Tela Bay (Loperena 2016a).

In retelling this history, Carla observed:

> At this time the municipal corporation began to sanction illegal land sales within Triunfo. The community was not aware of the plans they were hatching against us. As soon as we realized what was happening, we formed a committee of local researchers to investigate what was happening with our lands, which we later named the Committee for Land Defense. That was 1994—the birth of the community land defense movement. (interview, November 24, 2009)

Conflict surrounding the construction of the Marbella project generated a climate of violence and fear within Triunfo, leading to escalating threats, persecution, imprisonment, and the murders of several community leaders affiliated with Committee for Land Defense (CODETT, by its Spanish acronym): Jesús Álvarez, after numerous threats to his life, endured a fatal knife attack in downtown Tela in May 1997; Zacarías Santos was shot to death in his home in June 1997; Jorge Castillo Jiménez and Julio Alberto Norales were killed in October 1997 just after filing a police report denouncing acts of violence and intimidation against the community. Carla laid blame for their deaths on investors and municipal authorities who had a hand in the development of the project.

Marbella was finally halted in 2003 after the community filed a formal petition with the Inter-American Commission on Human Rights, in which it alleged state complicity in the violation of Garifuna collective property rights, which were protected by ILO Convention No. 169. Following a series of hearings in Washington, DC, the commission granted precautionary measures to key community activists, including Carla, but that did not stop developers and municipal authorities from aggressively pursuing their agenda.[14]

Although the Marbella project was placed on hold, pending a resolution from the commission, the community confronted several additional threats to their collectively held lands, as developers pushed forth with plans to transform Triunfo into an upscale enclave for elite mestizo families and visiting tourists. The conflict came to a head when the *empresarios*, backed by the municipal government, staged what some Triunfeños referred to as "a coup" against the *patronato* elected by the community in 2005.

Chepe, then president of the *patronato*, narrated the events that led to the schism. The community suffered extensive losses in the wake of Tropical Storm Gamma. The storm destroyed dozens of homes and hundreds of acres of cropland when gushing floodwaters cut a path through Triunfo's agricultural fields, leading to the formation of the "Gamma River." The government of Honduras promised to disburse foreign disaster aid equitably to affected areas of the country, including to Triunfo, but Chepe was wary of the government's motives. He believed the aid would be attached to conditionalities that would further threaten the community's autonomy: "If there is an emergency, we need to take the first steps to address it, because there are people in the community with sufficient resources to help, to give. We cannot help ourselves if we are only inclined to wait on help from outsiders" (interview, November 20, 2009). His insistence on self-help as a means of defending the community's autonomy built on a longer tradition of collective labor and mutual aid, in which Triunfeños bound together in times of need. But others in the community, namely the *empresarios*, adamantly disagreed.

According to Chepe, they wanted to exploit the crisis to rebuild and modernize their businesses and to seek debt forgiveness for previously obtained business development loans. The tension between the two groups was already brewing prior to Gamma, but the storm hastened the community divide. At its core was a conflict over who should benefit from the influx of development aid and tourism investments—individuals or the collective—and how these resources would affect Triunfo's autonomy.

Shortly after Gamma, officials at the municipality of Tela facilitated a meeting in the community purportedly to mend communal divisions. Both groups were invited to attend. Within minutes of the opening, the *empresarios* accused Chepe of mismanaging disaster relief funds and called for a vote to replace him. Chepe and his supporters, who were already suspicious of the municipality's motives, stormed out of the meeting. The municipality—in a breach of established legal protocol—certified Ricardo and his council as the new *patronato*. Meanwhile, Chepe's group remained registered as the legitimate communal authority in Tegucigalpa. Even after Carla was elected to replace Chepe in 2007, Ricardo continued to preside over the *patronato paralelo* with the full backing of municipal authorities.

In 2013, I met with Lorena—a development project administrator at the municipal headquarters in Tela. She worked for the Office of Governability and Transparency in 2006 when the *empresarios* formed the parallel governing council. Lorena began by sharing details about the projects the municipality supported in the community, including one intended to bring potable water to families who remained dependent on well water but that was the subject of intense debate within Triunfo. Triunfeños aligned with the land defenders feared the project would compromise the community's independent control over the management and distribution of water. Historically, an elected water board (*junta de agua*) was tasked with maintaining the water source and managing the community's water needs, without fee. Lorena said the system was not only antiquated but also ineffective and unsanitary; she dismissed the arguments in favor of the old system as "backward." I then asked her if she was aware of the existence of two *patronatos* in Triunfo. She said yes, describing Chepe and his successor Carla as radicals who were "antiprogress." The existence of two competing *patronatos* within Triunfo, both with some form of institutional legitimacy, further compromised communal land tenure security, which—for the duration of my research—was a hallmark of daily life.

Progress as Ruse

To *progress*, according to the *Oxford English Dictionary*, is to move forward in time and space; it is also to advance to a higher stage, and thus has inherent ethical and temporal connotations. Ricardo, leader of the *empresarios* and proprietor of the restaurant Rico's Place, understood this clearly; indeed, his political views drew liberally from prevailing discourses of uplift—namely poverty reduction and human development—and the rhetoric of communal autonomy used by activists opposed to large-scale tourism developments. In my first conversation with Ricardo, we sat on the patio of his restaurant, and he introduced me to his vision of Triunfo's bright future. I found myself nodding along, agreeing reflexively with his every, carefully chosen word. His networks were vast, both within the municipality of Tela and across development institutions, he assured me, and thus he was the leader with the capacity to guide the community toward future prosperity.

Most of the explicitly tourism-oriented businesses owned by Garifuna in Triunfo were aligned with Ricardo's *patronato*.[15] The economic clout of these businesses varied significantly, but business owners exercised additional political sway within the community due to their ability to lobby external institutions for financial support.[16] Among some factions, tourism businesses were deemed more valuable than other Garifuna-owned businesses, including *pulperías* (small convenience stores) and restaurants that served a primarily Garifuna clientele. The *empresarios* promoted a vision of Triunfo as tourism destination, which they believed would lead to economic and social progress.

A number of local tourism businesses in Triunfo have benefited from seed grants, loans, and hospitality training programs funded by international financial institutions, including the World Bank's Prosperity Fund (Fondo Prosperidad). Ricardo explained:

> In 2005, we had the good fortune of receiving a grant from the Prosperity Fund, a World Bank–funded grant that is managed by the Honduran Tourism Institute, and which forms part of the National Sustainable Tourism Program. Right now we are trying to determine how to secure

another grant from the Fondo Fomento al Turismo [Tourism Promotion Fund], which we would have access to via the [Interamerican Development ment Bank] loan that is being used to construct the Los Micos Beach and Golf Resort.[17]

Ricardo demonstrated a thorough knowledge of the institutions and programs dedicated to tourism development and together with other aspiring tourism entrepreneurs he was able to plug into these networks to materialize his business aspirations (fig. 3.1). His institutional ties to the municipality of Tela also gave him access to resources that were either out of reach for his rivals or outright refused, as a result of their staunch opposition to state-backed mass tourism development plans in Tela Bay.

Ricardo was also a trained consultant for business development and management. During our second meeting, he touted the efforts of his *patronato* to establish tourism businesses and specifically his role as adviser to aspiring business owners in Triunfo. When I arrived at his home office, Ricardo was seated at his desk assisting another Triunfeño in drafting a grant proposal for a project he sought to establish in Barrio Tiuna on the western

FIGURE 3.1: Flow of Money, Prosperity Fund (Fondo Prosperidad).

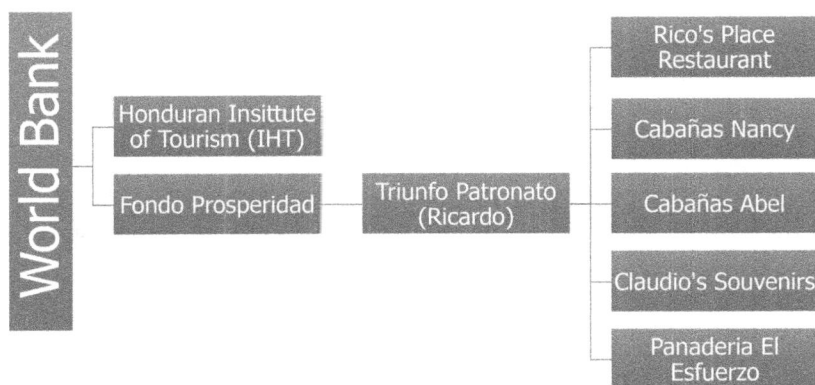

Source: Made by author. This chart represents only the beneficiaries identified by Ricardo. I was not able to fact check with World Bank documentation, but I wish to create a visual for how local tourism businesses link up to institutional resources earmarked for the promotion of tourism in the region.

end of the community. Ricardo's client, a tall lanky man who appeared to be in his late forties, told me he owned an *horno ancestral* (a traditional oven made of clay) that he used to bake Garifuna sweet breads, but he was meeting with Ricardo to develop a proposal to acquire an industrial baking oven to "improve quality and increase output." Ultimately, he sought to establish a café to sell baked goods, coffee, and tea to visiting tourists.

According to Ricardo, community-led tourism development was the only means of confronting the "monster of tourism."

"What is the monster of tourism?" I asked.

"The Los Micos Project," he replied—referring to the Indura Beach and Golf Resort—"it is the only way to survive—by establishing our own businesses, we can eradicate the high levels of unemployment in our community and promote local development. This is the course of the local economy." When Ricardo talked he reminded me of the project brochures written by the World Bank that touted the poverty-reducing, job-making potential of tourism. His promotion of tourism businesses was in essence an ethical project underscored by the need to improve the community's economic outlook and posited as an alternative to the "monster" that threatened to further disenfranchise the community. Tourism, he asserted, was the only viable path forward.

Ricardo's criticism of the Indura project, and its cannibalistic vision of tourism, was impassioned. And yet at the same time, he also supported the ODECO-sponsored negotiations with the developers of the resort, in which Garifuna communities located along Tela Bay would be included as *accionarios* (stockholders) in the project.[18] The five communities—Miami, Tornabé, San Juan, La Ensenada, and Triunfo—signed a memorandum of agreement with the state and investors on April 12, 2008, in which 7 percent of the government's stockholdings in the resort would be redistributed to the affected communities for local development projects.[19] With reference to this agreement, Ricardo asserted, "It gives us an opportunity to be more than just objects." His language echoed the rhetoric of ODECO's founding director, Celeo Álvarez, who in a prior conversation told me: "[Investors] have used and reused our people impulsively to serve their needs. We must change the dominant way Afro-Honduran people are seen. We need to be seen as humans and not like simple objects" (interview, September 11, 2009).

Celeo and Ricardo's comments demonstrate how Garifuna can be willing development subjects while also rejecting the forms of "thingification" that make Black people into mere instruments of production (Césaire 2000).

I asked Ricardo to explain what he meant. He said, "Well, Garifuna could work as receptionists and in other positions at the resort, not just as dancers for the tourists." While a receptionist position might offer steady income, it was still a low-paying job and thus not likely to meet the desires of Garifuna youth to "obtain a future." But for Ricardo, access to a wide range of formal employment opportunities on the resort would ensure full Garifuna participation in the tourism economy as opposed to being included in purely subordinate roles or, worse yet, entirely excluded from the promised riches. At the end of the meeting Ricardo admitted that he might be wrong: "Not all of the community is an agreement with my actions." This admission seemed to me a tacit recognition of escalating communal concerns regarding the impact of tourism on Garifuna land rights.

Our meeting helped me to glean a deeper understanding of Ricardo's perspective on development and his commitment to promote tourism as the way forward for the local economy. He desired to instill administrative discipline in the community and, in his words, "to exploit the capacity of each individual" in the creation of a tourism-friendly business environment that could solidify Triunfo's position as a global destination. The disciplinary component of his vision resonated with leading development discourses, such as the ethical mandate to be self-actualizing (Han 2012; Freeman 2014), which was deemed a respectable aim even among his detractors. It is further embedded in an ethico-political regime that promotes individual participation within the tourism economy as a means of achieving well-being. I contend that this possibility is promoted by the state and multilateral institutions through development policies that enable small-business creation—contingent on the acquisition of credit or debt—and that hinge on an autonomous Indigenous subject with the capacity to harness market opportunities for self-improvement.

Programs like the Prosperity Fund and environmentally friendly projects that promote "sustainable and participatory" development all shed light on the larger moral principles advanced by multilateral development institutions in the 1990s and early 2000s. Ricardo's commitments to this moral mandate—progress—was illustrated through his intent to make tourism into a viable local industry, but the question whether he was making errors loomed large. It became clear that development was at the root of community conflicts over land and, more importantly, the future. Indeed, debates over the future were deeply enmeshed with interpretations of the past and struggles over what it means to be Garifuna, as an identity and a way of living ethically. In this vein, statist development schemes presented the community with an ethical dilemma (Zigon 2007), between a perceived traditional way of being and a newly introduced modern ethos that would allow young Triunfeños to be legible as subjects of development and, in turn, capable of progress.

Garifuna inclusion within coastal development plans rested on the ability to be self-directed participants in the tourism economy, aided by small-business lending programs and technical trainings. This racialized political-economic calculus presumed Black and Indigenous peoples lacked the financial know-how and training to be full subjects of development. To achieve this lofty goal, they would need to learn how to turn dormant assets—land, beach, and culture—into capital via the creation of small businesses.

The Program for the Integral Development of Autochthonous Peoples (Desarrollo Integral de los Pueblos Autóctonos, or DIPA) was funded by the Inter-American Development Bank and formally launched under the administration of Manuel Rosales Zelaya in 2008. One branch of the program was administered through the Office of Autochthonous Peoples, and the other branch operated as a subdivision of the Honduran Social Investment Fund (FHIS, by its Spanish acronym). According to the DIPA's FHIS coordinator Omar Cacho, the general objective of the DIPA program was to "contribute to the betterment of the life conditions of the autochthonous peoples of Honduras and to the sustainable and integral development of the economic, social, cultural and environmental spheres" (interview, January 25, 2010).

Cacho said the creation of businesses was not only a means to alleviate poverty reduction but also a necessary component of land defense strategies: "For Garifuna to be able to stay in their communities depends on local conditions. If there is a source of employment, the logical conclusion is that they will return to the community" (interview, January 25, 2010). This sentiment was shared by Hugo Galeano, director of the UN Small Grants Program, who said, "Opportunities to wield political influence [in issues pertaining to land rights] will emerge from these productive processes" (interview, March 9, 2010). In other words, one must demonstrate business skills and the capacity to manage their territory to be able to defend against land dispossession. He posited business acumen and the values of free enterprise as prerequisites for inclusion in "development" and for land defense. Through the Small Grants Program, the United Nations has funded small-business initiatives in several coastal Garifuna communities. Given the huge investments in tourism, many of these projects have been earmarked for the creation of tourism microenterprises.

Lumagadien Trompu was an ecotourism project spearheaded by the women's cooperative Voz de las Mujeres and funded by the United Nations in Triunfo de la Cruz. The project included the construction of three ecotourism *cabañas*, a dining facility, and a meeting space, which received US$30,000 in funding. The project was conceived in part as a land defense strategy, because it was built on the same stretch of land where foreign investors were planning the luxury Marbella resort. Lumagadien Trompu was thus an effort to unite the goals of business creation with a political agenda advocating territorial rights. In this vein, Galeano asserted, "Tourism is a way to demonstrate presence in the territory so that Garifuna can influence politics, but this cannot be achieved solely on the basis of ancestral rights." From this observation, we can see how foreign aid was used to render the land economically productive in accordance with prevailing understandings of property (see chapter 1) while also upholding the aims of community members aligned with the land defense movement. In her description of the UN-funded project, Carla stated:

> We have a small hotel project [*cabañas*], which is a women's initiative to look for other economic alternatives, to generate a little bit of income. We were trained by OFRANEH and with their help we solicited the funds for the project. We were able to execute the construction of the project on our own, with our own efforts, but with money from the [UN]. We were able to administer and run the project successfully.

Despite Carla's characterization, Mr. Galeano classified the project as a "failure." He placed responsibility for the project's failure on OFRANEH's misuse of project funds and the alleged technical deficiencies of the women overseeing Lumagadien Trompu.[20] When I discussed these critiques with Carla, she offered a quick-thinking retort: "The project was established on disputed lands and thus served its purpose—demonstrating our presence and ownership over the land to refute illegal encroachments by developers." She also held the municipality of Tela responsible for obstruction, as it refused to run electricity cables to the project site. Without electricity, the project drew few tourists, and in 2009—only a few months after opening—the project was destroyed by a storm (fig. 3.2).

The Food and Agricultural Organization (FAO) of the United Nations has also supported a number of business creation projects in the Garifuna communities, all geared at strengthening local tourism development. In an interview with Carlos, a senior FAO official, he reflected on his previous

FIGURE 3.2: Picture of storm damage to the Cabañas "Lumagadien Trompu."

Photo: Christopher Loperena.

experiences working with both Garifuna and Miskito communities. "From my perspective, the Miskitos are stuck at a level of serious primitivism. In my opinion they have not evolved much since the times of colonization" (interview, February 24, 2010). This unusually candid display of racism was followed by the disclaimer "And neither do we (Westerners) understand them." He seemed to have a more favorable perception of Garifuna: "It is easier to work with the Garifuna population, because they integrate more easily into the occidental logic." The tension—as articulated by Carlos—is one of fundamental differences in value systems. For Carlos, "occidental logic" correlates to the acquisition of technical skills, and the capacity to successfully administer productive projects or small businesses. Again, the key issue underlying inclusion is the ability to play by rules set forth by the development establishment and NGO bureaucrats. It brings attention to the contemporary operations of cultural racism, which reinforces the racial subordination and exclusion of Black and Indigenous peoples at the same time that it holds promise for inclusion.

Under the supervision of the FAO, the Proyecto Comunitario Garifuna supported the creation of several tourism businesses in Triunfo by giving participants access to small-business loans. It purported to "make them into clients of the financial system so that they could aspire for better things." The microenterprises supported through the credit included: a trash pickup business (benefiting eight families), a cultural museum (nine families), an artisanal fishing cooperative (eight families), a baker's cooperative (twenty-four families), and an association of restaurant owners (eight families).[21] By and large, these productive projects support the creation of Garifuna entrepreneurs, through either individual or collective business models that promote local development. The project produced a clear improvement in the lives of some of the participating families, but on the whole it has served only to weaken—albeit unintentionally—the unity of the community.

The development *migajas* (crumbs) offered to Black and Indigenous beneficiaries of productive projects work in function of state development priorities, creating a bridge between macroeconomic initiatives and local economic desires to tap into these emerging markets.[22] In short, the creation of small businesses helps to sustain anticipation and hope for the tourism economy. They also sustain communal conflict, as opposing factions vie for access and control over the means of production. The extent of these development projects, from the funding through the training, are intended to render the land productive, either through its transformation into leisurescapes or, as we saw in chapter 1, into farms.

"Our Culture Is Holding Us Back"

Lucas, whom I met through Ricardo, invited me to visit his business in Barrio Tiuna. After greeting me, he walked me to the center of the patio and pointed to his recently completed oven. The large dome-shaped clay oven bulged out from under an oxidized tin roof. It had smooth rounded walls and a front "door" used to prevent heat from escaping. Lucas referred to the oven with pride, but he was quick to note that this was just the "humble beginning" of his more ambitious goal—to purchase an industrial oven. His business plan, if realized, would allow him to pay for the new oven and construct a small storefront café where tourists could come to have coffee and Garifuna sweet breads. The industrial oven would offer him a competitive advantage over other bakers in the community, and it would also be more "efficient." I asked him to explain what he meant by efficiency, since I assumed an electric oven would require more energy to operate. "It is more efficient, because it will place fewer strains on local resources [firewood] and make my business more profitable." In other words, it would be more environmentally friendly and at the same time increase his earning potential.

Lucas's business aspirations rolled off his tongue in a semi-rehearsed manner, demonstrating his mastery of development know-how; it seemed like he had been practicing how to sound just like the ideal business owner that Ricardo was trying to cultivate. He had a good command of the jargon of "scientific capitalism," carefully framing his business aspirations in the economic rationale of efficiency and self-help, two drivers of individual wealth creation. As Ferguson (2006, 80) observes, the technical and ostensibly nonmoral discourse of scientific capitalism is underscored by "notions of the inviolate rights of individuals, the sanctity of private property, the nobility of capitalist accumulation, and the intrinsic value of 'freedom' (understood as the freedom to engage in economic transactions)."

Lucas's neutral tone slowly morphed into a political screed, as he steered the conversation toward the larger questions of development within the community. He was very critical of the prevalence of "conservationism"[23]—a word he used to describe the "problem" of Garifuna culture. Lucas insisted, "We have to find a way to confront the monster of globalization," emphasizing "the need to find a way to overcome within this system," as opposed to being left behind or—to use his metaphor—flattened by the monster.[24] Although Ricardo had used this same metaphor to describe tourism, his use was somewhat different in that he imagined the community to be in a battle of epic proportions, in which failure to act would not only relegate them to the margins of the tourism economy but also potentially lead to their annihilation.

Lucas strongly opposed Carla's *patronato*, which he referred to as the "real *paralelos*."[25] He claimed their group was illegitimate, since it was not officially registered with the municipality of Tela, and insisted that its politically "conservative" (meaning: traditional) emphasis was impeding development. He continued to critique the group's tactics, arguing that it would ultimately "stunt the community's growth." Visibly upset, he remarked that this was not "any of my business," as I was not a *comunitario* (from the community). He went on to offer a blunt appraisal of what he perceived as my alignment with Carla, arguing that Ricardo was the real authority on community development. I acknowledged my ongoing work alongside the land defenders and then explained, somewhat meekly, that I desired to gain a clear understanding of both perspectives and visions.

Lucas smiled smugly, then began rattling off specific projects that Ricardo had spearheaded, such as the roof replacement at the *centro básico*. He used the school repairs to launch another criticism at Carla and her supporters: "They do not have the *capacity* to generate projects for the betterment of the community." This was an important, and oft-repeated, derisive remark that underscored two recurring themes in community politics: who is *capacitado* to lead and, relatedly, who has the ability to generate projects that will result in material gains. Ricardo's assumed superiority was proved through his successful navigation of the development terrain and his ability to channel funds to local projects and business initiatives. Projects that improved community infrastructure buttressed his authority in the community, even though he was also widely scorned for allegedly sanctioning illegal land sales.

When speaking about the development of the community, Lucas used the term *metamorphosis* to describe the change necessitated by the onslaught of tourism. He said, "A cocoon is difficult to break." In other words, change was imminent, but the community was still having difficulty breaking free from the cocoon. "Why?" I asked. "*Por nuestra cultura* [because of our culture]. It is difficult to explain, but our culture is holding us back. We are too busy looking back." He referred to the "hegemony of the ancestors," and in what seemed like an internalization of market discourse, complained about the failure of "morenos" to make progress.[26]

Lucas framed Garifuna culture as a problem to be overcome, reflecting a belief system that was widespread among the *empresarios*.[27] The cocoon metaphor thus had useful implications for Ricardo's larger vision: the development he sought for the community was an inherent good, if one could see past the shell. All that anyone needed to do was allow the butterfly's latent beauty to fully emerge.

The sudden interest in tourism as a means of livelihood was influenced by the precipitous rise in tourist arrivals, the simultaneous commodification of Garifuna lands and culture, and the surge in externally funded projects focused on the creation of tourism entrepreneurs. But the local tourism industry was still "in diapers" according to Lucas, and very few Garifuna had managed to successfully carve out a living as tourism entrepreneurs. Citing a lack of training in business administration, many Triunfeños echoed the complaints of tourism officials in Tela. For instance, Joel, the owner of a small cluster of *cabañas* under construction, told me, "The *morenitos* don't know about business."[28]

Joel insisted Carla's group was *contra el progreso* (antiprogress), but, according to him, "evolution" was inevitable. In our conversation, he repeatedly stressed the conflict over collective and individual property regimes and also the importance of having business savvy in order to facilitate investments and lead the community out of *el monte*—the bush, or lands that remained underdeveloped. Again, the *empresarios* deemed themselves more prepared to lead the community down the path of progress, whereas members of Carla's group were labeled conservative and inept. This political narrative mirrored the racialized discourse of development officials and mestizo entrepreneurs in Tela and Tegucigalpa, many of whom considered Garifuna incapable of productive participation in the national economy, aside from a few standout community leaders. These ideas reverberated within the community, especially among the *empresarios*, who sought to distance themselves from the perceived backwardness of the land defenders.

On April 2, 2009, in my second formal interview with Ricardo, he clarified his understanding of development:

> *Ricardo:* Development is first and foremost, to prepare oneself. A disc jockey at the local radio station, Faluma Bimetu, always said, "A people without education is inept." So, that is what we must aspire to—prepare ourselves, become trained [in marketable skills], encourage the youth to study, to go to school, to high school, to the university. One must dedicate oneself to one's studies, because it is the best way to *prepararse*.
>
> *Chris:* In terms of economic development, what do you consider to be the most appropriate mode of development for the community?
>
> *Ricardo:* The best way to achieve economic development is to make yourself into a small-business owner. Why? Because those people that have the capacity and know-how to become self-employed and generate their own income, will do so by becoming a business owner. We have seen that the best way to better the local economy is through the creation of small businesses.

He offered a personal anecdote on how he became a business owner to demonstrate the possibilities inherent in entrepreneurship:

> We saw that people were coming to the community in search Garifuna food. They came, visited the beach and then, because we live facing the ocean, they would come here during lunch time and ask for traditional Garifuna foods. And well, we visualized a business plan and we built a small makeshift house on the beach to meet the needs of tourists. At the end of that season, we realized that it was really worth it. We worked in that way for three consecutive years, only working during Holy Week,

but then I realized that the business could meet my financial needs during the entire year.

Ricardo's success highlights his own agency in recognizing an opportunity and acting to reap the benefits. His "will to improve," to echo Tania Murray Li (2007), was reiterated by other Garifuna entrepreneurs, such as Nancy, who explained:

> The tourists began arriving in 1992. They were mostly European tourists and a smidgen of North Americans. They lived in tents on the beach and we decided to construct six casas *típicas de manaca* [palm huts]. Little by little we grew the size of our business, making improvements along the way.

Today the hotel consists of eighteen rooms ranging in size from one to three beds. The entire hotel is constructed from cement *bloque*, which is a more durable construction material and widely recognized as a sign of progress and upward mobility. The success of her business is also a testament to her hard work and ability to self-actualize her development desires.

Autonomy as Refusal

Shortly after my arrival in Triunfo in 2008, Carla engaged me in a conversation about community divisions. Ricardo, she said, "is a *vendido* [sellout] and is not sufficiently conscious to develop his own critique of development." I was struck by her use of the word *sellout*, a term Triunfeños used to ridicule certain Garifuna: those people who were embarrassed of their culture or not sufficiently knowledgeable about their history or who sold land to non-Garifuna. Ricardo did not speak Garifuna and he was born in the city, which also fed arguments regarding the inauthenticity of his claims to place. During a communal meeting at 22 Manzanas (see chapter 4), Carla proclaimed, "Ricardo has the vision of the city—he was born and raised in the city of Tela. He does not have Garifuna *pensamiento* [ways of thinking], and that is why he wants to make Triunfo into an appendage of Tela." By calling into question his identity as Garifuna, she sought to undermine his vision for the development of Triunfo and, more critically, his ability to protect communal autonomy. Garifuna, she argued, were a culturally distinct people and thus should not be lumped together with mestizo city dwellers, or adopt their ways of thinking and living.

Similar to the *empresarios*, Carla's vision for the future was guided by an explicit ethical orientation to the community's future prosperity, which had been greatly reconfigured by the prospect of tourism in Tela Bay. Carla, however, pitted Garifuna modes of living and ancestral land use practices against the accommodationist strategies employed by her adversary, and she was quick to dismiss critiques from her opponents, especially the attempts to undermine the intelligence and capacity of the so-called *viejas* (elderly women) that constituted her base. "Capacity for what? What does that have to do with anything?" she asked indignantly. "Our ancestors were not *capacitados!*" Her assertion not only challenged the racist logics embedded within state development schemes, regarding the deficiencies—educational, cultural, and moral—of Garifuna, but also underscored the importance of ancestrality to people like Carla figuring out very modern visions of collective self-determination. The spirits of their ancestors were a guiding force in the struggle to defend Garifuna territory and, for many, a source of pride.

Both *patronatos* proclaimed to be the legitimate communal authority, and both professed to struggle for Triunfo's future, but there were key differences in their approaches to working with the community, and more importantly, key differences in how they aligned politically with external institutions. Members of Carla's group refused to work with the municipal authorities, because the authorities had on many occasions undermined Triunfo's autonomy through the authorization of illegal land sales, as well as ongoing attempts to establish fee-based utility services within the community. At that time, water and trash management were run by community elected committees, but the *empresarios* saw a need to modernize communal infrastructure to increase tourism.

The tense relationship between the community and the municipal government was the result of Tela's unrelenting attempts to expropriate Garifuna lands. Some feared the municipal government would make Triunfo into a suburb (*barrio*) of Tela.[29] Puntito, a taxi driver with dreadlocks that reached below his shoulders, told me, "If they make us into a suburb of

Tela, our lives will become much more difficult. We will have to start paying taxes, water, everything. They want to take the little bit that we have for their pockets." Thus to defend communal autonomy in the face of *barrioization* was also a struggle to ensure community members could continue to afford and manage their own services and utilities, such as the *represa comunitaria* (community-managed dam), the *centro básico* (public grade school), and the community health clinic. Although the local government provided some financial and technical support for these services, Triunfeños operated and maintained communal infrastructure through a system of collective work and established kinship and neighborhood networks. Autonomy thus was not reducible to the conservation of "traditional" ways of being, as argued by the *empresarios*, but rather a practice to fend off the incursion of state bureaucracies into communal life. Efforts by the government and private enterprise to capitalize on Triunfo's resources could potentially erode long-standing communal structures that were vital for the survival of Triunfeños. It was in essence an assault on the tenets of autonomy that are of crucial importance to Indigenous struggles throughout the Americas.

In an interview with the mayor of Tela, David Zaccaro, he complained to me about the "tributary problem" in the community, stating that Triunfeños refused to pay taxes to the municipality:

> Where you live, you have to pay taxes, many types of taxes—municipal taxes, state taxes, you pay to use services that you want. When there are problems, you can make claims, because you pay for the services. So, together with Ricardo and other *progressive* leaders, we have tried to combat this idea of *auto-marginalization* that some of the communities have—under the guidance of certain leaders—but it is a long journey, that demands lots of strength. The only way to grow is to grow together, which can happen when we have it clear in our minds that we are one government and one team. And this is something that we have been able to achieve with some of the younger leaders that have a different mentality. But I try to be very discreet in this, because I don't want to offend the sensibilities of others. I am being very honest and I am not playing politics. (interview, April 2, 2009)

Zaccaro's complaint about Garifuna who refuse to pay taxes reveals a deeper discomfort with the community's claims to autonomy, which he derisively refers to as "auto-marginalization." Refusal manifests not as mere resistance to state bureaucracies but as a generative reorientation to communal self-determination and an insistence on "a certain grounding in the world" (McGranahan 2016, 321), one that animates social cohesion among *comunitarios*. Moreover, a regulatory framework does not exist for the taxation of communally held lands, something that was threatened by state efforts to map Indigenous and Black territories and that land activists sharply opposed.[30]

Community members, including those who avoided making public proclamations of allegiance to Carla's group, frequently debated the stark contrasts between Carla's and Ricardo's perspectives on communal development. Angel and Janet, two of my closest friends in the community, explained to me that the same *grupito* (little group) is behind land sales, all of whom were affiliated with Ricardo's *patronato*. Janet's elderly mother, Doña Norma, was sitting on the patio fanning herself with a thin piece of cardboard as we discussed the problem of land sales. She was quiet at first, but she spoke up to clarify the issue of communal land tenure in Triunfo.

> *Chris:* Before land was donated, right?
>
> *Doña Norma:* Yes, people did not have much, so when someone showed up in need of land, a local family would donate land to that person, but things have changed.
>
> *Chris:* Now land is sold, right?
>
> *Janet:* Yes.
>
> *Chris:* But even among native Triunfeños?
>
> *Janet:* Yes, and it is expensive to buy land.
>
> *Angel:* Just that parcel that is there by the restaurant owned by Justina's son is selling for 350,000 lempiras [US$19,500].
>
> *Chris:* Wow, that is a lot of money! But only another Garifuna can buy the land, right?
>
> *Angel:* An *indio* [mestizo] will probably have a Garifuna purchase the land and then take over the parcel. That is what happens often.
>
> *Doña Norma:* No, then we will take it back!

Angel: Ricardo, as president of the *patronato*, has legitimated the sales. Look at Marbella.

Chris: And what about Playa Escondida [a private beach community adjacent to the Cerro Triunfo de la Cruz]?

Angel: Beto Guillén, the same person who sold 22 Manzanas, sold that land. He was *indio*.[31]

Doña Norma: He inherited the land from his father.

Janet: Before, his house was the only one located out there. It was *monte* and jungle.

Chris: So, was it always owned by *indios*?

Doña Norma: No, that land belonged to Blacks. I am Triunfeña. I know the history of my people! And there where Professor Abel has his *cabañas*, those lands were owned by my family. We donated the land to Abel, and when the family wanted to recuperate it, he said no.

According to Doña Norma, individuals sometimes take over lands belonging to another family without consultation. To avoid conflict, the original owners simply acquiesce to the loss. In other cases, mestizo investors have bought into the community by using Garifuna as proxies for the purchase of land.

Although women elders—the so-called *viejas*—were the most vocal advocates for communal autonomy, the land defenders also swayed increasing support from community youth. When I first met Selvin, he had a muscular build, a broad smile, and a full Afro. He earned a living as a construction aide in Triunfo and at times he joined his father, a respected fisherman, on short fishing expeditions. Selvin, as I explained earlier, aspired to become a seaman, which is a common pursuit among young men in the community. Indeed, it was a group of *marineros* (seamen) who requested I offer an English class to community youth, because all seamen are required to pass a basic English literacy test before they can "ship out" (gain employment on a cruise ship).

About two months into the class, Selvin found work at a *maquila* (factory) in San Pedro Sula. His dream of landing employment on a ship was beginning to fade, and he felt growing pressure to find a source of steady income. He eventually took a position as at a factory owned by Miguel

Facussé—one of the most notorious business leaders in Honduras, and the country's largest landowner before his death in 2014. However, after only a few months, Selvin returned from San Pedro Sula, having quit his job due to what he described as "abusive" conditions.

Selvin had lost a significant amount of weight. His hair was shaven close to the scalp, and he was more demure than I recalled from my class. I asked him about his work experience: "I worked from 7 a.m. to 7 p.m.; it was horrible." He said he was treated like an "animal," and confessed, "It's not worth it, Chris." After a short pause he continued, "Here we *live free*, we eat well—*machuca, albóndiga*—food that gives you strength." As mentioned previously, the importance of the land and the geographic privilege of living by the sea with access to plentiful seafood and fish was often brought up in conversations with community youth.

He went on to complain about the state of the community, the divisions in the leadership, and the problems these conflicts posed for the future of the community:

> The *empresarios* think they are the *cabezas* [heads] of the community, and many agree. But I think they are ignorant, because they are deeply indebted to the banks, which have financed their businesses. They really don't have anything, and in order to pay their debt they are willing to sell communal lands.

He was unmoved by their leadership and questioned their concern for the welfare of the community. "It is more about protecting their individual interests," he said. His words mimicked Carla's, who often critiqued the individualistic motivations propelling alienation of communal property. He also faulted the mayor of Tela, who, he alleged, had taken over lands on the eastern edge of the community. "That is why it is in the interest of the mayor to support Ricardo, because Ricardo and him legitimate each other's business interests."

Selvin chuckled as he gestured toward the beach, "This would be like pollution for the big hotels," he said pointing to the locally owned *cabañas*—many in need of repair—and the dugout canoes scattered along the beach. "All of these houses (pointing behind us) would be removed." This version of "paradise" he refused. He continued, "If it wasn't for Carla, we would not have land. If she says, *hasta aquí llego*, then we will remain landless." In other words, if Carla were to retreat from the land defense movement, the process of land privatization would reach its logical conclusion—total displacement.

Conclusion

The ethical struggle among the state, multilateral institutions, local *empresarios*, and land activists plays out both within the abstract realm of development discourse and the very concrete realm of beaches and streets and neighborhoods. And in both realms, the two sides of the conflict represent dramatically distinct visions of the future. People on both sides claim to be future oriented, or *futuristas*, but they have very different political aims, which I believe are loosely encapsulated by the politics of communal autonomy and the politics of progress. Thus, to be Garifuna is split into two dominant strands: progressive (modern) and conservative (ancestral), pitting individual freedoms against the autonomy of the collective and creating unprecedented challenges for unity. Of course these two views cannot capture the nuances in peoples everyday actions and political orientations—indeed, elements of each are creatively incorporated in local people's imagination of an autonomous Black future.[32]

For community members aligned with Carla's *patronato*, state-backed tourism development policies were bound up with the erosion of collective property regimes, and in that way, they presented real threats to collective survival. And yet projects like Indura are heavy with ethical contradictions, precisely because of their potential to generate employment opportunities and infrastructural improvements, including paved roads, potable water, and electrification—improvements that are widely coveted and which some community members view as modernization. How, then, can Carla and the land defenders, who are staunchly opposed to megatourism developments, articulate a political vision that is in favor of both autonomy and progress?

Finally, it is necessary to analyze the contradictory ethical standings of Garifuna, or what Faubion (2010) terms "ethical complexity." With reference to the prospect of mass tourism in Tela Bay, Nancy—the Garifuna hotel owner I introduced in the opening vignette—said:

> On the one hand, land sales are bad, because our children will not have a place to build their houses. On the other hand, maybe it can be a way to generate employment . . . so that people from the community could stay here and work, without having to take the risk of moving to San Pedro Sula or Tegucigalpa.

Nancy was not in favor of land privatization per se, nor was she wholly against development, which she acknowledged had the potential to generate jobs. She maintained hope for the promise of tourism but fretted over the implications for future generations of Triunfeños, particularly their ability to subsist on the lands they inherited from their ancestors.

4   RESCUE THE LAND, DEFEND THE FUTURE

My inspiration to participate in the struggle? I find inspiration in the history of my people, in their principles, in their suffering and their aspirations.

EDGARDO, land defender (2009)

ALBA CALLED AT ABOUT 10:45 P.M., her voice shaky. "Chris, sorry to wake you, but there is a serious problem," she said. "Carla and Miguel are surrounded by armed men at Barrio Indomables."

"What! How do you know?" I blurted as I jumped from my bed. She had received a call from Carla a few minutes earlier. They were on night duty at the site when a white double-cabin pickup truck showed up. Several men carrying guns jumped out of the back. "I am worried they may be in serious danger," she said. There was a short pause. "Chris, do you think you can go over there?" she asked reluctantly.

She was referring to a sandy stretch of land, dubbed Barrio Indomables— Land of the Unconquerable. The property had been seized five days earlier, the latest in a string of land recuperation efforts led by Carla and other community activists—primarily women—opposed to the privatization of communal lands in Triunfo. In light of the violent history of conflicts in the community and bloody confrontations over land in other areas of the country, such as the

Aguán Valley, I knew Alba's fear was well justified.[1] As I grabbed my camera and flashlight, I nervously scrolled through my cell phone contacts until I arrived at Leticia, my closest confidant in Triunfo. She immediately called her uncle Carlos, who agreed to accompany me to the site.

Neither of us spoke as Carlos drove toward Indomables; our heavy breathing was offset by the rattle of his rusty pickup speeding along the pitted dirt roads. We parked in front of Lucil's Store, about a kilometer from the property, and then walked down a dark and overgrown footpath until we reached the clearing. I dialed Carla. The field was empty and silent. There were no trucks in sight. "Carla, we just arrived. Where are you?" I whispered. "The truck left, Chris. I just got back home with the kids, but Miguel is still there. Be careful, because the hitmen may return."

We crossed the clearing cautiously and waded into an abyss of darkness. Eventually a flashing light signaled us toward Miguel and the rest of the group. The men, about ten in total, excitedly recounted the details of the night. A white double-cabin pickup with bright strobe lights arrived at about 9:30 p.m. As the pickup approached the clearing, one of the night watchmen—a closely allied *indio* (mestizo) by the name of José—blew into his blow horn repeatedly to ward off the unwanted company. They were certain the truck belonged to Toño Fuentes, a wealthy congressman from Tela who allegedly purchased the disputed land from the María Claret Credit Union. A Garifuna hotel owner had previously owned the property, but he forfeited ownership to the bank after using the land as collateral to acquire a loan. After the invaders heard the horn, the truck pulled into a house adjacent to the site, which was occupied by a group of men purportedly hired by Mr. Fuentes to watch over the parcel. Several heavily armed men exited the truck, keeping their strobe lights directed at the open clearing, and disappeared from view. About two hours later they left.

Eventually a police car from the City of Tela arrived at the scene. The officers spoke briefly with Miguel, scribbled some notes, did a half loop around the clearing, and exited on the road back toward Tela. "What are they going to do for us?" Miguel asked dismissively. "The officials in Tela want this land for Tela!"

This heart-pounding episode has multiple meanings. First, it demonstrates the ways in which racialized violence stemming from tourism development is intimately tethered to ideologies of progress, because this particular parcel was designated to become an upscale housing community—yet another attempt by elite mestizo investors to transform Triunfo into a beachside resort. It also sheds light on the multiracial coalitions forged in the struggle to defend communal lands, and the networks of women involved in the land struggle, the stakes they have in the movement, and the risks they confront as participants.[2] Explicit commitments to the land struggle do not preclude women from participating in the tourism economy, as I explained in the previous chapter; however, it does entail an ethos of relationality[3]—a sense of belonging to the land and vice versa, which is a central tenet of land recuperation tactics.

Industrial development in energy, agribusiness, and tourism after the 2009 coup d'état has coincided with a surge in violent repression against Indigenous and Black activists opposed to the state's economic agenda. State-sanctioned repression demonstrates the government's growing disregard for laws and protocols established to protect the ancestral rights of Indigenous peoples; it also underscores the significant risks borne by Black and Indigenous peoples, and especially women land defenders, in the defense of their territories. Their dedication to the *lucha* (the struggle) exposes their bodies to what social movement activists have begun to call the "death system"—the murderous economic model consolidated by the Honduran state and multinational capital in the postcoup conjuncture.[4]

Women's bodies are often on the front lines of efforts to recuperate expropriated communal lands in Triunfo. Their leadership positions them as the arbiters of the land struggle, allowing them to strategically mobilize gender difference and narratives of ancestrality to garner communal authority over matters of crucial political import. But the land defenders' leadership, as I demonstrated in the previous chapter, is staunchly opposed by the self-proclaimed *empresarios* (businessmen) who refer to them as "invaders." They view land recuperation as an affront to private property and a barrier to progress.

I begin with an analysis of land recuperation tactics. I then move into a discussion of ancestrality, a relational mode of living and being with the land that stands in contradistinction to the so-called progressive agenda of the *empresarios*. This leads into an analysis of women's work and the crucial role women play in the land defense movement. The labor of mothering, in particular, is a political and territorial praxis through which the land defenders build community cohesion in the struggle to contest the destination-making strategies of multinational capital on the Caribbean coast. Finally, I interrogate the forms of gendered anti-Black violence women activists confront and the larger implications of the *lucha* for Garifuna survival.

Rescate Territorial: Land Defense or Invasion?

Understanding "what land *is*," to cull from the work of Tania Murray Li (2014, 590), requires a deeper engagement with how land, "as an assemblage of material substances and social relations," is both constituted by and constitutive of larger social formations. For the land defenders, land is the axis around which notions of self and collective belonging cohere. Thus, a coordinated strategy of land defense and recuperation was necessary to stave off what some Garifuna referred to as "cultural genocide."

Land defenders use the verb *rescatar* (to rescue) to describe the act of recuperating lands that have been privatized, either through illegal sale or through theft. The *Oxford English Dictionary* defines the term *rescue* as "to set free" or to "deliver a person from the attack of, or out of the hands of, enemies." To rescue signals both the agentival capacity of the land as provider and the symbiotic relationship between the land and the people—one that is founded on principles of reciprocal care, of mutuality. Karuka (2019, 20) argues that "indigenous relationships in and with place are concrete, not just mystical." This is not to dismiss the mystical as irrelevant to Indigenous struggles in defense of their land, but he seeks to underscore how relationships between Indigenous people and their territories serve as a basis for materialist critique. Susana, a Garifuna elder and celebrated land defender, explained:

> If we sell the land, we will no longer have a territory and the ancestors will no longer be with us, because the Garifuna have a history. Garifuna have their culture, beliefs, there is a spirit that guides us, which is inseparable from the land. We no longer toil the land, we no longer fish, we no longer make *ereba* [a staple food made from cassava flour]. . . . Other

people are buying our culture and we will be left with nothing, without a soul.

Her comments gesture toward the significance of land to social reproduction and to Garifuna survival as a distinct people. The defense of land and its other-than-property value was thus critical for life now and in the future.

This sentiment was reiterated by Doña Gloria, a midwife and elder. In describing Garifuna childbirth practices, she told me: "The placenta, the umbilical cord, everything that comes out of the womb after [the mother] gives birth, is buried into the land, and in this way a connection is created." According to Doña Gloria, burying these parts of the body in the land "gives strength to the woman and the newborn" and ensures that both mother and child are free of illness. She likened this practice to the necessity of caring for the land by maintaining ancestral farming methods, most often the domain of women, and founded on principles of collective labor.

Women typically sowed, maintained, and harvested crops in collective work groups; each family laid claim to an individual plot within a larger communal farm (*trabajadero*) where they would work for a period of two to five years. They would then allow the land to lay fallow for ten to fifteen years to avoid overfarming. This system, known as *barbecho colectivo*, was necessary to ensure the land would maintain its fertility and vitality. Women's farming practices are resonant with the relational understanding of land as agent and giver of life. In this vein, severing access to lands may also endanger the possibility of a collective future. This understanding of the land stands in stark contrast to the economic logics that govern private property ownership and possession, in which land is simply a vehicle for rent or profit.

Who could rightfully claim the land and on what basis could such claims be made were key points of contention between the land defenders and the *empresarios*. Labeled as "invaders" by the opposing communal faction, the land defenders, rather than developers, were imagined as greedy interlopers who sought to disrupt the bedrock principle of capitalism—that individuals could (and should) own property. To counter these accusations, Carla and her allies couched their political actions, particularly the practice of *rescate territorial*, in ancestral presence and collective belonging—a point I develop more fully later in the chapter—in dialogue with international legal norms pertaining to the collective rights of Indigenous peoples. This two-pronged strategy also served to mitigate pervasive tropes of Black immorality and Indigenous primitivism that circulate at all levels of Honduran society. These dynamics came into sharp relief following a conflict over an area dubbed 22 Manzanas.

In January 1997, a few years after extending its urban jurisdiction over Triunfo, the municipality of Tela granted 22.87 *manzanas* (approximately sixteen hectares) of communal land to the municipal labor union in payment of a previous debt.[5] Individual plots were distributed among union members without prior consultation with the community, even though the lands were located within the boundaries of Triunfo's collective title. The municipality alleged that the lands were idle, that is, not in productive use, and therefore appropriable. The community rose up to impede the land transfer.

Land rights activists, organized by the Land Defense Committee of Triunfo de la Cruz (CODETT), launched a successful recuperation of the area. The rescue mission entailed establishing a permanent presence on the disputed land, dividing it up into plots for participating families, and clearing it for residential or agricultural use. A few months later, in what appeared to be an act of reprisal, Honduran authorities arrested Miguel, then president of CODETT, for his alleged participation in a drug-trafficking ring.

The land defenders accused the government of fabricating the charges against Miguel to undermine his moral authority and leadership of the *lucha*. Miguel's case garnered international attention when the Black Fraternal Organization of Honduras (OFRANEH) brought a petition to the Inter-American Commission on Human Rights.[6] The court, citing a lack of definitive evidence, ruled in favor of Miguel: "His right not to be subject to an arbitrary and illegal arrest or imprisonment was violated."[7] Immediately following his release, after serving seven years in prison, Miguel resumed his militancy in the land defense movement.

Miguel, along with his wife, Carla, and their five children, endured significant hardships because of their dedication to the struggle; their suffering became symbolic of the collective suffering endured by the entire community. Suffering for territory, to echo Donald Moore (2005), was a form of political labor and a means of staking claims to rights. As such, Miguel's lengthy detention and subsequent exoneration infused the land struggle with greater legitimacy.

During Miguel's imprisonment, Carla took on increasingly prominent roles within the movement to defend Triunfo's lands. In 2007 she was elected president of Triunfo's *patronato*. Upon assuming the presidency, she immediately set out to protect against further incursions from outsiders and to recuperate lands that had been previously privatized via illegal sales or theft. Notable for its multiracial composition and largely female base of support, Carla's supporters included Garifuna who were allied with the movement to defend communal lands and landless mestizo peasants (commonly referred to as *indios* or *blancos*) who had been granted permission to settle the area located at the entrance of the community, just off the main coastal highway. Although most of the indios could not claim Garifuna ancestry, they were considered to be Triunfeños by virtue of their commitment to issues of communal concern and allyship with the land defenders. What does this multiracial alliance signal, particularly in light of allegations from municipal authorities and the *empresarios* that Garifuna are racist against the mestizo population? Moreover, how might we rethink Black geographies, not just as places where Black peoples reside but also as spaces of radical imagination from which emancipatory epistemologies emerge (Kelley 2002; McKittrick 2006; Woods 2017)?

To answer these questions, I delve further into the history of territorial defense in Triunfo. Community land defenders have met mounting pressures to privatize communal lands with both legal proceedings against the state and direct action in the form of land rescues. Analyzing the interplay between these two strategies and the ways in which rights talk is folded into the everyday politics of autonomy in Triunfo is necessary to make visible the ethical and legal grounds on which land recuperations are executed.

Land of the Unconquerable

Carla's close alliances with OFRANEH, CODETT, and a cohort of militant women elders emboldened her to spearhead several land rescue missions over the course of my stay, including a contentious fight over the tract of land that would eventually be taken over and renamed Barrio Indomables, as we saw at the chapter's beginning.[8] Before the recuperation, and amid mounting concern that the parcel would be transformed into a resort-style residential community, Carla began to consider a land rescue mission. She knew that first she would need to gain sufficient support from the community because rumors about a potential takeover had already begun to raise questions about the rightfulness of such an action.

On June 9, 2009, the communal assembly, at Carla's suggestion, voted to conduct a community poll about ongoing land recuperation efforts, and specifically to the conflict over Barrio Indomables. The new owners, the family of the Honduran legislator Toño Fuentes, had begun clearing the land for future development, which heightened the concerns of community members opposed to the land sale. Over the course of three days, a team of surveyors walked door to door to determine whether there was sufficient communal support for the land recuperation. A community poll concerning the land situation in Triunfo de la Cruz included the following questions:

1. Do you agree we should continue to recuperate communal lands and what can we do to achieve this goal?

2. What can you do to support the unity of the community?

3. Do you want [Triunfo] to be a suburb of Tela?

4. The municipality of Tela insists on maintaining Ricardo's parallel communal governing council, to consolidate Tela's urban jurisdiction over the community and so that Triunfo becomes a suburb of Tela. Are you in agreement?

5. Do you support taking legal action against those who have sold communal lands to outsiders?

6. Are you prepared to support and participate in the recuperation of lands usurped within the community, as is the case of Nueva Delicias [later renamed Barrio Indomables]?

At the bottom of the survey there was a space provided for the surveyor and the surveyed to sign.

At the next week's meeting, Carla spoke emphatically about the survey results. The respondents, according to her, overwhelmingly supported the recuperation of the disputed parcel: "That land is ours and we are not going to let them come from Tela to invade!" Her assertion inverted the rhetoric of invasion Ricardo and others, as well as officials in Tela, used to refer to the land recuperation movement. By doing so, she positioned Triunfeños as the rightful owners of the land.

Following Carla's impassioned speech, Miguel informed the participants that Fuentes was trying to sway support for this project by paving the main access road—a project that had been stalled for over a year and that nearly all Triunfeños desired, given the deteriorating state of community roadways, which became nearly impassable during the rainy season. But, he warned, this was a ploy by Fuentes to convince community members to sell their lands. He said the same construction equipment being used to repair the entrance road was being used to level and fill the disputed land parcel. This allegation was followed by a rash of hisses and jeers.

On the following Tuesday—prior to the start of the meeting—one of the land defenders reported seeing armed guards at the site. Carla's eyes flared: "We will not let them intimidate us!" That same morning, under a cloudless sky, the assembly participants banded together to confront the security guards. The group was composed of Garifuna, *indios*, women, men, and children, about forty in total.[9] They shouted: "The people united! Will never be defeated!" We marched into the clearing and found only a single guard. Miguel ordered him to surrender the lands to the community. Placing his hands firmly on his shotgun, the guard took several steps back: "Mario Fuentes bought this land," he stammered. "He is the owner now and he sent me to protect his property." Shaken by the confrontation, he pleaded, "I am not at fault."

The guard watched helplessly as several youth allied with the struggle began uprooting the rickety wooden posts that had been erected along the outer perimeter of the property. Next, the group gathered together under a lone mango tree in the middle of the clearing. "We will begin to measure individual plots today," said Miguel. "What size shall we allot for each plot," he asked, "Twenty-five by twenty-five?" Meanwhile other participants began to imagine the layout of the land. "Over there will be a soccer field," said one woman. "And here a park," interjected Carla as she pointed to the space under the tree. "A street will run down the center of the clearing," added another, "and it will be lined with Garifuna-owned businesses!" In addition to the partitioning of the land into equal plots, the imagined layout of the space included an area for leisure and spaces for communal gatherings and cooperative work; it was therefore a powerful instantiation of a Garifuna vision of autonomy—a freedom gained via collective struggle and reciprocal care.

Carla was fully aware of the critiques circulating among her adversaries—that she was merely *aprovechando* (exploiting) communal divisions for personal gain, or that she was in fact stealing private property. But for the land defenders, this was not theft; it was justice. Land recuperations, such as the one at Barrio Indomables, were motivated by larger concerns about freedom and survival in the face of a racist and brutal state apparatus. Carla understood this intimately. She then called the participants together for a prayer: "This is God's will. This land belonged to our ancestors and therefore it belongs to us. It is our cultural inheritance. It is our future."

About an hour after we arrived, a police patrol car showed up. The entire group gathered to confront the four officers as they stepped out of the car. Miguel addressed them firmly, "You cannot come here and kick me out of my house." He reiterated: "We are not invading. These are our lands, and we have the documentation to prove it. Furthermore, we have a case before the Inter-American Commission on Human Rights and they have yet to pass a resolution; thus, there can be no legal transactions involving land in the disputed area."

The next day, when I arrived at Barrio Indomables, a construction crew was installing concrete posts around the perimeter of the property. According to Miguel, a group of mestizos hired to repair the entrance road were commissioned by Toño Fuentes to begin putting up the fence. They had also erected signs that read Propiedad Privada (private property) along the road running adjacent to the property. Miguel ordered the land defenders to tear down the signs. Meanwhile, a small group of *empresarios* gathered on the other side of the road, shaking their heads in disapproval. Doris, one the more colorful members of the group, cried out to them: "Stop fucking with us! Triunfo for Triunfeños, Tela for Teleños! You're selling out the community!" She then spit in their direction before turning toward me with a mischievous grin.

Some of the women collected firewood to begin cooking, while the others worked to build a thatched-roof shelter, or *galera* (fig. 4.1). Undeterred, two armed security guards slowly moved in our direction with a large reel of barbed wire that they were using to erect a temporary fence. Carla summoned the land defenders to put a stop to the construction, once and for all. The entire group marched up to the guards. "You cannot erect a fence here!" exclaimed Miguel, while vigorously waving the community's land title in their faces. He then signaled to the others to come up along the right and left side of the guards. The guards began backing up slowly, their fingers hovering nervously on the trigger of their shotguns. Miguel warned, "If you kill a Black person here, I promise that you won't make it to the exit."

For the land defenders, the prohibition against land sales to outsiders was not only mandated by the ancestors and thus crucial for their collective survival; it was also a central tenet in international jurisprudence pertaining to the rights of Indigenous peoples. Notions of ancestral being and occupation coarticulate with the emergence of international laws and norms created to defend the collective rights of Indigenous and Black peoples. As noted by Tianna Paschel (2016, 3), to understand the making of Black political subjects in Latin America, we must attend to the "global ethno-racial fields" in which movements and claim making are embedded. Garifuna claims to land are refracted and amplified through these larger political fields, including globally circulating discourses of ethno-racial rights. The Colombian Constitution of 1991 was pioneering in this regard,

FIGURE 4.1: Barrio Indomables. Photo taken shortly after the recuperation began. This structure became the main meeting space for community participants aligned with the land defense movement. The Garífuna flag is waving in the background.

Photo: Christopher Loperena.

because it recognized rural Black communities as a culturally distinct group with collective rights to land.[10]

Women's Work?

At first glance Garifuna communities look very traditional in terms of their gender roles—the men do the fishing, the women do the farming—but as I lived with them for longer, I learned that these traditional roles that women occupied were part of what infused their activism with a greater sense of purpose and urgency. Frequently derided for being antiprogress, women land defenders tied the struggle against land sales to gendered labor practices and ancestral ways of being.

Garifuna women have historically worked the land, harvesting crops that are central to the Garifuna diet, such as yuca (cassava), sugarcane, and plantains. Yuca in particular is crucial to household sustenance, as it is used in the production of *ereba*, a nutrient-rich flatbread prepared almost exclusively by women in collective bakehouses.[11] Making *ereba* is difficult and time consuming; it entails stripping the outer skin of the vegetable, grating, and then pressing the flour in a long, woven sieve, or *luguma* (snake), to squeeze out the bitter juices, which can be toxic. The flour is then dried, sifted, and baked on a large round metal surface to produce hard, flat tortillas. Women elders continue to make *ereba*, but there is less and less of it these days. Younger Garifuna women are more inclined to look for paid jobs, and there have been sporadic but scary bits of violence in the farms along the coast that means less yuca is grown and less *ereba* is produced.

Lands that have been privatized at the western end of the community—where the much-maligned Playa Escondida development now stands—were once filled with fruit trees, including mango and coconut, and home to many wild animals, such as wild pigs and tapirs, which were hunted to supplement household diets. Importantly, the community also used *reservas* (reserve lands) for the collection of construction materials, medicinal plants, and other goods necessary to sustain Garifuna spiritual and material well-being. For instance, the sieve used in the production of *ereba* is made from a sinewy plant referred to as *balaire*, and which is in short supply due to the rapid expansion of tourism.

Reflecting on these challenges, Toya told me: "Even though we are no longer going to kill ourselves [toiling the land], because, after all, development is here, right? We have education, professionals, secretaries and even doctors here in Triunfo, which is a source of development, but we must also use the land in the way of our ancestors to develop." Her statement points to the need to preserve the culture of labor that existed in the past to ensure the livelihood and survival of the people, while also recognizing that many community youth have educations and may be disinclined to do farm work. While there are persistent and powerful external forces—investors, multilateral development institutions, state laws, and policies—forcing these individual communities to change, there is also an emerging desire within these communities to do things differently. This tension, as I have mentioned, pits the imagined future to which many Triunfeños aspire in tension with the ancestral (recall Lucas's statement about the hegemony of the ancestors). The *empresarios* have capitalized on these divergent aspirations to further their agenda within the community, arguing that agricultural labor is less lucrative than, for instance, formal employment in the tourism economy, which was aligned with the inevitable march of progress. To their opponents, Carla and the land defenders were a rowdy group of women who were incapable of thinking beyond the immediacy of daily communal life.

Nevertheless, Carla has found ways to strengthen her authority within the community by strategically deploying narratives of the past and ancestrality to forge a broad-based alliance of Triunfeños opposed to the sale of communal lands. During an assembly meeting on May 5, 2009, Carla reiterated Triunfo's historical foundations to distinguish Garifuna land tenure practices from the private property market and to push back against growing pressures to sell, which stemmed in part from the municipal government's willingness to sanction illegal land transactions in the municipal property register. She reminded participants of the struggle endured by their ancestors to establish themselves in Honduras, after they were exiled from St. Vincent in the Lesser Antilles. Carla skillfully tethered Garifuna belonging to ancestral practices, including the practice of collective farming and the tradition of gifting lands to Garifuna newcomers. She stated:

> In those times, they designated a parcel of land for their houses and another for their agricultural plots. The land is not a commodity! That is what we're fighting against . . . the culture of commodification. The patrimony of the communities is different—collective property!

Garifuna could sell or gift their individual parcels to other Garifuna, as I explained earlier, but land sales to non-Garifuna were strictly prohibited. Moreover, the transfer of land between Garifuna, when sold, was usually for a nominal sum of money in recognition of the land's value to the collective life-worlds of the community. The collectivist ethos governing the exchange of land within Triunfo was one premised on principles of mutuality and guided by an awareness that the land gives life and texture to autonomy.[12]

Carla's rendering of the past bound Garifuna identity to histories of struggle and dispossession. Resort tourism development in Tela Bay, contingent on fracturing the community's collective title, had the potential to displace them yet again, unless they were willing to fight, and fight together. Carla concluded with an emphatic statement, "No one can come here and tell us how to run our house—as a *people*, they cannot put us in the same sack as the rest." In this manner, she addressed the dual issues of peoplehood and autonomy. Garifuna are a distinct people with distinct cultural beliefs and material practices pertaining to land and labor, both of which had come under threat by the continued pressures of developers and municipal authorities in their quest to solidify Tela's standing as an international tourism destination.

Women in the community were involved in activities organized by both *patronatos*, depending on the benefits to be derived from participation, a pragmatism stemming from the need to feed their children and maintain their households. However, nearly all the women I interviewed faulted the *empresarios* for the privatization of communal lands and hailed Carla as the true defender of the community.[13] Doña Susana, an elder who is also a member of the Laguira Dance Group, summed up the conflict bluntly: "The problem is land. One [*patronato*] sells the land and the other rescues the land. The one that rescues the land loves their community." She continued, "But the community our ancestors left us is not for sale. It is our inheritance." Inheritance, in this sense, established a particular relationship between Triunfeños and their territory, but also between the present inhabitants of the land and their ancestors who struggled to defend the land.

In a subsequent conversation, I asked Doña Susana to help me understand the significance of land loss for Garifuna culture. She began with a stern assertion: "We are not going to lose the land. We will fight until the end to protect her!" She then explained, "If we lose the land, where will we live? In the city? There we'd lose our language, we'd lose the *buyei* too." Her emphasis on the *buyei* (a Garifuna spiritual guide) was of particular importance, because Garifuna spiritual practice is premised on maintaining a reciprocal relationship between the present inhabitants of the land and their ancestors. Elaborate ceremonies such as the Dügü entail building temples from natural materials (e.g., palm fronds and *balaire*) and preparing foods that are specific to the Garifuna diet—again products of the land. In this vein, selling the land was perceived as a profound transgression—

not only to the land, which provides for the community, but also to their ancestors and the struggle they waged to secure the land for the present inhabitants. The maintenance of these relationships, between the ancestors and their descendants, lied at the crux of the vision espoused by the land defenders, demanding an orientation to development and progress that challenged the dominant ethos of resource exploitation.

On a sweltering evening in July, as daylight slowly gave way to the night, I sat with Ricardo, leader of the *empresarios*, in the patio of his beachfront restaurant. I asked him to explain his stance on communal conflicts over land in Triunfo:

> *Chris:* The Los Micos Beach and Golf Resort [Indura] is a controversial project. If the opportunity to build a similar project here emerged—maybe on a smaller scale—what would you do?
>
> *Ricardo:* We have that vision here! We have a project here on the Black Lagoon, which is not on the same scale as the [Indura] Project, but with extensive possibilities and [backed by] Garifuna. But since we don't have funds, well, the progress is very slow, and there is the situation of collective land tenure . . . that is a double-edged sword. We can't leave it [the land] too open, but it also creates barriers for us who have ambitions, another vision of development.
>
> *Chris:* In what way?
>
> *Ricardo:* For example, [the Black Lagoon] project will entail the construction of traditional condominiums—it is an ecotourism development tied to the environment. But within the clause of our communal land title, there can be no sales.

According to Ricardo, Triunfo's communal property title was a "double-edged sword" and a barrier to the project he envisioned. Because the owners of the Black Lagoon residences would be owners of the land as well, and the communal property title prevents the sale of lands to non-Garifuna, the project was at a standstill. Although he did not say so explicitly, progress on the Black Lagoon project would require developers to obtain the rights to the land and then sell the condos on the open market, most likely to outsiders.

Ultimately, Ricardo's business projections were defined in tension with collective land tenure and ancestral ways of being with the land. The opposing visions promoted by Ricardo and Carla reflect deep communal divisions regarding not only land, but also seething contests over the meaning of the future. For the land defenders, the community and the land that sustains it is conceived of as an autonomous space, one that will provide refuge to future generations of Triunfeños.

I do not mean to imply that ancestral ways of being with the land are unanimously shared in Triunfo. Rather, following the work of Audra Simpson (2014, 31), I argue for a "critical, democratically inflected tradition" to trace the ways ancestrality is dynamically lived and imagined in the present and at times in pursuit of politically divergent futures.[14] Accordingly, we must understand the *lucha* as an expression of the will to survive, which is contingent on living with, not off, the land. Living with the land is to live ancestrally, or in ways that continue to foment relations of reciprocal care and love. The land defenders' efforts to rescue privatized lands was more than an act of repossession; it was a means by which to reestablish relationships that were critical to sustaining collective life.

Amar el pueblo, or, On Territorial Mothering

It was the end of the rainy season and the roads in Triunfo had deteriorated drastically. Wary of damaging their vehicles, taxi drivers from Tela refused to enter the community, leaving Triunfeños with little recourse to get to and from town to handle basic shopping needs, trips to the municipal hospital, and to the bank. In spite of repeated pleas for support, municipal authorities in the nearby city of Tela refused to help. While Ricardo continued to haggle with the municipality, Carla decided to take matters into her own hands by leading an autonomous effort to address the deepening transportation crisis.

On the morning of January 21, 2009, a group of about twenty-five Triunfeños—mostly women—gathered on a grassy strip of land at the edge of the Laguna Negra (Black Lagoon). An old dump truck covered in rust was positioned alongside large mounds of broken concrete, stones, and rocks (fig. 4.2). Some of the rocks were as big as a football and weighed upward of ten pounds. We labored under the scorching sun to pile the

FIGURE 4.2: Collective labor as autonomy.

Photos: Christopher Loperena.

rocks one by one into the back of the rusty dump truck, which we used to infill the craterlike holes lining the dilapidated roadway.[15]

On the second day of work, more men joined the women on the bank of the Black Lagoon. Doña Juana, a Garifuna elder and land defender, shouted, "We must speak the truth. Today there are eight *plátanos* in our midst!" gesturing to the men who heaved rocks with pursed lips. One of the women asked, "Are they green or ripe?" Juana replied with a chuckle, "Green, still," eliciting raucous laughter from the women and a few disapproving head shakes from the men. Her humorous retort positioned the women activists as more seasoned, a subtle—but universally understood—undermining of the sexual and political dominance assumed by men in the community.

After filling the dump truck for the third time, we paused for a break. Sitting on the rocks next to Justina, I asked her about the role of women in the community. I expressed my surprise at the overrepresentation of women and the ostensible lack of support from men, especially considering the demanding nature of the work. "That is the way it is, always," she said nonchalantly. She continued, "We, the women, show more concern for our community."

On the other side of me sat Mari, who, after taking a swig of *aguardiente* (moonshine), jumped in and said, "To love your community is expressed through actions, not through words." She likened this communal sensibility to the love between two people: "You cannot think only of yourself, you must also consider the well-being of your partner, and that is how we must think of the community and how we should serve the community." Mari's sentiment was shared by many of the land defenders I interviewed. By demonstrating their ability to resolve community needs free of state intervention the land defenders also staked a claim to their ancestral territory, defying the presumed authority of municipal officials and tourism investors.

Mari and Justina's comments were not only a declaration of women's corporeal autonomy but of communal autonomy, because infrastructural improvements and land defense were obtainable only through these forms of collective labor and reciprocal care. Indeed, women often articulated their commitments to the community in terms of care not only for the land and fellow Triunfeños but also for their ancestors and for the unborn sons and daughters of the community (*hijos de la comunidad*).

The importance of reciprocal obligations between adult children and their mothers can be framed more broadly as a relationship between the practice of mothering and survival. As noted by Kerns (1997, 1), "Links with and between women as mothers provide the stable framework of social life" within Garifuna communities. Kerns demonstrates the ways in which the mother-child bond is perceived as a means of survival, insofar as children are expected to care for their mothers (financially) in their old age. Throughout my fieldwork in Triunfo, I came to understand mothering in broader terms, as an expression of love and living in reciprocal relation with the land, that cut through dichotomies of gender, culture, and nature. I refer to this as "territorial mothering."[16]

Consuela, a Garifuna woman who was born in La Ceiba but came to live in Triunfo in the early 1990s, said: "I always struggled to support my children. I washed clothes, *cargué pan* [sold bread] and I went to sell my product in Tela, Triunfo, even in San Pedro Sula."[17] Consuela proudly narrated the sacrifices she endured for the survival of her family, noting that her son Efraín is now a schoolteacher. But her temperament shifted when she began talking about her daughter, Paola. She is also a mother but refuses to wash or sell bread for a living: "Paola does not want people to see her doing that type of work." Sucking her teeth, Consuela sneered, "I am not ashamed to work. Let them see me working! She doesn't want to *cargar pan* [sell bread], but she doesn't feel embarrassed to come and ask me for money!" Carla, who was sitting nearby, affirmed Consuela's frustrations and commented on the ingratitude of her daughter: "She saw how you struggled to raise her and now it's her turn!"

Just as women are expected to care for their children, *los hijos de la comunidad* (sons and daughters of the community) are expected to care for their mothers and, by extension, for the community through collective labor, participation in community life, and the basic upkeep of family landholdings. In this vein, the practice of everyday life was bound up with notions of territorial mothering—not merely biological reproduction, but a political and social praxis that undergirded wider practices of social reproduction and that men contributed to as well through their participation in the struggle to defend communal lands. Those who did not contribute to the struggle were labeled "sellouts," and in more severe cases their claims to communal belonging were explicitly called into question.

Land defenders often spoke of their children and the children of their children as the beneficiaries of the present struggle. Dora, a fixture at the weekly meetings of the Land Defense Committee, observed:

> It is precisely because we have family, a home that women are more concerned for the future generations and for what we will leave to our children. So, this makes us feel much more committed and concerned with what happens within our community. We commit ourselves to one another for survival and to ensure we leave a patrimony for those that are yet to come.

Thus, to understand the dynamics of land defense and the important role played by women in the *lucha*, one must interrogate ideas around motherhood and mothering, underscoring the centrality in Garifuna life of not just the individual relationships within families, but the broader relationship across the community as a whole. Goett (2017, 91) has documented similar dynamics among Creole women in Nicaragua: "Women's sociality and mutual aid are not simply strategies to cope with inequality but vernacular practices that build community and promote self-valorization."

Sheyla was a sharp-witted high school graduate and community youth organizer. She was publicly aligned with Carla's *patronato*. I asked Sheyla to describe the role played by women in community affairs. "The Garifuna woman is the mother of culture, the one that makes sure her children get ahead in life, the one that makes sure her people make progress, and the one that labors daily to ensure our collective well-being," she responded.

"Mother of culture?" I prodded.

"Yes," she said, adding, "She is the mother of culture, because thanks to her our culture is still alive. Thanks to her we are still on this land and we continue to make progress as a people, because she is the one that makes sacrifices so her children can have an education, so her children can become something in this life, to see them through their educations.

She is the one that puts that huge basket of bread on her head to go sell in her community, on the beach to tourists or in the city. She is the one that bakes *ereba*; she is the one that dances punta . . . the woman is everything."

In some ways, Sheyla's mention of progress is resonant with normative understandings of progress, as in educational advancement, but it is also contingent on relationships of mutuality and of reciprocal care. In this sense, women—in their roles as mothers and as agents in the land struggle—are often credited for the collective survival of the people. This is so precisely because they wear so many different hats and offer various visions of what mothering can be, from ways of living to ideas about caring for children and community. [8]

Instead of thinking of maternal responsibilities as a limitation or self-sacrifice, many women uphold their roles as mothers to forge collective power, a long established political tradition in Latin America (Martin 1990; Stephen 1995; Aretxaga 1997).[9] And perhaps most importantly, mothering provided women with a platform from which to critique the ethos of resource exploitation called for by the state and represented locally by Ricardo's vision for the future of the community.

Territorial mothering extends far beyond the domestic sphere, and in many instances it involves making demands for entire communities, protesting on the streets, and participating in land recuperation movements. It is therefore a political praxis that is crucially bound with the discourse and embodied practices of land defense, and that is not exclusively hinged to gender. Rather, collectives—men, women, and children—must come together to defend against privatization and ensure access to land for future generations. This point was made clear to me by a past president of the Land Defense Committee, as he recounted the story of a Garifuna activist by the name of Reymunda Amaya.

Reymunda was the first to stand up to incoming tourism developers. In his words, "The men were her soldiers because she was the *mera mera* [the real deal] and that is how the land defense movement began." Women land defenders, like Reymunda, established a culture of struggle that is carried on today by their descendants and that continue to animate the *lucha* for Garifuna past, present, and future. This ethical commitment to one another and to the land was reiterated following the June 2009 coup d'état against Manuel Zelaya when large delegations of Triunfeñas and Triunfeños joined the anticoup resistance movement in Tegucigalpa.

I was again struck by the large number of women elders that chose to participate in the protests. They went despite the threat of violent repression at the hands of the state. Some of the women explicitly tied their participation in these acts of resistance to the future well-being of the nation. "Manuel Zelaya favored us, the poor. The constituent assembly [proposed by Zelaya] would have been good for the Garifuna and also for the future of our children in this country, because it is not possible for them to live under a dictatorship," explained Leticia. She continued, "But as Garifuna and as women, we have shown much support [for the resistance]. We have left our families, our children, our homes there in the community to come to Tegucigalpa and be involved, with our natural medicines, and in many other ways." They joined the resistance as mothers, as Hondurans, and as a Black Indigenous people with a stake in the political crisis unfolding in the nation's capital and with a commitment to combating the systematic deprivation of social goods, rights, and privileges necessary to sustain life, not only within their communities but also for the entire country.[20]

Land grabs by elite mestizos and state authorities have deepened the ethos of struggle established by earlier women activists, such as Reymunda, which binds individuals to collectives and future life to an ethos of relationality. These forms of living are powerfully disruptive of the moral paradigms embedded within the dominant development agenda and are therefore targeted for destruction by state and parastate agents.

Poner el cuerpo

Women land defenders have increasingly assumed leadership positions in the movement to defend Garifuna territory both within Triunfo and in representative organizations, such as OFRANEH.[21] Gregoria Flores is a native Triunfeña. She was one of the founding members of the Land Defense Committee of Triunfo de la Cruz. In 1994, she joined OFRANEH's leadership council, and in 1996 she was elected president and general coordinator. For almost a decade Gregoria was on the front lines of a fierce struggle to defend Garifuna territorial rights in all forty-six coastal communities.

And then, on May 30, 2005, Gregoria was shot at point-blank range. She had just left OFRANEH's central office in La Ceiba to collect affidavits from several key witnesses for one of the cases the organization filed before the Inter-American Commission on Human Rights. While waiting at a traffic stoplight, an unknown assailant approached her vehicle and shot her with an exploding bullet that pierced her upper right arm and torso. The attempted assassination followed several threats against her life and forced Gregoria to flee to the United States, where she was eventually granted political asylum. She reported: "They told me that if I stayed in Honduras, I would only have seven days to live. I had to come [to the US] immediately, take my kids out of school and university, relocate my mom to a different community and come."[22]

Targeted acts of repression, arbitrary arrests, and murders of Garifuna activists have become increasingly common, particularly in the first few years following the 2009 coup d'état. On April 7, 2011, to cite one of numerous examples, unidentified arsonists set fire to the home of Carla and Miguel. The attack took place as Carla and her five children were sleeping. One of the children smelled the smoke and alerted his mother, narrowly averting a devastating tragedy.

More recently, on September 9, 2019, two armed men assassinated Mirna Teresa Suazo, president of the communal governing council for the Garifuna community of Masca. OFRANEH publicly denounced the attack and indicated that it was politically motivated due to Suazo's leadership role within the community and her alignment with the struggle to defend Garifuna lands.[23] On October 12, 2019, just over one month later, the Garifuna teacher María Digna Montero was assassinated in the Garifuna community of Cusuna. She was also a member of OFRANEH and allegedly targeted for her work on behalf of the organization.[24]

Rita Segato (2014, 345) has described this uptick in violence against women's bodies as a form of unconventional warfare, in which the battle is not between states but is state and parastate agents brutalizing its most vulnerable citizens: "In the parastate action of these groups, the need to demonstrate the absence of limits in the execution of cruel acts is even more critical, since there are no other documents or insignia to designate who has jurisdictional authority. On the one hand, savage brutality is the only guarantee of control over territories and bodies, and of bodies as territories, and, on the other, the pedagogy of cruelty is the strategy for the reproduction of the system."[25] This new pattern of war, via the control of territory and women's bodies as territory, is visible throughout the Americas, but it is particularly sharp in Honduras, which was declared the "murder capital of the world" in 2011 (for every hundred thousand citizens of the country, ninety-two were killed). And in 2017, the international human rights organization Global Witness named Honduras the "deadliest country in the world for land and environmental activism."[26] According to the report, over 120 land rights and environmental activists were killed in Honduras between 2010 and 2017. The true figure is probably much greater.

Violent crimes against women have also increased significantly; nearly 3,500 Honduran women have been murdered since 2009.[27] The majority of these crimes remain in impunity or unresolved. Nonetheless, Garifuna women continue to wage their struggle against the state, knowing full well that their actions may result in death. Why? Because Black mothers, as Christen Smith (2016, 32) maintains, reproduce and preserve Black life and as such Black women directly challenge the racist (anti-Black) ideologies that undergird the state's structure.

Conclusion

National economic advancement is contingent on the transmutation of land, water, and forests into commodities for individual accumulation and the making of morally autonomous subjects with the capacity to achieve progress. This is precisely what land recuperations, like the one at Barrio Indomables, were meant to forestall. For some Triunfeños, however, the actions taken by Carla and her supporters equated to an invasion. Crecencia, a shop owner in Barrio Centro, said, "I'm not in agreement with the recuperation. Why did they wait until [Mario Fuentes] cleared and leveled the land? This land *has an owner* and he has invested a lot of money." Her disapproval was rooted in the logics of private property; that is, private ownership is determined not only by who buys the land but also by who puts the land to productive use—material improvements is one means by which this relationship is established. This increasingly persuasive way of thinking about land and ownership was dramatically incongruous with the modes of relationship forged through collective acts of "rescuing" or freeing the land.

In the fight to rescue privatized lands from the grips of developers, Garifuna women land defenders enacted an oppositional spatial praxis, which Sarah Ihmoud (2019, 515) in her discussion of Palestinian women's resistance in Israel, refers to as a "politics of staying in place." Their efforts insist that the nature of the problem, as well as the potential responses to it, are shaped by lived experiences of gendered violence and race. Crucially, women land defenders harnessed gendered narratives of the past, of ancestrality, to refuse the antiprogress label levied on them by developers, state authorities, and the *empresarios* and to reclaim control of their territories and bodies.

In this sense, collective futures are made possible by cultivating reciprocal relationships—with one another, and with the land, sea, and forests that produce life. To live ancestrally, therefore, is a way of being in relation with the land that refuses the supremacy of progressive time, the violence of development, and that enables other visions of community to emerge. This disposition toward one another, and toward a collective future, powerfully contests the presumed "unimaginability" of Black geographies (McKittrick 2006).[28]

5 THE LIMITS OF INDIGENEITY

Pueblo Garifuna v. Honduras

> *Just because the issue of development has been raised does not mean we have to simply disappear.*
>
> ALFREDO LÓPEZ, OFRANEH[1]

I RETURNED TO HONDURAS IN June 2013 after being away for over a year. When I arrived, the land defenders were deeply immersed in their own research into the history of conflicts over Triunfo's ancestral territory. A small team led by Carla was hard at work collecting documentary evidence, photos, and any other details they could muster to strengthen their decade-long case before the Inter-American Commission on Human Rights. The filing deadline was imminent.

I found Carla weary eyed and drinking a bottle of *malta* under a palm-covered patio. For two weeks she had been holed up in a tiny one-room office, rented by OFRANEH, where she and one other woman by the name of Cely worked day after day in what was clearly a tedious and emotionally draining task. The office was full of overstuffed three-ring black binders, strewn across every available surface, alongside stacks of dusty manila folders, tattered newspaper clippings, and other documents stamped with official insignia. A bulky desktop computer droned loudly in the background, as if taking one lingering gasp for air.

For the next seven days, I worked alongside Carla and Cely to compile a comprehensive database documenting illegal land sales, stolen lands, unresolved conflicts over disputed parcels—such as the one at Barrio Indomables—and the long history of violence against community land defenders. The more I delved into the history of the land conflict, the more I became aware of the stakes of the *lucha*, the lives lost, and very real threat of further violence. This threat made our work and the pending court hearing all the more urgent.

In this chapter we are going to jump ahead to one of the most impactful moments of recent Garifuna history—appearing at the Inter-American Court of Human Rights on May 20, 2014, in San José, Costa Rica. The result is a deepened understanding of how Garifuna harness the law to defend their lands and autonomy against the state's extractivist development agenda, as well as the limits of recognition as a means to resolve struggles over Black collective rights.

Although Garifuna are one of nine officially recognized "ethnic" groups, state authorities have repeatedly denied their status as a people native to Honduras, thereby calling into question the legitimacy of their territorial claims and raising concerns about how these claims infringe on the rights of the majority mestizo population, as well as those people recognized by the state as authentically Indigenous.[2] This negation, which featured centrally in the state's arguments before the IACHR and during the Court's in situ visit to Honduras in August 2015, stems from two interrelated issues: the historically rooted and willful incapacity, on the part of mestizos, to perceive of a Black people as indigenous to Honduras, and government collusion with private capital to extract resources from Indigenous and Black territories.[3]

State officials not only have undermined the possibility of Black Indigeneity but also have exalted the rights of officially recognized Indigenous peoples—in a strange and circuitous logic—to defend mestizo property rights in the zone. This politics of (mis)recognition thus tethers Indigenous subjectivity to the mestizo nation-building project and ideologies of whitening. It also reinforces the popular perception that Black people are foreigners in Honduras, despite ample historical evidence to the contrary. Echoing the extractivist logics of multinational capital, state authorities have sought through legal and extralegal means to extract and render invisible the affective, spiritual, and material attachments Garifuna have to their ancestral territory, while at the same time denying the existence of anti-Black racism.

Garifuna contested this campaign of legal expulsion through the articulation of a counternarrative that firmly anchored their place-based claims to self-identification as a Black Indigenous people and by arguing that the forms of dispossession they faced on the coast were imbricated with the disenfranchisement of other marginalized populations, including landless mestizos, who are, given the history of agrarian reform in the country, often positioned as rivals in a contest to secure control over scarce resources.

I begin with a brief chronology of Triunfo's Inter-American Court case. This is followed by an ethnographic analysis of the courtroom proceedings, in particular the testimony of the key witnesses. I demonstrate how their testimony both disrupts and reinforces conventional representations of Indigenous difference upon which rights to territory are typically predicated. I then present an account of the court's site visit to Triunfo de la Cruz on August 21, 2015, which I use to further my analysis of the arguments used by state officials to defend mestizo property rights and to counter their purported victimization. I conclude with a discussion of how Black autonomy, a central tenet of Garifuna political imaginings, encompasses affective and spatial relations that refuse the normative underpinnings of freedom.

Anatomy of the Case

As we have seen, conflicts over land in Triunfo go back several decades, but they intensified with the emergence of tourism as a state development priority. The passage of Hurricane Mitch in 1998 created the conditions of possibility for a dramatic expansion of tourism along the Caribbean coast. I have elsewhere referred to this as the first stage of a longer experiment in disaster capitalism (Loperena 2017a), through which the government of Honduras together with multinational capital concretized the extractivist economic model that is in place today.

Following decentralization measures in the 1990s, the municipality of Tela extended its jurisdiction over portions of Triunfo's communally titled lands, and then with the backing of the Honduran Institute for Tourism began sanctioning illegal land sales to non-Garifuna investors. This further weakened land tenure security for Triunfeños. The first significant violation was tied to the Marbella Beach Club, a multimillion-dollar resort housing development to be built on the community's eastern edge. Between August 1993 and July 1995, the municipality sold approximately forty-four hectares (109 acres) of land previously titled to the community to the company IDETRISA (Empresa Inversiones y Desarrollos El Triunfo SA de CV), which was backing the construction of the resort (described in chapter 3).

Then, in January 1997, the municipality of Tela granted 22.87 *manzanas* (approximately forty acres) of Triunfo's communal land to the Municipal Workers Union. The land was conferred to union members in the form of private property titles without consultation and without the permission of communal authorities, fueling seething conflicts between Triunfeños and the municipal employees who received lots within the disputed area. On February 4, 1998, the community filed a complaint before the National Agrarian Institute (INA, by its Spanish acronym) in which it accused the municipal government of unlawful usurpation. INA eventually conceded the validity of the community's claim, in September 2001, but conflicts over land continued to intensify and subsequently spread to other disputed tracks—including Barrio Indomables (see chapter 4), Playa Escondida, and a large plot of land belonging to the women's agricultural cooperative El Esfuerzo—all designated for tourism and residential real estate projects.[4]

Government-sponsored tourism initiatives on the coast coarticulated with regional conservation proposals and the overall destination-making politics of elite investors and their allies in the National Congress (Brondo and Woods 2007; Loperena 2016a). Zones designated for conservation, such as the Punta Izopo National Park and the Cuero y Salado Wildlife Refuge, further constrained the historical land use practices of Garifuna living in the region, deepening their resolve to seek official recognition of their rights to the land they have historically occupied.

In response to this state of siege, community activists in Triunfo de la Cruz, with the support of the Garifuna organization OFRANEH, brought a formal petition to the Inter-American Commission on Human Rights in

2003. The community's case was built upon the aforementioned disputes, the persistent and ongoing loss of territory, and targeted acts of violence and harassment carried out against land rights activists, including the murders of Jesús Alvarez, Óscar Brega, Jorge Castillo Jiménez, and Julio Alberto Morales. Following a decade of deliberations, the commission finally advanced the case to the Inter-American Court of Human Rights. The public hearing, held on May 20, 2014, provided a stage for the contestation and negotiation of the rights-worthiness of differently racialized subjects, as well as of competing sovereign claims, between the state of Honduras, mestizo investors, and the Garifuna.

The Audacity of Black Indigeneity

On the morning of the hearing, OFRANEH representatives and a bus full of Garifuna supporters from Honduras gathered in front of the stately neoclassical headquarters of the Inter-American Court of Human Rights, in the upscale barrio of Los Yoses in San José, Costa Rica. They arrived early, intent on making their presence known as court officials and the international press arrived. The court's ruling on the case would set a precedent for all member states of the Organization of American States, and thus it generated broad interest on the part of Indigenous and Black social movements across the Americas.

Triunfeños were cautiously optimistic. The commission had made it clear that it found evidence of state complicity in human rights violations against the community, methodically documented in the Merits Report, which community activists frequently cited to justify land recuperation efforts back in Honduras.[5] If, however, the court ruled in favor of Honduras, Garifuna land activists would lose significant political ground at home, potentially forcing them to concede recuperated lands to developers. The stakes were high.

Before the start of the hearing, a *buyei*, or spiritual guide, conducted a traditional ceremony on the steps of the courthouse in which he called on the ancestors for accompaniment (fig. 5.1). The Garifuna swayed gently to the beat of the *tambores*, singing in harmony, while the *buyei* lit a large cigar and then wafted the billowing smoke over the participants. Spiritual incantations, such as this one, were vital to the land struggle, because the

FIGURE 5.1: Buyei performs spiritual ceremony before the hearing at the Inter-American Court of Human Rights in San José, Costa Rica.

Photo: Christopher Loperena.

ancestors were regarded as present-day guides and protectors. The ceremony, as I discuss later, was also an important political enactment, given that Indigenous rights to territory, within the framework of international law, are often premised on the logic of cultural difference (Hale 2006; Loperena 2020). In accordance with new legal procedural codes, Indigenous communities garner rights by proving that their culture is imperiled or in jeopardy of being lost altogether, and thus the performance of cultural alterity was indispensable to the community's larger legal strategy (Loperena, Castillo, and Mora 2018). Over the course of my research, I had come to expect ceremonies, like this one, at Garifuna political manifestations. This time, however, the stakes felt different. At the conclusion of the ceremony we filed quietly into the courthouse knowing that this day, regardless of the outcome, would be historical.

Once inside, the Garifuna delegation—two witnesses, two representatives from OFRANEH, a Garifuna interpreter, and the lead lawyer—took their seats before the judges' bench. The state representatives sat on the opposite side of the courtroom, watching closely as we shuffled into the gallery. Last, the seven presiding judges entered, ceremoniously taking their seats at the front of the courtroom.

At the start of the trial, the commission provided an overview of the case, including the primary findings from the Merits Report and a summary of the specific human rights violations committed against the community. The lawyer representing Triunfo, Cristián Callejas, then called forth the first of two witnesses, José Ángel Castro. Ángel offered his testimony in Spanish, providing clear and concise answers to the questions. When asked if the community would accept lands in another part of the country as a concession for the lands it had lost, he responded: "The answer is no, because our lands are not fungible."

Next the court called forth the second witness, Clara Eugenia Flores. Although Clara, then president of Triunfo's communal board, spoke fluent Spanish, she opted to present her testimony in Garifuna and thus spoke through an interpreter, who was also a native of Triunfeña.[6] Clara donned a gold, black, and white dress—the colors of the Garifuna flag—and wore her hair in carefully manicured twists, which were tucked meticulously below a matching gold headband. She responded to the questions with extraordinary clarity and composure. When asked about her relationship to the land, Clara paused for a moment and then said, "Land, as my mother taught me, is my life; it is sustenance, what gives me life, and I care for it as I would for myself." The land invasions, she alleged, began in the 1970s, and then picked up pace again in 1994, with the massive Marbella tourism development on the community's eastern border. Slowly, year after year, the boundaries of their community grew smaller and smaller.

When asked how she had been affected by the loss of communal lands,

Clara fell silent and then started to sob. Many Garifuna in the audience also wept quietly, men and women alike. Gasping heavily, she said:

> This has caused tremendous damage to our community, culture and customs. Parents can no longer take their children [to the fields] to show them how to cultivate, how to sustain themselves. . . . My mother took me with her to cultivate the land—rice, yuca, corn. We had trammel nets for fishing. . . . We had everything we needed in the house and enough to share with our neighbors and extended families. There was no need to emigrate to find work, to find opportunities to live. We shared with everyone in the community, and this is a component of our culture that has been lost. . . . Migration and the lack of land has caused changes in attitude among our people, because when they come back, they come with an individualistic outlook, no longer in solidarity, and if this continues, we will lose everything.

Clara's testimony emphasized the necessity of caring for the land by maintaining ancestral farming practices; these life-giving activities are imperative for sustaining the communal ethos that, for many Garifuna, was a constitutive feature of their culture. In this vein, cutting off access to lands used for the cultivation of staple foods and for the maintenance of cultural and spiritual practices posed an existential threat to their survival as a people, she argued. Her testimony elucidated the material and affective attachments Garifuna have to land, crucially important components of their contemporary claims to place.

With a stoic gaze, Clara continued, "From within the community they promote divisionism to exploit our resources, and when we question these third parties about why they are doing this, they say they do it with permission from the municipality." This was followed by quiet affirmations from the audience, which created a palpable sense of collective grievance, an affective disposition and mode of belonging that powerfully narrated the history and experience of dispossession.

After her emotional testimony, the lawyer for the state began his cross-examination. At one point, he asked Clara whether she was aware that one of the disputed touristic developments included in the case was spearheaded by a Garifuna businessman. She responded: "Yes, I know that person. He has our same color, but he doesn't speak Garifuna, nor was he raised among Garifuna."

He then asked cynically, "Then do you consider the woman who is serving as your interpreter to be more Garifuna?"

"Yes, she's Garifuna," she replied. "She speaks Garifuna, she is the daughter of a Garifuna woman, and she has Garifuna within her blood. Put that other person alongside her and *I will show you* who is more Garifuna, him or her!"

The interpreter, Teresa, was of mixed Garifuna and mestizo descent; she had long straight black hair and tan skin. She could pass for mestiza—that is, non-Black—prompting the state lawyer to publicly probe her racial and ethnic identity. This, I suggest, raised larger questions concerning social group membership. If Teresa, who is visibly mixed race, is recognized as a member of the group, why are others excluded and how are such decisions made? Government efforts to amplify internal political divisions—especially intracommunity discord over group membership and the governance of land use—was ultimately an effort to undermine Garifuna claims to collective self-determination. Through this line of questioning, the lawyer also alluded to liberal values, such as freedom of choice and individual autonomy, which he contrasted dramatically with collective land tenure regimes.

Clara's defense of Teresa, at least superficially, was based on ethnic markers (e.g., language) as well as ancestry, but her unequivocal retort also speaks to the political basis of identity—a criterion that is often excised from the legal logics of race and identity operating within the courtroom. Teresa's long-standing commitment to communal land defense and to Garifuna autonomy positions her as more Garifuna than the businessman referenced by the state lawyer, who has worked alongside municipal authorities and developers to advance the government-sponsored tourism agenda in Triunfo. She is thus, in the eyes of her peers, a *comunitaria*—someone who is committed to communal autonomy. This was likely inscrutable to the government lawyer, but it certainly factored into Clara's rebuttal.

This paradox—the repeated performance and accentuation of ethnic difference to legitimate claims before the court and the ways the testimonies and performance of difference simultaneously undermine these ethnic characterizations—illuminates the slippery conceptual grounds on which Indigeneity is constituted in the space of the court. Following this terse exchange, the lawyer asked Clara whether she was aware of other Indigenous peoples who were in the zone of Tela Bay before 1797—the year Garifuna arrived on mainland Honduras. The implication of the question was clear: that Garifuna are not native to Honduras, because they are not of pre-Hispanic origin.

Clara said, "Yes, I know of this history, but I also know that when the Spanish arrived, they had to leave their lands and flee to another area." Again, the state lawyers attempted to deny Garifuna Indigeneity by prioritizing the Indigenous past over the vitality of the Indigenous present in Tela Bay. This legal strategy was used to counter Garifuna claims to territory and ultimately to defend the land rights of non-Indigenous mestizos living in the area. The existing dispute did not involve other Indigenous peoples, but rather mestizo investors who had illegally acquired lands within the community's ancestral territory, lands that were previously conferred to Triunfo and that are protected by international legal conventions ratified by the Honduran state in 1995.[7]

The state lawyer concluded his questions with a troubling assertion. He argued that Garifuna can live and circulate freely in other parts of Honduras, while non-Garifuna are discriminated against when they attempt to live within Garifuna communities. His provocation speaks to the ways whiteness gets coded as property and Blackness as dispossession, since, from his perspective, mestizo settlers should be entitled to establish roots within Black territories in spite of legal conventions that uphold the inalienability of collective property rights.[8]

In Defense of Mestizo Property Rights, Act I

The exteriority of Blackness to the nation is itself an outcome of mestizo nationalism (Hooker 2005) and the historical ideology of Indo-Hispanic racial mixture, or *mestizaje* (Euraque, 2003; Portillo 2011). Garifuna, in particular, have been subjected to accusations of being foreigners in their natal lands, both by state officials and in popular discourses on Honduran national identity, which stands in contradistinction to Indigenous peoples of pre-Hispanic origin. Blackness, I contend, stands at the limits of Indigeneity, and Black peoples, in turn, are subjected to ongoing threats of legal and spatial expulsion from the nation.

Understanding the ways in which Black peoples are understood as exterior to and, at the same time, of the national body politic is necessary to make sense of the legal arguments presented by the state in response to the territorial pretensions of Garifuna in Triunfo. In a letter to the court, the Honduran deputy attorney general argued:

> The jurisprudence of the Inter-American Court of Human Rights regarding indigenous peoples is not applicable in this case due to the fact that the Garifuna community Triunfo de la Cruz does not constitute an indigenous or original people, but rather an ethnic group with its own cultural, social and political characteristics that reached the intended area after it had already consolidated its status as an independent state. The jurisprudence [of the Court] refers to original peoples, which is not the case here, and to apply it to this case could be contradictory and potentially harmful to an indigenous people, considering that the territorial demands of the Garifuna community Triunfo de la Cruz could enter into conflict with lands previously conferred to an original people, the Tolupán. (August 11, 2014)[9]

Here, the deputy attorney general acknowledges the unique ethnic characteristics of the community but bluntly denies the Garifuna's status as an Indigenous people, arguing that their territorial demands could infringe on the rights of others. The Tolupán (also called Xicaque), one of seven officially recognized Indigenous peoples in Honduras, once laid claim to the lands in and around Tela, but—after the arrival of Spanish colonists—resettled in the mountainous region to the south of the coast. The deputy attorney general also argued that the cultural orientation of Caribbean peoples is toward the sea, not *tierra adentro* (inland areas), thus the community's land claim was considered invalid on both historical and cultural grounds.

I contend that the legal negation of Garifuna Indigeneity sheds light on the racial logics undergirding dominant notions of Indigeneity in the

Americas more broadly (see also Loperena 2020). Authentic Indigenous peoples, positioned rhetorically as the rightful heirs to the nation, are deemed to be of pre-Hispanic origin with distinct racial and cultural characteristics, ones that predate the arrival of Afro-descendant peoples and the emergence of the modern mestizo citizen-subject.[10] Therefore, Garifuna, perceived as Afro-Honduran, cannot make legitimate claims to national territory.[11]

This letter was typical of the state's entire legal argument—a tangled web of historical fallacies and racial bias. State authorities not only eschewed responsibility for the rampant racism faced by Indigenous and Black peoples in present-day Honduras; they aggressively undermined Garifuna demands for control and ownership over the resources concentrated within their territories. Indeed, by underscoring the rights of non-Garifuna living within the community's land claim or with titles to lands Garifuna claim as their ancestral territory, the state furthered its own territorial mandate and sovereign pretensions. This was reiterated by the state when detailing the potential impact of reinstating the existing communal titles that had been slowly eaten away at by developers: "The process of titling land to the Garifuna communities involves three stages: titling, extension and clearing the title of encumbrances (*saneamiento*). Regarding the last stage, [the state] emphasized that it should be taken into account that in the area intended there are several non-Garifuna occupants with legal documents that recognize their property, who are also protected by national legislation."[12] Again, the key questions are whose rights are at stake and how might titling Garifuna ancestral lands jeopardize the rights of mestizo property holders.

Ultimately, the denial of Black property rights is predicated on the negation of Garifuna placeness within the nation, which serves to protect and expand the claims of mestizo or white property owners with overlapping claims to land. In this manner, the state, with support from multilateral development institutions and private investors, can ensure the success of the tourism industry and, in turn, make good on its promise to increase investments in related infrastructure, which is ostensibly of benefit to *all* Hondurans. This way of thinking about Garifuna lands—as up for grabs—was reiterated during the court's in situ visit to Honduras in August 2015.

Defending Mestizo Property Rights, Act II

The sun's relentless glare was no match for the giddy anticipation of my colleagues as we approached the exclusive Tela Mar Resort, where a select group of community leaders and OFRANEH representatives were scheduled to meet with court officials. It was August 21, 2015, the first day of the in situ visit and just over fifteen months after the public hearing in San José.

At the resort entrance, we encountered two armed security guards. "Are you guests of the hotel?" one asked abruptly. Miriam Miranda, the president of OFRANEH, informed him of our scheduled meeting. She then provided them with a copy of the invitation letter printed on official court letterhead. Unmoved, the guards insisted that only guests were permitted to enter the resort grounds. She pleaded in vain, "If we can just enter the lobby, we will be able to supply any additional details you need." Again, the guards refused. Frustrated, Miriam snapped back, "What if we wanted to make a room reservation, wouldn't we be allowed to enter the lobby just as any other guest of the hotel? This is a hotel, right!" Meanwhile, several cars, occupied by well-heeled mestizos, drove through the security gates without incident. One of my friends turned to me and sighed, "The same as always," referring to the everyday forms of anti-Black racism they confront. About thirty minutes later a representative from the municipality of Tela arrived to inform the delegation of a change in plan. Instead of one-on-one meetings with the judges, we would be meeting as a group in the former headquarters of the Tela Railroad Company, five minutes away by car.

Upon arrival, we encountered a large crowd of mostly mestizo employees of the municipal labor union, their lawyers, state officials, and representatives from the municipality of Tela (fig. 5.2). They were gathered just to the right of the building entrance, eagerly awaiting the arrival of the court officials. Some glared at us suspiciously, while others completely ignored our presence. Minutes later a small white van flanked by a police motorcade pulled up, eliciting cheers from the unionists and other curious onlookers.

The meeting room was equipped with dozens of plastic lawn chairs, a long table where the judges were seated, and an old sound system with a

FIGURE 5.2: Former headquarters of the Tela Railroad Company, Tela, Atlántida, August 21, 2015.

Photo: Christopher Loperena.

microphone and two tattered speakers. On entering the cavernous room, the unionists, municipal authorities, state officials, and the Garifuna delegation hurriedly filled the available seats. After a brief introduction by the president of the court, the mayor of Tela was invited to address the judges. During his speech, he described several development initiatives spearheaded by the municipal government in Triunfo, which he used to refute Garifuna allegations of racial discrimination. After speaking about the ways his government supported neighboring "Afro-descendant" communities, he shifted his attention to the growing *ladino* (mestizo) population living within the boundaries of the Garifuna territorial claim. Echoing the arguments presented by the lawyers representing the state before the court, he questioned, "What would happen to these people if the court ruled in favor of the community?" After a dramatic pause, he said, "Then, would we have to remove the Garifuna from the city of Tela?" He concluded his speech with a plea: "As Tela's authority, I am sure that no segregation or racism is being practiced here, and we must be very clear about that. . . . Please do not divide this society in which we live, because we are all brothers," insinuating that the real victims are the mestizo inhabitants of Triunfo.

Beatriz, a respected elder from Triunfo, was the first member of the Garifuna delegation to approach the microphone. Visibly flustered by the mayor's comments, she fervently described the history of territorial conflicts in Triunfo and the challenges facing the women's agricultural cooperative El Esfuerzo. In July, a tourism consortium forcibly dispossessed the women of their lands for the construction of a new upscale residential community. Her account rendered visible the forms of racialized dispossession executed by tourism companies in Triunfo with support from state and local government institutions. At the end of her presentation, she exclaimed, "And we are not Afro! We are Garifuna, of the Garifuna race. I'm not from Africa. I'm from Honduras!"

Despite the state's official recognition of Garifuna cultural difference, and the repeated denial that the country had any "problems of a racial nature," the argument that Garifuna are not Indigenous is racist, precisely because it has been used to disavow them of their material rights in order to protect mestizo property and commercial interests in the region. Moreover, it exacerbates existing tensions between Garifuna and non-Garifuna on the coast, an age-old tactic, but with particularly menacing implications, given that Garifuna represent a tiny minority when compared to the mestizo population—less than 5 percent of the total population of nearly ten million people—and are often rendered as a nonnative people or as foreigners. This resonates with Arjun Appadurai's (2006) argument about the "fear of small numbers;" nationalistic anxieties about minority groups, he reveals, can generate violence and even lead to ethnic-cleansing campaigns.

Aware of the potential for violence, OFRANEH's president Miriam Miranda approached the microphone. In a passionate plea to the non-Garifuna participants in the audience, she said:

Who says that you are enemies of the Garifuna people? No one has said that. The impression that here there are two opposing groups is untrue.

We are not picking a fight with you, because we are not enemies. We brought this to the international level because the state has repeatedly violated the human rights of the Garifuna people. We went [to the court] to demand respect from the state for the rights of the Garifuna people, because many call us *arrivants*—that's the word being used now—they question why we are fighting for our rights if we've only been here for two-hundred-plus years, when the ones who control this country haven't even been here for one hundred years, and no one calls them foreigners![13]

Hardly pausing to catch her breath, she exclaimed, "Well, that's what the state representatives have been arguing, that we're fighting against you—campesinos, poor people—and it's not true! . . . It is very important to make this clear, because otherwise we are left with the impression that we, the Garifuna people, are trying to impose our rights over the rights of the rest of the population." With this intervention, Miriam sought to remind them of their shared structural positions in relation to the mestizo elite, which is responsible for the dispossession of Garifuna lands, and for the exploitation and disenfranchisement of the predominantly mestizo peasantry. Attempts to sharpen divisions between these two groups absolves the government and the mestizo elite of their responsibility for the lack of opportunities for upward mobility plaguing the country. But the disavowal of anti-Blackness (see Vargas 2018) also renders inscrutable the shared structural positions of differently racialized populations in Honduras, thus reinforcing the assumed antagonism between mestizo campesinos and Garifuna, and between Afro-descendant peoples and officially recognized Indigenous Hondurans.

Mestizo Victimhood as Denial of Anti-Blackness
Miriam's frustration was well founded. The government had been relying on this antagonism for decades. And Honduras is not alone. In neighboring Nicaragua, Courtney Morris has identified a very similar exploitation of racial differences. In her analysis of regional autonomy measures on the Caribbean coast of Nicaragua, she demonstrates how Afro-Nicaraguan claims to land are perceived as an affront on mestizo rights. She terms this

"mestizo victimhood," which essentially positions mestizos as victims of discriminatory laws designed to redress the land tenure insecurity of Black and Indigenous peoples: "Rather than address the structural causes of land dispossession and displacement, the state increasingly relies on the Coast as a site for poor Mestizos in the Pacific who have become the excess, surplus labor of a neoliberal economy that has no use for them" (Morris 2016, 360). Similarly, in Honduras, state officials exploit the plight of landless peasants to drum up empathy and racial affinity among mestizo Hondurans and an imagined national citizen-subject who is threatened by the territorial claims of Black Hondurans, who for many are not legitimate heirs to coastal lands, because they are from "another place."

This racial logic is deepened by the official terminology used to categorize non-mestizo Hondurans. It is for this reason that Beatriz was so adamantly opposed to the use of the term *Afro*. For many of my colleagues, the government's persistent use of *Afro* was seen as an attempt to displace the Blackness around them onto some other faraway place, rather than acknowledge it as an inherent part of the nation. This sentiment was widely echoed by Garifuna in Triunfo and by representatives from leading Garifuna organizations.[14] In April 2014, the Garifuna organization Gemelos lobbied the government to annul African Heritage Month and to eliminate the words *Afro-descendant* and *Afro-Honduran* from all official documents, decrees, and other texts. They argued that the use of these terms had "substituted their true origin in Honduras with an African nationality."[15] This argument speaks to a different narrative of belonging, one that firmly anchors Blackness to Honduras, to the land, as well as to freedom, since Garifuna often distinguish themselves from other people of African descent with the simple adage, "We were never slaves." Thus, to be Garifuna is to be Black Indigenous, to be free, and to be Honduran. Opposition to the term *Afro-descendant* was not a denial of Blackness; rather, for organizations such as Gemelos and OFRANEH, it was an attempt to counter the politics of expulsion imposed by the state. This political strategy reinforces an oddly amorphous vision of Afro-descendant people as by definition placeless, making it that much easier to ensure the property rights of whites.

In popular use, mestizo or *ladino* references people who are neither Indigenous nor Black. Yet this racially ambiguous category still allows for white Hondurans to tether their claims to national belonging to the pre-Hispanic past (see Brondo 2010), because they are the purported descendants of the original Indigenous inhabitants of the land, whereas Garifuna are not. But the term *ladino* also lacks internal coherence, which allows for the absorption of other non-Black peoples into the nation, as in the case of Arab-descendant migrants who arrived in Honduras in the nineteenth century.[16]

Now I will return to the moment in which Miriam proclaimed, "The ones who run this country haven't even been here one hundred years and no one calls them foreigners!" Her protest speaks to the fact that the new drivers of capitalist accumulation—the service and *maquila* (manufacturing) industries—are controlled almost exclusively by a handful of Arab-descendant families. This group, principally Palestinian Christians, sometimes referred to as *turcos* in popular discourse, are nonetheless easily recognizable as Hondurans with the full rights and privileges of citizenship. Perhaps then we should understand mestizo as an aspirational racial category that is tethered to capital but always exclusive of Blackness, whereas, Black peoples cannot be recognized as Indigenous to any place but Africa.[17] Black expulsion allows elite mestizos to have final say over who can and cannot be a member of the nation, and to what degree. Indeed, Garifuna are members of the nation to the extent that they contribute to the national economy, that is, through tourism, and by virtue of the benevolence of state actors who "allow" Garifuna to be in Honduras despite their presumed foreignness. In this way, anti-Black racism is shrouded in benevolent discourses of multicultural inclusion.

Inherently anti-Black logics of governance render invisible the ways in which racist governmentality is enacted and allow for state institutions and the dominant racial group to argue that any laws or policies deemed to redress historically rooted racial inequities in the present are actually racist. The charge of reverse racism becomes a key governing logic in itself, one used to "classify populations and exclude people of color from the categories of citizenship and the imagined community called the nation" (Grosfoguel 2004, 327). Further, this logic can be mobilized to incite anti-Black violence and to discipline unruly subjects, those who challenge the supremacy of the dominant racial order. The allocation of resources and access to rights and privileges of citizenship are mediated through the color of one's skin.

Blackness and Indigeneity: A False Antagonism

The court's site visit ended inconclusively on August 22; more meetings, more papers to sign, and then they were gone. On October 8, 2015, after two months of excruciating suspense, the court revealed its verdict, ruling in favor of the community. It said that the state was responsible for the violation of Article 21 of the American Convention on Human Rights, specifically citing the state's failure to adequately protect the community's right to collective property. Although the state had previously titled lands claimed by the community, the Inter-American Court of Human Rights (2015, 30) ruled that the state had not adequately "guaranteed effective use and enjoyment" of the community's collective property rights. This had created a situation, the court recognized, of sustained land tenure insecurity for Triunfeños, jeopardizing their ability to exercise effective ownership over their lands and producing significant impacts on communal land use practices, territoriality, and cultural values and ways of knowing.

The logic of cultural difference was central to both the legal rationale used by the court to adjudicate the case and the framing of land claims by Garifuna plaintiffs before the court. As I mentioned earlier, to secure territorial rights, the Indigenous community or people in question must demonstrate deep cultural ties to the land, which corresponds to their "particular way of being, seeing and acting in the world." That way of being must both be foundational to them—in other words, constitutive of their "worldview, religiosity, and in turn, their cultural identity"—and must also be threatened by the loss of territory.[18]

Judges, lawyers, human rights defenders, and anthropological experts all build upon the established legal definition of *Indigenous* as articulated within international laws and conventions. The most prominent example is International Labour Organization Convention No. 169, adopted in 1989, which states that *Indigenous* applies to:

(a) tribal peoples in independent countries whose social, cultural and economic conditions distinguish them from other sections of the national community, and whose status is regulated wholly or partially by their own customs or traditions or by special laws or regulations;

(b) peoples in independent countries who are regarded as indigenous on account of their descent from the populations which inhabited the country, or a geographical region to which the country belongs, at the time of conquest or colonisation or the establishment of present state boundaries and who, irrespective of their legal status, retain some or all of their own social, economic, cultural and political institutions. (Article 1, Convention 169)

While self-identification as Indigenous is an important component of how Indigeneity is defined in the courtroom, so is the notion of descent from the original inhabitants of the country or "geographical region to which the country belongs." This definition binds cultural difference to biological ancestry, and in the case of Latin America, to pre-Hispanic origins (read: non-African). Within these parameters, Garifuna may lay claim to Indigeneity on the basis of their sociocultural characteristics and yet—because of their African ancestry—are not fully recognizable as such. Thus, the question whether Garifuna are actually "Indigenous" became a crucial point of debate between the "community" and the "state" in the *Garifuna Community of Triunfo de la Cruz v. Honduras* and loomed large in the final deliberations of the court.

Scholars of Indigenous social movements have noted that Afro-descendant populations in Latin America have difficulties making claims for collective rights (Hooker 2005; Anderson 2007).[19] This is attributed to the fact that most Afro-descendant populations are concentrated in urban areas and, therefore, well integrated with the national culture (Van Cott 2000). However, the Garifuna case presents a nuanced opening insofar as the Garifuna are both Black and Indigenous. Dual racial and ethnic identification enabled Garifuna activists to harness international legal mechanisms designed to protect the territorial rights of Indigenous peoples.

Ultimately, the evidence presented by the Inter-American Commission on Human Rights in support of Triunfo's claims before the court outweighed the objections of the state. Not only did the court recognize the

Garifuna as an Indigenous people with legally sound claims to ancestral rights, but it detailed how and why Garifuna constituted an Indigenous people. For this, the court drew upon the extensive evidence compiled by the Inter-American Commission, historical and anthropological records, and the expert testimony of the legal scholars José Aylwin and James Anaya, as well as the written testimony I provided for the *Case of the Garifuna Community Punta Piedra v. Honduras.* Culture and its internal coherence was indispensable in the determination of the rights-worthiness of Garifuna. In this regard, the ruling furthers the power-laden discursive fields through which Indigenous difference is constituted (Loperena 2020). As Jennifer Hamilton (2008, 4) argues, "Rather than having a specific referent (indigenous cultural practice and epistemology), Indigeneity refers to the idea that the content and meaning of indigenous difference is produced in particular contexts, in response to a variety of social, political and economic forces." In this sense, Indigeneity is produced vis-à-vis these courtroom deliberations and through the fraught union of anthropological knowledge production on Indigenous peoples and the law.

This myopia in legal discourse disfigures the complex nature of Indigenous subjectivity and elides more substantive political claims. Indeed, the culturalist logics used to secure recognition from the state are essential in "maintaining the structure of colonized/colonizer relations," as argued by Glen Coulthard (2007). Nonetheless, the IACHR remains an important site of struggle for Indigenous peoples throughout Latin America and is increasingly bound up with the fight for territorial autonomy (Loperena, Hernández, and Mora 2018; Sieder, Schjolden, and Angell 2005). As such, establishing a stake on a place-based identity, both culturally distinct and imperiled by external forces, was crucial to the legal strategy employed by the community to secure rights. The state representatives undermined these arguments by juxtaposing Garifuna to other Indigenous peoples who not only preserve distinct ways of being and normative systems but also lay claim to a pre-Hispanic past, which constitutes the cornerstone of Honduran national identity.

Ultimately, the state's arguments were too weak to sway the court, but the judgment still served to buttress Honduran state sovereignty, because the state is positioned as the ultimate arbitrator of rights and justice. In this way, Garifuna placeness is partly contingent on recognition from the sovereign, a process that holds great menace for racialized populations because of the limited political possibilities and constraints of the law (see Coulthard 2007).

On the Question of Sovereignty

The court's ruling raises several important questions: What are the broader implications of this judgment for Indigenous and Black territorial struggles? Is the court the primary vehicle to realize Indigenous and Black autonomy? How does the judgment address or redress the condition of anti-Black racism in Honduras? Many Garifuna land activists were critical of the law and its limitations, yet they still opted to bring their petition to the Inter-American Commission on Human Rights, because legal recognition remains an important means to demand redress for historical wrongdoing and to garner attention from the international community for the extraordinary violence perpetrated by the state against these communities. Audra Simpson (2014, 24) observes: "We could see this as a political strategy that is cognizant of an unequal relationship, understands the terms of bondage, and chooses to stay within them in order to assert a greater principle: nationhood, sovereignty, jurisdiction by those who are deemed to *lack* that power, a power that is rooted in historical precedent but is conveniently forgotten or legislated away." In other words, a willingness to operate within this theater of recognition is necessary to make certain claims on the state as a people, one that is historically, juridically, and culturally constituted. This reality of course exists alongside a deep skepticism about the radical potentiality of the law, which was well merited given the court's failure to recognize Garifuna maritime rights and refusal to extend the boundaries of the existing land title to include areas held in "reserve" for future population growth.

Triunfo's ancestral land claim includes beach and sea areas, which the state lawyers objected to: "The appropriation of such zones is not possible, nor is it possible to issue a title of ownership over them, as they are not open to trade by individuals, but rather are of use to the entire nation," as stipulated in the "Theory of Public Goods."[20] Moreover, Article 617 of the Honduran Civil Code provides, among other things, that "the adjacent sea and its beaches, are called national goods of public use or public goods."[21] Here we see how Honduras asserts its sovereignty over land and maritime resources "for the use of the entire nation" while also positioning the rights claims of Indigenous and Black peoples as an affront on Honduran national sovereignty and the use rights of the normative Honduran citizen-subject. What is of significance, in my reading of the state's arguments, is the extent to which national sovereignty stands in for mestizo sovereignty, since the resources—land and maritime—of Indigenous and Black Hondurans are always up for grabs, as is amply visible from government backed development policy and legislation. This claim also ignores the specific ways elite mestizo families have privatized the eastern edge of the community's previously titled lands. Recall that the resort enclave Playa Escondida is almost completely inaccessible to Garifuna, as many of the luxury homes are fortified with guards and walls to prevent outsiders from entering.

The contrast between the state's legal arguments before the court and the on-the-ground realities in Triunfo makes visible how the logic of private property trumps all other claims. This legal arrangement protects the propriety of those with the capital to buy land and to use it in a way that is deemed to be productive—in terms of national economic growth—or in ways that cohere with dominant racial-spatial regimes of progress. Elite mestizos demonstrate their ownership over land in a variety of ways, from the creation of profitable infrastructures (e.g., luxury homes, fortifications, pools, hotels) to the large-scale exploitation of the resources concentrated in these zones, as seen in the massive usurpation of lands along the Caribbean coast for African palm plantations and by the fishing industry. Exploitation of maritime resources by fisheries is permitted and folded into the logic of development—for the benefit of the nation—while small-scale fishing by Garifuna in protected areas, such as Punta Izopo and the Cuero y Salado Wildlife Refuge, are rendered threats (Loperena 2016a). But threats to what? Precisely to the tourism imaginary of the state, which sees these environmental resources as vital to the establishment of large-scale eco-destinations such as the Indura Beach and Golf Resort.

Despite the many limitations, the court's favorable judgment is a significant victory for the community, morally and legally, because now the ethical standing of communal land defenders—which state authorities and community members aligned with the opposing faction often questioned—has been legitimated by an international court of law. Court-mandated reparations included the effective demarcation of lands granted to the community; new measures to protect titled land; the investigation and prosecution of those deemed criminally responsible for the deaths of four community land activists; and the establishment of a $1.5 million development fund to cover pecuniary and nonpecuniary damages to the community. Not surprisingly, the state has failed to comply with the reparations called for by the court, other than the creation of an interinstitutional commission charged with implementation of the sentence. This failure to comply speaks to the limits of legal strategies for justice and redress for structural racism.

Conclusion

The negation of the Indigenous status of the Garifuna people in the *Garifuna Community of Triunfo de la Cruz v. Honduras* is not only a legal argument advanced by the state to dispossess them of their ancestral lands but also a prerequisite for the government's extractivist development agenda on the Caribbean coast. In this manner, state institutions, with support from international financial institutions like the World Bank, the Inter-American Development Bank, and private investors, can ensure the success of the national tourism industry. The representatives of the state also relied on fixed ideas about cultural alterity, the pre-Hispanic past and Indigenous racial difference to position Garifuna as external to the nation. This legal strategy substitutes a hybrid and highly nuanced Black Indigenous subjectivity for one that is intelligible within the framework of racial domination of mestizos over communities of color and excludes Blackness from the nation both spatially and temporally.

Although the court's verdict upheld the territorial rights of the community and acknowledged the state's responsibility for the violation of these rights, the ruling elided the most substantive political claims, including maritime rights that could have secured communal rights over key economic resources for generations to come, but would also challenge too forcefully the sovereignty of the mestizo state. I believe the court's refusal to recognize Garifuna maritime rights as well as rights to lands designated as "communal reserves" is due to the inability of the law to see beyond the narrow culturalist logics undergirding the legal definition of Indigeneity. The ruling has the unintended effect of sustaining essentialized representations of Indigenous difference. The conferral of rights is premised on past ways of being, and as such, these rights coarticulate with the larger framework of racist governmentality, responsible for denying Indigenous placeness within modernity. Thus, even when Garifuna can obtain legal recognition as an Indigenous people, the juridical boundaries of Indigeneity make it nearly impossible for them to fully secure the resources they lay claim to.

Audra Simpson (2014, 16) has written brilliantly about the limits of recognition, and juxtaposes this political objective to "refusal," which entails "a willful distancing from state-driven forms of recognition and sociability in favor of others." The Garifuna struggle for territorial autonomy employs both strategies; Garifuna demand legal recognition of their land rights while also acknowledging the law's inherent bias toward the state and the dominant settler society. The legal case is therefore only one component of a larger strategy to contest the extractivist economic model pursued by the mestizo elite that also imagines Garifuna lands as appropriable. Refusal materializes through a politics of spatial obstruction, refusal to pay taxes, and the expression of nonnormative political desires.[22]

Garifuna ways of being on and with the land are essential for group cohesion and future livelihood, particularly within a society that views them as interlopers or as *arrivants*. In this vein, the demand for autonomy exceeds the legal ruse of recognition. As I have argued in the previous chapters, autonomy cannot be achieved through the mere recognition of rights, but rather the recognition of rights is a means to buttress the ethico-political standing of the *defensores de la tierra* as they engage in a politics of refusal that ultimately seeks to unsettle the very notion of what it means to be "free" within a racist and brutal state apparatus. Freedom is not reducible to liberal rights; rather, autonomy is an affective disposition premised on the struggle for a collective future, as Clara made clear in her testimony, one that supplants the moral and temporal mandates of progress with values such as solidarity and reciprocal care. Much of this is lost within the legal realm. It does not appear in the court transcripts, nor does it factor into the exacting legal reasoning outlined in the sentence, yet it continues to animate the struggles of the *defensores de la tierra* and their wager for a different future.

CONCLUSION

If we leave this land, it would lead to our demise, because this land is our inheritance, which our ancestors left us. Here we live in peace, we do what we like, we are free. We are free.

DOÑA TOYA, Garifuna buyei (2013)

ON MARCH 2, 2016, five months after the Inter-American Court of Human Rights (IACHR) issued its historic ruling against the state of Honduras, Berta Cáceres was murdered. Her murder is not an isolated act—dozens of Indigenous and Black activists have been killed since the IACHR ruling. But her murder was particularly brutal and particularly painful. As cofounder and general coordinator of the Civic Council of Popular and Indigenous Organizations of Honduras (COPINH, by its Spanish acronym), Berta worked tirelessly to halt the expansion of extractive industries within Indigenous territories, often in close collaboration with OFRANEH. At the time of her death, she was leading a daring community uprising against the development of a large hydroelectric project that was slated to be built on the Gualcarque River in the Lenca community of Río Blanco. Funding for the project—as with many of the development initiatives we have seen throughout this book—hinged on loans from multilateral development banks and private financing. The Agua Zarca dam was backed by a consortium including the Honduran renewable energy company Desarrollos Energéticos SA (DESA) and Sinohydro, a massive state-owned Chinese hydropower engineering and construction company.

In April 2013, Lenca community activists, organized by COPINH, blocked the main access road to the Agua Zarca construction site. The government responded by militarizing the entire community and surrounding area. Four months later the military opened fire on a group of peaceful protesters in Río Blanco, which resulted in the death of Lenca community leader Tomás García and injured his son, Alan García. Subsequently, DESA accused COPINH and Berta of multiple crimes, including usurpation of land, coercion, and causing over $3 million dollars of damage to the company's private installations. The criminalization of protest has become an increasingly common method of repression used by state and parastate actors, including private security companies, to silence opposition to the larger postcoup economic agenda. Berta's brutal assassination on March 3, 2016, implicated not only DESA but also state-backed extractivist developments in energy, agribusiness, and tourism.[1]

Extractivism today, as in the past, is tethered to a vicious political-economic calculus that renders Black and Indigenous peoples and their territories into capital. This happens in two primary ways: through the dispossession of land, where what is extracted is the ability of Indigenous and Black peoples to use and possess the land in ways that are resonant with their own epistemologies and sacred practices, and through the generation of surplus value via the exploitation of nature, bodies, and culture, as realized through the creation of large tourism projects like the Indura Beach and Golf Resort. In other words, both culture and the body are naturalized—made into a "natural" part of the landscape—from which the mestizo elite extract immense wealth.

The generation of huge profits can come only with the annihilation of life. This life-annihilating impulse, which social movement activists in Honduras refer to as the *sistema de la muerte* (death system), has a particularly anti-Black valence. This is because extractivism is inherently racialized and refigures sites of Black survival, community, and home into commodities for elite accumulation. But the *sistema de la muerte* is simultaneously a settler colonial project; at the same time that it situates Blackness as foreign and disposable, it exiles Indigenous peoples to a mythical "otherwhere"—outside the time and space of the present.

The death of Berta Cáceres prompted a global response. Allied movements from across the world, including human rights organizations, fifty-eight members of the US Congress, and the European Parliament all demanded accountability for her murder. The outpouring of grief and the clarion call for justice was a testament to her larger-than-life struggle, to her vision of a world in which equality and environmental sustainability is lived, not just proselytized. She lived this way until her final days.

The news of Berta's death was shocking, not only because of the international accolades she had received and that many believed would offer her protection, but also because she was a friend and mentor. I met her in 2003 during my first stint working in Honduras. She inspired me to do research on social and environmental justice in Indigenous territories and to do this work while committing myself to sustained political engagement. This is why her loss was so profoundly unsettling for me. But as with all great leaders, her vision transcends the boundaries of the present; it germinates and reproduces itself. The continuing manifestation of her spirit speaks to the strength and courage of the larger realm of Indigenous and Black land and environmental activists who, like Berta, in the face overwhelming violence, continue to fight for a greater good.

I have written and rewritten these pages, knowing that my words will be inadequate to capture the profound impact of her loss. Instead, what I offer here, in these final pages, is necessarily incomplete. It's an offering, a few fragments of her work and vision, which I share in honor of her memory, while also recognizing that my words are not sufficient. Words never are.

Seven years have now passed since the IACHR ruling against the state of Honduras for the violation of Garifuna communal property rights. Little has changed. The government has failed to comply with the reparations called for by the court. And violence against Garifuna land defenders has spiked dramatically. This violence has produced a state of nearly permanent crisis in the communities, where conflicts over land—nearly all targeted by developers either for African palm cultivation or for tourism developments—continue to gnaw at Garifuna territorial autonomy.

On July 18, 2020, in a brazen act of terror, four Garifuna men from Triunfo de la Cruz were forcibly disappeared. At around 5:30 a.m. the men were violently abducted from their homes and forced into three unmarked vehicles. The assailants had bulletproof vests and brandished weapons. They were dressed in police uniforms. The government, as expected, has categorically denied any involvement.

The victims of this vicious attack—Alber Snider Centeno, Suami Aparicio Mejía, Milton Joel Martínez, Gerardo Rochez—have not been seen or heard from since.[2] As president of the *patronato* (communal governing council), Snider Centeno was actively engaged in several investigations into stolen lands within Triunfo. Three out of four of the disappeared men, including Snider, were members of OFRANEH and aligned with the broader struggle in defense of Garifuna territorial rights. Many Triunfeños allege that this odious act is another attempt on the part of state authorities to nullify the land defense movement.

OFRANEH believes the crime is directly related to the community's successful IACHR case. They note that the forced disappearance of these four men follows a troubling trajectory of violence and intimidation against Garifuna land defenders, which has proliferated in recent years. Moreover, the Bureau of Police Investigation attempted to divert attention from their alleged participation in the disappearances by spearheading a smear campaign against the victims, accusing them of being involved in an organized crime ring.

On July 31, 2020 OFRANEH issued a press release highlighting the questionable circumstances surrounding the case and the criminal investigation. The abduction took place during a state-imposed curfew designed to mitigate the spread of COVID-19:

> On Saturday, July 18, the country was under a curfew, which theoretically prevented the movement of vehicles without the permission of the authorities. In this sense, it is impossible for us to believe that the mobilization of three vehicles transporting heavily armed men has gone completely "unnoticed."

... The state of Honduras claims to be "guarantor" of human rights; unfortunately, the statistics indicate the opposite. In the last years, more than a dozen Garifuna have been assassinated for defending their ancestral territory, and to date the state has not presented concrete results, and instead has committed itself to discrediting arguments that relate these crimes to territorial defense. (OFRANEH, July 31, 2020)

OFRANEH's apprehensions about the state's motives and potential involvement in the crime are warranted given the well-documented participation of state officials and the national police in acts of repression against land and environmental activists in other parts of the country.

The forced disappearance of Alber Snider Centeno, Suami Aparicio Mejía, Milton Joel Martínez, Gerardo Rochez—like the murder of Berta Cáceres—echoes a disturbing pattern of state-sanctioned violence against human rights campaigners and Indigenous and Black environmental activists throughout the Americas. Juliet Hooker (2019) has characterized this new conjuncture as a period of "racial retrenchment," an era in which formally recognized rights for racially minoritized peoples are being rolled back, sometimes violently, which has simultaneously revealed a deep seated racial animus against Black and Indigenous peoples. Hooker, in collaboration with the Anti-Racist Research and Action Network, argues that the past four decades of expansion of rights is coming to an end, and in some cases these hard-fought victories, including collective rights to land, are being undone (Hooker 2019, 3).

The surge in violence amid seemingly huge victories has several explanations, including the rising wealth and influence of elite sectors of society and their tightening grip over the economy; the "organized abandonment" of social welfare prompted by neoliberal state reorganization (Gilmore 2008; Hooker 2019); and the contaminant rise of far-right politics globally. In this context poor but racially dominant groups within multiracial societies have come to blame their own disenfranchisement on the rights gains made by Black and Indigenous peoples. This might help illustrate why, even after the historic IACHR ruling against Honduras, Garifuna land defenders are facing a barrage of violence.

In spite of the devastating and racist violence they face, Black and Indigenous peoples continue to organize in defense of the life-sustaining resources that abound within their territories, but within the crucible of extractive capitalism, even ordinary forms of living and survival are acts of defiance. This is what Audra Simpson (2014, 3) refers to as the "labor of living in the face of an expectant and a foretold cultural and political death."

Throughout this book, I have narrated the labor of living that Garifuna engage in, the stakes of their decades-long struggle to defend their lands against the profit-driven plunder of their territories. These projects—hydroelectric dams, industrial farming, resorts, mines—threaten their presence in Honduras today and also their ability to exist in the future. The collective future is what is at stake—a future wholly under threat by a political and economic system that has little regard for life, or at least, for the realms of life that cannot be rendered productive or profitable. Thus to *rescue the future*, for my interlocutors, entails a commitment to nurturing the relationships that exist between Garifuna and their territory, as well as those that sustain life between and across the present, past, and future inhabitants of the land.

Similarly, in his discussion of Indigenous resistance against the Dakota Access Pipeline in the United States, Nick Estes elaborates on the relationships between Lakota and Dakota peoples and their more-than-human relatives—land and water. To defend the land and protect the water is necessary to ensure the "the continuation of life on a planet ravaged by capitalism" (Estes 2019, 15). In this sense, the interrelationship between human and more-than-human life stands in direct contrast to capitalist exploitation and the profit-driven alienation it demands.

Garifuna understandings of land are cohesive with those espoused by other Indigenous peoples throughout the Americas. However, because Garifuna are Black, they are often accused of strategically usurping Indigenous identity (and cosmology, for that matter) for material rights, or more specifically, to claim land. As I have demonstrated, this allegation is an argument used by the Honduran state to extend its sovereign control over the coastal lands that Garifuna have inhabited for over two hundred years. Garifuna self-identification as Black Indigenous is more than a legal strategy in pursuit of rights. It is a substantive claim, rooted in Garifuna life and space-making practices, which emphasize living with rather than off the land. Relationships between and among Garifuna and their coastal territory are of course constantly shifting, in part because of the sway of development ideology, which has been used to dispossess Garifuna lands and to generate acquiescence to "liberal-capitalist systems of private property and commodified real estate markets" (Nichols 2018).[3] But for the land defenders, the land is not reducible to its commodity form; it is the axis around which notions of self and collective belonging cohere.

Through their activism, collective organizing, and the everyday labor of living, land defenders enact a different way being in space, one that powerfully contests the extractivist logics undergirding the coastal development agenda, and, to echo Ruthie Gilmore (2002), that underscores the "geographic imperative" that animates all struggles for social justice. This is because racism is a project of spatialization, which displaces Blackness and Indigeneity to what Fanon (2008) termed "zones of non-being." The land defenders are keenly aware of this, often proclaiming: "Without the land we will cease to be Garifuna." This simple but powerful statement illustrates the central import of the land to Garifuna ways of life and future survival. It suggests that land is more than an abstract means of production, which, as Marx reminds us, always expresses a social relationship of exploitation. As such, Garifuna understandings of land defies the core principle of capitalism—that *individuals* can (and should) own property—and thus ruptures the proprietary relationship upon which liberal personhood is based.

As an anthropologist aligned with larger struggles for social justice, I am committed not only to documenting catastrophe but also to documenting—and celebrating—life and the otherwise. Elizabeth Povinelli (2011) has described this ambiguous but essential part of our world as "forms of life that are at odds with dominant, and dominating, modes of being." These forms of life—or alternative socialities—don't exist outside of the political and economic structures of society but rather emerge from them. They become visible and therefore able to be documented by virtue of their friction with hegemonic social forms and modes of being. Part of our work, then, is to shed light on alternative ways of living that emerge from the ruinous encounter between capitalism and its Other. This is what Sadiya Hartman (2019, 33) refers to as "the beauty that resides in and animates the determination to live free."

I have endeavored to document the workings of extractivism in Honduras, which in the pursuit of profit threatens all life but that has particularly dire impacts on Black and Indigenous peoples and their territories. I have shown the mechanisms by which this racialized profiteering operates in one specific corner of the globe, as well as the battles waged by racially minoritized peoples—both against this destruction and also in pursuit of another world. Their struggles, it turns out, have much broader implications for our world—a world in which the conjoined crises of racism and environmental plunder are eating away at our shared future.

In narrating their history, Garifuna frequently reminded me, "We were never slaves." This is not just a means to distinguish their history from that of other African diasporic peoples in the Americas; it is a declaration of a humanity that refuses appropriation and of the possibility of Black placeness in the Americas. "We were never slaves" invites the question, then, What does it mean to be human, to be free, under capitalism?

I suggest that the claim of Black placeness is an act of rebellion, in the way McKittrick (2016, 85) defines it: "to honor Black life as an ongoing struggle against . . . objecthood and placelessness." It encompasses staking a claim to Black life and Black futures that challenges us to think beyond the confines of normative spatial epistemes and to grapple with the limits of conventional understandings of freedom. Freedom here is not the liberal rights notion of freedom, nor is it the freedom to appropriate, or to buy and sell property. Rather, freedom is that which ensures collective survival, contingent on an ethical orientation to one another and to the land.[4] The collective future to which Garifuna land defenders aspire enables a more expansive notion of freedom—a freedom to do and be otherwise. This freedom grows in twisty knots; it is of course always constrained and yet worth fighting for.

NOTES

Introduction

1. Quoted in Jackie McVicar, "Indigenous Men in Honduras Are Being Abducted. Are the Police to Blame? America Magazine," *America: The Jesuit Review*, August 5, 2020, https://www.americamagazine.org/politics-society/2020/08/05/indigenous-men-honduras-are-being-abducted-are-police-blame.

2. There are seven officially recognized Indigenous peoples in Honduras—the Lenca, Miskito, Tawahka, Pech, Maya Chortis and Tolupán—in addition to the English-speaking Blacks (or Creoles) and the Garifuna, who also identify as Indigenous but are most often classified as Afro-Honduran.

3. February 15, 2003, was a massive antiwar action that took place in cities across the globe.

4. The Free Trade Agreement of the Americas, or FTAA, was a trade agreement backed by the US government, steeped in neoliberal economic thinking of the time, and strongly opposed by left-leaning parties and politicians. The late Hugo Chávez, then president of Venezuela, was among the most outspoken critics of the plan, which he argued would be used to undermine the sovereignty of Latin American nation-states. He subsequently proposed an alternative trade block, the Bolivarian Alliance for the People of Our America (ALBA, by its Spanish acronym). In close alliance with Brazil, ALBA became an emblematic policy objective of leftist governments throughout Latin America.

5. This is evidenced in the popular protest chant "¡Otro mundo es posible!" (Another world is possible). It was also the slogan for the World Social Forums, which had wide resonance among grassroots groups in Latin America. According to Arturo Escobar, alternative imaginings of the future are rooted in actual existing worlds and

territorial struggles. In *Pluriversal Politics*, he (2020, 69–70) argues the epistemologies and struggles of Indigenous, peasant, and Afro-descendant peoples are pathways to transformation which require thinking outside the space of Western social theory.

6. I am inspired by the work of Sadiya Hartman, who in *Wayward Lives* (2019), illustrates how young Black women in the early twentieth-century United States made life in the face of death, including the everyday acts of resistance they engaged in simply by daring to experience pleasure or freedom, however compromised.

7. Contrary to popular belief, much of the capital for these initiatives actually comes from within the country, as is the case in Aguán Valley, where land grabs for oil palm production have been orchestrated by mostly domestic investors with support from multilateral development institutions (Edelman and León 2013, 1700).

8. This is so even in "pink tide" states, where extractivism has coincided with more progressive, and presumably anti-neoliberal ideologies (Ruiz Marrero 2011).

9. Braudel and Wallerstein (2009) have encouraged social scientists to think beyond the temporal immediacy of the event, and in doing so to locate old habits of thought and action that animate the "current reality," which is actually "a conjoining of movements with different origins and rhythms."

10. Interrogating the tourism-extraction nexus, Davidov and Büscher (2014, 6) argue that tourism ventures within rural Indigenous communities entail both the commodification of nature and the extraction of dance, food, and local crafts for the consumption of visiting tourists. Córdoba Azcárate (2020, 13) argues that capital intensive infrastructure development associated with tourism "exhausts places, bodies, and resources in order to satisfy short-term consumer demand." Tourism, she asserts, is "reengineering" the earth. My work is conversant with these authors but centers race as an analytic for understanding the extractivist character of tourism. By analyzing tourism development through the lens of race and racialization, we can establish clearer linkages between colonial practices of resource plunder and the destination-making politics I detail in this book.

11. The Honduran state is not a bounded or singular entity. Rather, it is constituted by a heterogeneous set of actors, institutions, and social practices that are tethered to other "statelike" spheres of power; this complexity undermines its utility as a coherent object of study (see Abrams [1977] 2006; Trouillot 2001). Nonetheless, social movement activists often experience "the state" as an antagonistic force, and thus it remains a meaningful referent and target of their activism.

12. I use the phrase "Black and Indigenous peoples" to refer to the full spectrum of racially minoritized populations in Honduras. Throughout Latin America, Black and Indigenous protest movements in defense of their territories and collective rights have been met with brutal repression. This worrisome pattern has enabled scholars of the region to draw clear linkages between the resurgence of extractivism and "racial retrenchment" (Hooker 2020).

13. In her study of care in neoliberal Chile, Han (2012, 5) demonstrates how the state, through orchestrated acts of social divestment, transposed responsibility for the care of its citizens onto individuals. In the neoliberal conjuncture, discourses of "self-

care" and "self-improvement" become dominant, and, she argues, they are premised on a self that is both sovereign and morally autonomous.

14. Douglas MacRae Taylor's *The Black Carib of British Honduras*, published in 1951, is a notable exception.

15. Historical works by Bourgois (1989), Euraque (1996), Putnam (2002), Chambers (2010), and Gudmundson and Wolfe (2010) have helped to counter this misconception regarding African heritage in Costa Rica and Honduras.

16. Ethnographies by Mark Anderson (2009), Keri Brondo (2013), and Jennifer Goett (2017) have helped shape these emerging debates, shedding light on the gendered and raced politics of diasporic Blackness in Central America, as well as the varied modes of political subjectivity that have emerged in response to the erasure of their histories and larger claims to place. Because of the particular social and historical ties between Caribbean Central America and the Caribbean islands, the Atlantic coasts of Honduras, Nicaragua, and Costa Rica are often imagined as exterior to the formation of the contemporary Central American states, which reinscribes the exteriority of Blackness to the Central American isthmus.

17. Paul López Oro (2016) has contributed substantively to this emerging formulation through his foundational chapter "Ni de aquí, ni de allá" in which he argues that Garifuna New Yorkers live within multiple diasporas and are thus simultaneously Black, Indigenous, and Latinx, which defies dominant ideologies of racial categorization. He has furthered this analysis by highlighting the various terms Garifuna use to describe their identities (e.g., *Black Indigenous*, *Afro-Indigenous*, *Black Carib*), which he says points to the "multiplicity of geographies informing Garinagu racial identity formations" in Central America and its diasporas (López Oro 2021, 250).

18. The notion that Garifuna are Indigenous-like may hold in place the analytic distinctions between Blackness and Indigeneity.

19. In her study of Mexican postcolonial racial geographies, Saldaña-Portillo (2016, 124) demonstrates how through the extension of liberal rights and politics, the Mexican state effectively "cut off Indigenous peoples from their spatial practice." In other words, liberalism was a tool to sever Indigenous peoples from what she calls their "territorial difference." Similarly, Ybarra's (2018, 15) account of resource conflicts in Guatemala shows how racial liberalism "subsumes Indigenous collectives in logics of individual rights and needs."

20. Aside from being conceptually provocative, Black Indigeneity has important implications for the on-the-ground political work and aims of antiracist struggle.

21. I provide a much more thorough engagement with these dynamics in chapter 4.

22. Restrictions on resource use and extraction within the park's "core zone" (see map on p. xiii) have infringed on the rights of Garifuna living in the area, and in some cases they have been rendered into environmental threats (see Loperena 2016a).

23. Similarly, Macarena Gómez Barris (2017, 3) argues that extractivism facilitates the "reorganization of territories, populations, and plant and animal life into extractable data and natural resources for material and immaterial accumulation."

24. Fernando Coronil critiques Marx's unitary focus on labor as the source of ex-

change value. Centering the physical materiality of the commodity, he argues, "makes it possible to view the specific mechanisms through which capitalist exploitation extracts surplus labor from workers and as well as natural riches from the earth under different historical conditions" (Coronil 2000, 356). An additional critique of Marx's focus on labor is relevant, that is, the distinct status of the slave as property in preemancipation plantation society (see Hall [1980] 2019, 213), and more recently with regard to the profits that derive from financialization.

25. Mestizo is generally used to reference people of mixed Indigenous and European descent; it is the dominant racial category in Honduras. Garifuna refer to mestizos as *indios, ladinos,* and *blancos* (whites), which underscores their exclusion from this racial category.

26. In her examination of Canadian tar sands mega-projects, Preston (2017, 356) uses the phrase "racial extractivism" to highlight the colonial roots of neoliberal resource extraction within the oil and gas industry specifically. She analyzes how race-based epistemologies are embedded within social relations of production and consumption and serve to normalize settler claims to Indigenous lands.

27. See Sadiya Hartman's (1997) discussion of the fungibility of commodities as it pertains to the captive body.

28. Cheryl Harris's (1993) foundational work "Whiteness as Property" has been fundamental to my own understanding of the relationship of land, property, and modes of racial subjugation.

29. Global Witness, "Defending Tomorrow," July 29, 2020, https://www.globalwitness.org/en/campaigns/environmental-activists/defending-tomorrow/.

30. In her ethnography of Afro-Nicaraguan activism, Goett (2017, 3) theorizes Black autonomy as "an expression of African diasporic identification and gendered political consciousness," which she defines as a vital social practice that permeates and extends from the most intimate spheres of life. It is thus greater than the legal recognition of rights to territory or self-determination.

31. Lisa Lowe (2015, 107) demonstrates how the tenets of liberal governance grew out of the colonial encounter, securing "freedom" for the colonizers through the despotic denial of liberty to those deemed to be incapable of self-determination. Thus the prevailing notion of political liberty enshrined within Western democracies was entangled, from its inception, with the subjugation of those who were presumed to be incapable of self-governance and progress. Similarly, Chakravartty and Da Silva (2012) address the ways that the condition of indebtedness precludes racial others from the possibility full moral and economic personhood.

32. Historical entanglements between anthropology and colonialism have been well rehearsed by preeminent scholars, including Faye Harrison, Edward Said, and Talal Asad.

33. For example, leaning the native language is a hallmark of anthropological research practice, but I chose not to learn Garifuna. Many elders in Triunfo de la Cruz expressed concern about the political implications of outsiders speaking Garifuna.

Since most Triunfeños are also fluent in Spanish, it was not necessary for me to learn Garifuna to do my research.

34. *Antropofagia* was a Brazilian cultural movement associated with de Oswald de Andrade. Through acts of cultural cannibalism, Andrade spawned a uniquely Brazilian artistic aesthetic.

35. Ryan Jobson (2020, 5) powerfully critiques the notion of field site as bounded culture area, which he argues is often deployed possessively as a currency for professional advancement.

36. In its judgment, issued in October 2015, the Inter-American Court of Human Rights determined the Honduran state to be responsible for violation of Garifuna collective property rights.

37. Yarimar Bonilla (2015) has contributed to this debate in her reclassification of anthropological interlocutors as "cotheorists." I'm also inspired by the notion of fugitive anthropology, which entails "rethinking the contours of the political" in the cocreation of spaces for transformation (see Berry et al. 2017).

Chapter 1

1. Soto Cano (or Palmerola, as it was previously known) served as a base for US military operations during the 1980s, which targeted revolutionary movements in neighboring Nicaragua and El Salvador. These movements were deemed a threat to US security and economic interests in the region. Zelaya's ousting, as we will see, has resonance with this violent history.

2. According to the World Bank's (2018) latest estimates, Honduras's Gini coefficient, which measures income inequality around the world, is 52.1, making it the second most unequal country in Latin America. About 48 percent of Honduras's population lives in poverty, with most of the poor living in rural areas (60 percent). See "Gini Index (World Bank Estimate)—Honduras." 2018. https://data.worldbank.org/indicator/SI.POV.GINI?end=2018&locations=HN&most_recent_value_desc=false&start=1989&view=chart.

3. The term *banana republic* was first used by the writer O. Henry (1905) in *Cabbages and Kings*, which he wrote while residing in Honduras.

4. The provinces first gained independence as part of Agustín de Iturbide's short-lived Mexican Empire.

5. *Criollo* refers to descendants of the Spaniards, or those who were mostly of Spanish descent and who typically had access to higher social status within the postcolony.

6. Honduran immigration legislation was notoriously racist and specifically referenced the threat of Arab and Black peoples to the progress of the nation—see Barahona's (1991, 264) discussion of the 1930 Immigration Law.

7. See Suyapa Portillo's (2021, 41–44) account of how the aims of liberal reformers converged with the interest of foreign multinationals intent on transforming the Caribbean coast into a bastion of the new agro-export economy.

8. Anderson (1997) notes that Garifuna became known for their industriousness

and skill as laborers in the extractive economy of the coast—characteristics that distinguished them as more desirable workers relative to the Miskito population and that they used to curry favor from Spanish and English colonial forces.

9. Soluri (2005, 43) notes, "The Tela Railroad Company [a United Fruit Company subsidiary] received 6,000 hectares of national lands (including timber rights) for every 12 kilometers of railroad completed." By the 1930s United Fruit and its subsidiaries were in possession of approximately 120,000 hectares of land.

10. Euraque (1998, 152) contends the construction of a unified Honduran national identity was contingent on the notion of a homogenous mestizo race, which excluded "the West Indian immigrants brought by the banana companies but also the indigenous North Coast Garifuna populations." Colby (2011, 186–87) has analyzed similar processes in Costa Rica, where state politicians sought to halt the threat of "Africanization" by banning visas and visa extensions for the "negro race."

11. The US Alliance for Progress of the early 1960s also played a central role in encouraging land reforms throughout Latin America—a clear attempt to quell growing tensions between campesinos and the landowning elite and to prevent the growth of communism in the region.

12. "Se considera contrario a los principios de la función social de la propiedad e incompatible con el bienestar nacional y el desarrollo económico del país, la existencia y mantenimiento de tierras incultas ociosas" (Honduras National Congress, "First Agrarian Reform Law," No. 2-62 1962. Chapter 11, Article 9).

13. US fruit multinationals in coordination with the US military orchestrated a coup d'état Arbenz in 1954.

14. Sarah England (2006, 110–12) has written about the racialized ideological thinking that propelled the state's efforts to integrate the North Coast into the national economy, which hinged, at least partially, on development policies that promoted mestizo migration and resettlement onto lands claimed by Garifuna.

15. Some scholars see this progressive move as a continuation of early twentieth-century policies of *mestizaje*, since the inclusion of the peasantry into state modernization proposals was inextricable from the process of what Díaz Arias (2007) has referred to as *ladinización*.

16. *Ejido* titles, including those issued to Black and Indigenous peoples, conferred rights of use onto the communities, but these lands remained under the dominion of the state.

17. The law allowed individual landholders to sell their land once the debt with the State of Honduras for land adjudication had been paid in full. However, cooperatives were forbidden from selling or renting the land they owned collectively (Articles 93 and 106). Andres León Araya (2015, 85–91) argues that the law's primary objective was to replace noncapitalist modes of production (and by extension, small subsistence farmers) with peasant enterprises that could further propel the production of cash crops for export.

18. Miguel Facussé, who was of Arab-Palestinian descent, founded the Dinant Corporation, a multinational company that quickly rose in prominence following a wave

of industrial development in and around San Pedro Sula in the 1990s that unfolded in tandem the neoliberalization of the national economy (Euraque 2019). At the time of his death in 2015, Facussé was the largest single landowner in Honduras.

19. The main attraction of African palm is its status as a "flex crop," with several end uses. Biofuels is one, but much of Honduran production goes to the cosmetics industry and to food uses (Alonso-Fradejas et al. 2016).

20. Mollett (2016) has brought needed attention to the history of what she calls "*colono* land grabbing." The scholarly literature on land grabbing has tended to focus on large-scale land transactions, ignoring the ways working-class peasants are also complicit in land grabs within Indigenous and Afro-descendant territories.

21. *Ejidos* were the earliest form of titling accessible to coastal Garifuna communities, followed by *garantías de ocupación*. After the approval of the Agricultural Modernization Law in 1992, the communities received full property titles (*dominio pleno*) to a portion of their lands, but the vast majority of their ancestral land claims remained either untitled or with limited legal recognition. Full property titles were particularly limited in scope—they encompassed only the residential areas (*casco urbano*) clustered along the coastline and excluded lands used for agricultural production.

22. Chaotic land tenure registries and violent conflicts between Indigenous peoples and investors throughout the continent led the World Bank to draft an Indigenous Peoples policy in 1991. World Bank Operational Directive 4.20 established a protocol for the implementation of all projects to be carried out in Indigenous areas. A central feature of the World Bank's Indigenous policy was the right to consultation enshrined in ILO Convention No. 169.

23. Inspection Panel, "Bank Management Response to Request for Inspection Panel Review of Honduras Land Administration Project," Report No. 399933 (2007).

24. Significantly, the report fails to mention the Honduran government's role in fomenting communal divisions around land tenure, in particular the de facto practice of sanctioning individual land sales within the boundaries of preexisting collective titles.

25. The Organization for Ethnic Communitarian Development (ODECO), then under the leadership of Celeo Álvarez, was one of two Garifuna organizations consulted during the initial conversations with the World Bank.

26. Derek Hall provides an excellent assessment of arguments for and against titling, and the crucial role played by international financial institutions in fomenting the formalization of property rights throughout the Global South. He notes titling projects are often carried out without adequate research into the conditions under which current landholders came to occupy their lands, and thus may provide "state backed legitimation for early land grabs" (Hall 2013, 122). This concern in combination with the fact that negotiations over disputed lands between Garifuna and more powerful actors would not likely result in a favorable conclusion fueled OFRANEH's opposition to PATH.

27. During the second phase of PATH implementation, launched in 2011, the government agreed to title 12 percent of its national territory to the Miskitu people; how-

ever, the titling of these lands happened alongside the expansion of extractivist economic activities in the Moskitia, including the Patuca III hydroelectric project and petroleum exploration (see Mollett 2018; Galeana 2020).

28. Ferguson (1994, 254–56) argues that reducing structural issues like poverty to technical issues in need of technocratic interventions (e.g. land tenure security) also has a powerful depoliticizing effect that is bound up with the expansion of bureaucratic state power.

29. Foreign multinationals, such as Standard Fruit, received land concessions that guaranteed use rights to land but not outright ownership.

30. See Republic of Honduras, *Honduras Is Open for Business: Tourism Sector Investment Opportunities*.

31. The government also faced internal pressure from social movement actors and from the international human rights community, which voiced strong concern about the targeted killing of environmental activists, such as Blanca Jeannette Kawas who was killed for her efforts to conserve natural resources in Tela Bay.

32. The convergence of conservation and development goals was of course resonant with the rise of neoliberal conservation strategies in other areas of the globe (Igoe and Brockington 2007).

33. Importantly, the National Congress had previously passed Decree 90/90, permitting foreign investors to purchase coastal property in urban areas for the purpose of tourism development.

34. Zelaya came from an elite landowning family in the department of Olancho. His embrace of leftist policies positioned him as a class traitor, something that isn't easily forgiven in societies like Honduras.

35. For a full account of Alianza Cívica Democrática's role in mining reform, see Holland, "Dangerous Path towards Mining Law Reform in Honduras," http://www.coha.org/wp-content/uploads/2015/12/The-Dangerous-Path-Toward-Mining-Law-Reform-in-Honduras.pdf.

36. Zelaya's support for the moratorium did not include a pause on large-scale tourism development, such as the Indura Beach and Golf Resort in Tela Bay. Instead, Zelaya, ignoring the demands of Garifuna land activists, pushed forward the tourism agenda without hesitation.

37. US corporate and military dealings in Honduras have deep historical roots, beginning in the early 1900s when US fruit multinationals established semisovereign banana enclaves on the Caribbean coast and then in the 1980s when Honduras served as an outpost for US military operatives against revolutionary movements in neighboring Nicaragua and El Salvador.

38. See Loperena (2016c) for a more robust analysis of Garifuna participation in the anticoup resistance movement.

39. The ensuing crisis generated by Zelaya's ousting, in combination with the global economic recession, deeply affected the Honduran economy; the annual growth in 2009 was –1.9 percent (Perez and Argueta 2011).

40. These legislative measures included the following: Law for the Promotion of

Public-Private Partnerships, Law for the Promotion and Protection of Investments. Model City Law, and the Part-Time Work Law.

41. At the time of the event over 70 percent of new FDI in Honduras came from the United States (see http://honduras.usembassy.gov/pr-051311-eng.html).

42. HOB also included investment opportunities in agribusiness, energy, forestry, infrastructure, textiles and global services. Mining was not explicitly listed at the time, since in 2006 the Honduran Supreme Court declared sixteen articles of the 1998 mining code unconstitutional (Moore 2012).

43. Mainstream Honduran media outlets used the term *crisis* to refer to the coup and to downplay the extralegal activities of the de facto regime that took power following Zelaya's ousting.

44. A full discussion of Romer's ideas is beyond the scope of this book. Here, I focus on how the Lobo administration marketed the charter city plan as a means of fast-tracking reforms that were designed to benefit private enterprise at the expense of poorer sectors of society.

45. "Why the World Needs Charter Cities," *TEDTalks*, August 5, 2009, YouTube video, 19:39 mins., https://www.youtube.com/watch?v=mSHBmaoIthk.

46. Associated Press, "Honduran Judges Rule against Privately Run 'Model Cities' Project," *The Guardian*, October 4, 2012, sec. World news, http://www.theguardian.com/world/2012/oct/04/honduras-judges-reject-model-cities.

47. In the latest setback for ZEDE proponents, the Honduran Congress repealed the 2013 law at the behest of the current president Xiomara Castro. The ZEDEs cannot be totally dissolved until the relevant articles are removed from the constitution.

Chapter 2

1. *Negrito* is a derogatory term for "Black." I provide a full account of community-level dynamics of these larger processes in chapter 3.

2. The appropriation of Garifuna culture for Caribbean tourism development dates back to the 1970s, when the national government funded the Festival Caribe de Danzas Garifunas to promote tourism to La Ceiba (Anderson 2000). It's my contention, however, that this process of commodification was not fully realized until after the arrival of multicultural legislation in the 1990s.

3. For a more extensive historical account of tourism development in Honduras, see Stonich (2000).

4. The report does not explicitly mention the race of incoming tourists, but race figures centrally in the conceptualization and implementation of tourism development proposals throughout the Caribbean. These proposals are entangled with white imperialist desires to have "authentic" experiences with the exotic Other (see Alexander 2005; Enloe 2014; Kempadoo 2004; Sheller 2003), which becomes apparent as cultural tourism grows in importance.

5. Funding for the PNTS was provided by the Inter-American Development Bank, which, as we will see, also provided the Government of Honduras with a loan for the public works infrastructure for the Indura Beach and Golf Resort.

6. Inter-American Development Bank, *Programa nacional de turismo sostenible: Documento conceptual del proyecto*, 2004.

7. For more on bilingual education reforms in Honduras, see Jorge Alberto Amaya's (2004) dissertation on the emergence of pluriethnic nationalism in Honduras.

8. International Labour Organization Convention No. 169 is a legally binding instrument that protects the rights of Indigenous and tribal peoples. It includes provisions for the collective ownership and management of ancestral lands.

9. In his account of cultural heritage and preservation in the Pelourinho district of Salvador, Collins (2019) provides an analysis of how the district's decaying colonial infrastructure and distinctly Afro-Brazilian character came to be embedded within politics aimed at cultivating development projects around Bahia's distinct cultural heritage. The restorative project, he argues, "works in practice as an alienating and future oriented attempt to redeem a black population presented as needing civilizational improvement" (Collins 2015, 3). In this sense, cultural preservation is contingent on the simultaneous inclusion and displacement of Black peoples and culture. Escallón's (2019, 361) analysis of the Quilombo de Palmares, a national heritage site in northeastern Brazil, addresses similar dynamics wherein the present-day inhabitants are rendered as threats to the site's historical and cultural significance. In both cases, heritage projects uphold the historical significance of Blackness to the national imaginary, which is distinct from the processes I analyze in Honduras, where Blackness is not central to historical narratives of national belonging.

10. Tianna Paschel (2016, 208–16) details the controversy surrounding the Statute of Racial Diversity and the Law of Quotas, two pieces of legislation that proposed to implement affirmative action policies at the federal level in Brazil. Prior to this, many of the country's most prestigious public universities had committed to reserving a certain percentage of university spaces were reserved racial minorities.

11. The creation of the Ministry for the Promotion of Racial Equality and the Economic Development of Indigenous and Afro-Hondurans is one example of how this type of institutional reform is implemented.

12. UNESCO also contributed to the heightened visibility and touristic value of Garifuna culture when it proclaimed Garifuna language, culture, and dance Intangible Cultural Heritage of Humanity in 2001.

13. Here I am highlighting how the state and private investors promote Garifuna bodies as part of the touristic offering. It is a form of commodification that smacks of colonialism, practices that construct the Other as object of imperial desire (Alexander 2005; Gregory 2007; Smith 2016a).

14. I delve into these dynamics more fully in chapter 5, when I analyze the legal arguments presented by the Honduran state to counter Garifuna claims to land in the Inter-American Court case of *Garifuna Community of Triunfo de la Cruz and Its Members v. Honduras*.

15. Letter of April 6, 2006, authored by Jessica García and Wilfredo Guerrero, two Garifuna communal authorities from the community San Juan in Tela (translation by author).

16. In addition to funding the basic infrastructure for the Indura Project, in October 2007 the Inter-American Development Bank approved a US$40 million loan to upgrade and aid the construction of the Caribbean Tourism Corridor (CA-13), a highway connecting the cities of El Progreso and Trujillo. The first phase of construction was to create a four-lane highway connecting the cities of El Progreso and Tela. This project, when complete, will facilitate the increased movement of people and goods between San Pedro Sula (the industrial capital and airport) and key tourism destinations along the Caribbean coast.

17. The park covers 781.45 square kilometers, made up of 36 percent ocean area and 497.45 square kilometers (64 percent) land, including 6.5 percent freshwater. This makes it one of the largest national parks in Central America. PROLANSATE, *Plan de manejo: Parque Nacional Jeannette Kawas* (Tela: PROLANSATE, 2004).

18. Following tremendous pressure from Garifuna activists and the negative media attention surrounding negotiations for the creation of the resort, the Government of Honduras agreed to allocate 7 percent of its total shares to five Garifuna communities in Tela Bay. I provide more details on this agreement in chapter 3.

19. Opposition to the Agua Zarca dam project resulted in the murder of numerous Lenca activists, including Berta Cáceres.

20. EDSA, "Indura Beach & Golf Resort, Curio Collection by Hilton," https://www.edsaplan.com/project/indura-beach-golf-resort-curio-collection-by-hilton/.

Chapter 3

1. The *patronato* is the highest recognized political authority in each community, per the national government. Members of the *patronato* are elected to two-year terms. Legally, each community can elect one governing council, but beginning in 2005 and through the duration of my fieldwork, Triunfo had two parallel governing councils.

2. The *empresarios* were commonly referred to as the *paralelos*, an epithet used to underscore the questionable means by which they assumed their roles as communal authorities. I detail this later in the chapter.

3. Brenna Bhandar (2018, 4) examines the ways liberal subjectivity is premised on the basis of "one's capacity to appropriate." In this sense, individual rights to buy and sell land are often bound up with notions of individual autonomy.

4. My friends often used the English word *rough* (in English) to describe their experiences living in the city.

5. "Un lugar donde nos mandamos nosotras mismas."

6. Goett (2017, 91) has also explored these issues in her recent ethnography of Afro-Nicaraguan activism. She analyzes the vernacular practices of autonomy and the forms of women-centered sociality working-class Creole women cultivate, and which she says, "are not grounded in capitalist social values."

7. OFRANEH, "Territorio," http://ofraneh.org/ofraneh/territorio.html.

8. The *casco urbano* refers to the community's residential core, or the area where community members constructed their homes. Garifuna inhabitants of the commu-

nity typically build their homes close to the shoreline and reserve lands further inland for agricultural production.

9. Agricultural labor was historically carried out by women. They laid claim to individual plots within a larger agricultural site that was collectively cleared and cultivated in accordance with customary practice. As in other areas of the globe, collective rights regimes in Triunfo often involve a mix of collective tasks and individual rights.

10. The term *blanco* (white) was used by Garifuna to refer to mestizo Hondurans. They also frequently used the term *indio* and sometimes *ladino*.

11. Castellanos's (2021) recent ethnography of housing and Mayan indebtedness in Cancún, Mexico, offers a critical account of how financialization and neoliberal transformations in the housing market facilitate racialized dispossession.

12. Punto Izopo National Park is a designated protected area that encompasses 40 square kilometers of land on the eastern end of the community. A portion of this area is included within the community's ancestral land claim but has since come under the management of the state and the conservation organization PROLANSATE (Foundation for the Protection of Lancetilla, Punta Sal, y Texiguatl).

13. Article 14, Agreement No. 754, 1991.

14. The precautionary measures mechanism is designed to ensure a rapid response by the IACHR in serious and urgent situations where there is an imminent risk of harm to persons or groups of persons in the thirty-five member states of the Organization of American States. See Organization of American States, "Consultation on Module II: Precautionary Measures," https://www.oas.org/en/iachr/consultation/2_measures.asp.

15. While these businesses catered primarily to visiting tourists, they also received local patronage. Similarly, tourists occasionally patronized businesses that catered to the consumer needs of community residents, such as the local billiard hall and the dance club Arenas.

16. I was not able to measure the actual financial input of the businesses listed, since most Triunfeños were reticent about discussing income and matters of personal finance. However, I was able to observe which businesses were most frequented by tourists. Cabañas Nancy and Cabañas Colón were the most successful by this informal measure. They were also the largest, in terms of guest rooms and other amenities.

17. The Los Micos Project was subsequently rebranded Indura Beach and Golf Resort.

18. ODECO, one of the most prominent Garifuna organizations in Honduras, has a long history of mobilizing for the rights of Black Hondurans. Its close ties to national politicians and government institutions frequently garnered criticism from OFRANEH's leadership, as did this deal it brokered with the Indura Beach and Golf Resort.

19. Many Triunfeños doubted the government would actually follow through on its promises to the communities, and some claimed to have no knowledge whatsoever of the agreement signed by ODECO with the IHT. In 2015, OFRANEH filed a complaint with the compliance adviser ombudsman, the independent accountability mechanism

for the International Finance Corporation (a World Bank subsidiary), in which it claimed the communities had yet to receive economic benefits from the Indura project—funded partially by loans from the World Bank.

20. See Mosse (2005) for an analysis of the social production of "success" and "failure" in development.

21. From the FAO's project summary for Proyecto Comunitario Garifuna (2006).

22. *Crumbs* was used sardonically by my informants to reference the development initiatives created specifically to benefit Black and Indigenous Hondurans, typically very small in scope in comparison to the multimillion-dollar investments in projects like Indura.

23. The terms of conservativism and conservationism were often used interchangeably by supporters of Ricardo's *patronato* to reference the purportedly retrograde politics of Carla and her constituents. This linguistic slippage was indicative of their perceived inability to participate productively within the future tourism economy.

24. Steven Gregory's (2007) study of globalization in the Dominican Republic details similar struggles pertaining to the restructuring of local livelihoods that has accompanied neoliberal reforms in the country and how these processes are lived and interpreted by locals.

25. This was an inversion of the prevailing communal discourse reference the two *patronatos*.

26. Carla's supporters often exalted the importance of ancestral modes of living, particularly modes of reciprocal care that are necessary to sustain community life (see chapter 4). The term *moreno* in Honduras is a racial epithet with strong anti-Black connotations. In the subsequent chapter I revisit the ways internal conflicts over land and development are framed temporally and racially.

27. Pandian has documented similar patterns of thought among agrarian citizens in southern India. He says to be subjects of development, individuals must "submit themselves to an order of power that identifies their own nature as a problem and demands that they work to develop themselves in order to overcome the limits of this nature" (Pandian 2008, 160).

28. Again, the use of *moreno* or *morenito* is used to denigrate the character and qualities of Black (or dark-skinned) peoples in Honduras. In some cases, Garifuna used the term to refer to themselves, or specifically to refer to those aligned with Carla's *patronato*.

29. The threat of becoming incorporated into the city of Tela, as opposed to maintaining their status as an autonomous community, preoccupied many of my friends in the community, not only because it would imply a loss of communal autonomy but also because it would impose new taxation structures and lead to reduced control over communal resources.

30. Honduras, with support from the World Bank, sought to conduct a series of cadastral surveys in the Garifuna communities. On the one hand this would permit the formalization of land tenure in Black and Indigenous communities, and on the other hand it would further entangle Garifuna communities in state bureaucracies.

31. The 22 *manzanas* refers to an area of recuperated land that lies within the boundaries of the communal title.

32. Ashanté Reese (2019) speaks to this in her discussion of the self-reliance strategies used by urban Black residents in Washington, DC, which are used to ensure individual survival, but also to build community cohesion.

Chapter 4

1. The Aguán Valley has been the site of numerous conflicts over land between campesino groups and large landowners, leading to the deaths and disappearances of over 140 land activists, according to a 2014 Human Rights Watch report.

2. Keri Brondo's (2007, 2013) work on Garifuna women's activism and the gendered effects of neoliberal agrarian legislation on Garifuna communities in Honduras has been instructive to my own understanding of these issues. She has brought needed attention to the role of Garifuna women in land recuperation efforts as well as the violence they face. Brondo (2007, 101) has demonstrated that while Garifuna land is held in common, rights of use were passed through the maternal line, and "it is therefore women who were harassed into abandoning or selling their resources, and for the most part, their property was transferred to male hands."

3. Manu Karuka (2019, 60) demonstrates how Lakota collective life and modes of relationship, which he terms reciprocal relationality, defied the assumed dichotomies between human and nonhuman worlds, and served to obstruct the expansion of capitalism and US sovereignty on the Plains in the second half of the nineteenth century. Arturo Escobar (2018, 16) has also written extensively about "relational ontology," which is a way of being that understands territories as living beings with memories. His argument builds on Marisol de la Cadena's (2010, 341) analysis of Indigenous politics and antimining oppositional movements in Peru, which "enact the respect and affect necessary to maintain the relational condition between human and other-than-human beings" and in this way disrupt the prevailing ontological distinction between humans and nature.

4. The *sistema de la muerte* (system of death) is a phrase used by social movement activists to reference the government's extractivist economic agenda and the forms of violence and death it authorizes.

5. A *manzana* is a measurement of land equivalent to 1.75 acres.

6. The commission receives complaints, some of which it decides to elevate for consideration by the Court.

7. IACHR Judgment, February 2006, 39.

8. Community activists first referred to the disputed land as *la hipoteca* (mortgaged land) or as Nueva Delicias, because it was adjacent to Barrio Delicias, which was also subject to a land dispute in the 1990s. After the successful recuperation of the property, the land defenders renamed it Barrio Indomables.

9. The "indios," a small contingent of mestizos from Boquete, were regular participants in the meetings at 22 Manzanas. They have collaborated on land "rescues"

spearheaded by the community, and thus they have been granted use rights to land in areas of recuperation. Their opinions are welcomed, but the final decisions are made by consensus and since they are a minority, they are often sidelined. Moreover, the Garifuna leadership made it clear that the lands in recuperated areas were to be distributed first to Garifuna, then mestizos, and a violation of the rules governing collective land tenure would result in expropriation and redistribution.

10. See also Kiran Asher's (2009) discussion of Transitory Article 55 and political processes that led to the approval of Law 70, the Law of Black Communities.

11. The bitter cassava plant is caloric and high in nutritional value, containing calcium, potassium, and small amounts of protein.

12. Principles of mutuality and reciprocal care were also embedded within collective farming practices, as I explained earlier.

13. Although men were usually blamed for the sale of communal lands, women have also been involved in land sales. In some cases, women were coerced or cheated into selling their inherited agricultural plots, but there were also instances wherein women sold lands to meet immediate needs. There was often a sense of sympathy in these accounts, which blurred the definitional lines between so-called sellouts and defenders of the land.

14. Anthropologist Mariana Mora (2017) also tackles this issue in her brilliant discussion of the Zapatista cultural practice "mandar obedeciendo" (governing by obeying). Mandar obedeciendo entails "active processes of transmission, selection, and reappropriation of practices and concepts as part of collective political actions" and therefore cannot be reduced to a pre-established cultural form (Mora 2017, 197).

15. Carla's brother, who lived in Los Angeles, agreed to let the women use his dump truck to handle the street repairs

16. In her discussion of women-centered networks and the labor of Black motherhood, Patricia Hill Collins (2000, 178) expands the definitional boundaries of mothering beyond the notion of a biological relationship between a mother and her child. Within Black communities, "othermothers" are women who assist "bloodmothers" in their mothering responsibilities. Christen Smith (2016b, 32) builds off of this work to advance an argument around social mothering: "[Black mothers] are also Black women who practice social responsibility for collective care (which is of critical import to sustaining Black life." My understanding of territorial mothering builds on this work but centers land as both agent and recipient of care necessary to defend future life.

17. Women often bundle their product inside a plastic tub that they balance carefully on their heads—hence the expression *cargar pan*.

18. Motherhood is a fiercely debated theme in feminist scholarship. In her foundational essay "Is Female to Male as Nature Is to Culture?," the anthropologist Sherry Ortner (1972) contends that the universal subjugation of women is because women are viewed as closer to nature. Feminist thought has since critiqued the logic of biological determinism underscoring Ortner's argument (Glenn, Chang, and Forcey 1994), fo-

cusing instead on the nuances of patriarchy. Women's subordination is not universal, nor is it equal in form. Rather, it is "based upon the particular location of different communities in racial/class formations or heterosexual economies" (Visweswaran 1997, 595).

19. According to Lynn Stephen (1995, 807), social scientists have typically divided women's movements into a dichotomous framework: movements that are explicitly feminist in orientation versus feminine or "practical movements that focus on helping women to fulfill their traditional gender roles." The dichotomy, she argues, distracts us from understanding the situational experiences of gendered organizing. In other words, rather than placing a fixed label onto these movements, social scientists should pay closer attention to the interpretations provided by movement participants. In this way, we may garner a better understanding of the diverse personal and political concerns that motivate activism and avoid "slotting people into all encompassing, essentialist categories of identity" (824). This argument is helpful to think through how mothering as praxis differs from motherhood and biologically deterministic accounts of women's organizing.

20. Because Indigenous and Black women confront multiple structures of domination in their daily lives (Hernández-Castillo 2010; Collins 2000), their work as mothers and as caregivers blurs the lines between home and community, personal and political (Lorde 2007).

21. Following Barbara Sutton (2007), I believe it is necessary to theorize the body as a site of political subjectivity, one that both reinforces the hegemonic tropes of feminine embodiment (e.g., the mother) at the same time that it destabilizes these gender norms by positioning women at the center of political struggles in defense of life more broadly.

22. Diana Williams, "I Didn't Have an 'American Dream,'" MCC, January 24, 2019, https://mcc.org/stories/i-didnt-have-american-dream.

23. "Asesinan a una líder garífuna y presidenta de un Patronato en Honduras," La Vanguardia, September 9, 2019, https://www.lavanguardia.com/vida/20190909/472713 81262/asesinan-a-una-lider-garifuna-y-presidenta-de-un-patronato-en-honduras.html.

24. "Assailants Kill Garifuna Defender and OFRANEH Member María Digna Montero," Im-Defensoras.Org (blog), October 14, 2019, https://im-defensoras.org/2019 /10/whrdalert-honduras-assailants-kill-garifuna-defender-and-ofraneh-member -maria-digna-montero/.

25. Translated by author: "En la acción para-estatal de estos grupos es todavía más crítica la necesidad de demostrar esa ausencia de límites en la ejecución de acciones crueles, ya que no se dispone de otros documentos o insignias que designen quién detenta la autoridad jurisdiccional. Por un lado, la truculencia es la única garantía del control sobre territorios y cuerpos, y de cuerpos como territorios, y, por el otro, la pedagogía de la crueldad es la estrategia de reproducción del sistema."

26. "Honduras: The Deadliest Place to Defend the Planet," Global Witness, January 2017, https://www.globalwitness.org/en/campaigns/environmental-activists/hondur as-deadliest-country-world-environmental-activism/.

27. https://noticias.terra.com/mundo/latinoamerica/activistas-piden-justicia-por
-asesinato-de-mas-de-3500-mujeres-en-honduras,3fe449d7a9be7c92e7e31d8a04be92
dc61u2g2w7.html.

28. Katherine McKittrick (2006, 8) states, "Black geographies are often unimaginable because we assume they do not really have any valuable material referents, that they are words rather than places, or that their materiality is always already fraught with discourses of dispossession."

Chapter 5

1. Quoted in the 2016 Amnesty International report *We Are Defending the Land with our Blood: Defenders of the Land, Territory and Environment in Honduras and Guatemala*."

2. In Honduras, the term *ladino* is often used in place of mestizo, but the terms are commensurate in popular understandings of race. Garifuna refer to mestizos as *indio* or *blanco* (white).

3. During the presentation of closing arguments at the public hearing in San José, Costa Rica, the lawyer representing the state insisted that Garifuna are not an "original people" and thus "do not have a right to the ancestral property to which they claim" (IACHR Judgment, October 8, 2015, 9, para. 19). I do not mean to suggest that officially recognized Indigenous people have more success securing territorial rights from the state. This is not the case, as the argument presented by the state is ultimately about securing rights for elite mestizo property owners, a point I return to later in the chapter.

4. The Playa Escondido Beach Club, a 30 unit hotel-condominium project on the west end of the community, and the Punta Izopo Resort, a planned but subsequently abandoned project on the east end of the community, are two examples.

5. In the Merits Report, the commission outlines the merits of the case, determines whether or not violations of human rights occurred, and if so, makes recommendations to the state.

6. This eventually became a point of contention, because the state alleged Clara had misrepresented herself before the Court as a non–Spanish speaker. The state provided evidence of a recorded interview Clara gave in Spanish, which was broadcast on a local television station in Tela. As such, the state argued that she had violated the Rules of Procedure of the Inter-American Court of Human Rights, specifically "the oath or solemn declaration rendered" before the presidency (see IACHR Judgment, October 8, 2015, 14–15, para. 39). The Court dismissed these charges, since Garifuna language is "important expression of the cultural identity of said people" (IACHR Judgment, October 8, 2015, 14, para. 41).

7. "Con base en la Ley para la Modernización y Desarrollo del Sector Agrícola, el 29 de octubre de 1993 fue extendido gratuitamente a la Comunidad un 'título definitivo de propiedad en dominio pleno' sobre las 380 hectáreas 51 áreas 82.68 centiáreas otorgadas como ejido en 1950" (IACHR Judgment, October 8, 2015, 22, para. 69, 22).

8. Cheryl Harris's (1993) important article "Whiteness as Property" has been in-

structive for my own understanding of how racial identity and property are conceptually linked.

9. Translated by author: "Partiendo del hecho que la comunidad garífuna de Triunfo de la Cruz no sería un pueblo indígena u originario sino un grupo étnico diferenciado con sus propias características culturales, sociales y políticas que llego a la zona pretendida cuando este ya se había consolidado a su condición como Estado independiente, no sería aplicable la jurisprudencia de la Corte Interamericana de Derechos Humanos en materia de pueblos indígenas pues, la jurisprudencia se refiere a pueblos originarios, lo cual no sería el caso, y al contrario su aplicación en este caso podría ser contradictoria e incluso lesiva a un pueblo indígena, en atención a que las pretensiones territoriales de la comunidad garífuna Triunfo de la Cruz podrían entrar en conflicto con tierras otorgadas con prioridad en el tiempo a un pueblo originario como es el Tolupán."

10. Mestizo belonging is premised in part on their presumed descent from the original inhabitants of the land, a point I revisit later in the chapter.

11. The Miskito people also lay claim to an Afro-Indigenous identity but have garnered greater recognition from the state. This discrepancy is partly due to the conflation, as Darío Euraque (1998) argues, of Garifuna with foreign Black laborers who came to Honduras to work on banana plantations in the nineteenth and twentieth centuries. But it is also because of the more visible Blackness of Garifuna, which, owing to their location within majority mestizo regions of the country, positions them more firmly as Afro-descendant, and thus nonnative. Their lands are also of greater immediate value to state development priorities.

12. IACHR Judgment, October 8, 2015, para. 96. "[El Estado] señaló asimismo que el proceso de titulación de tierra a las Comunidades Garifunas conlleva tres etapas: titulación, ampliación y saneamiento. Respecto a la última etapa enfatizo que debe tomarse en cuenta que en el área pretendida hay varios ocupantes no garífunas con documentos legales que acreditan su propiedad, quienes también se encuentran protegidos por la legislación nacional."

13. The Arab-descendant population, the so-called *turcos*, began immigrating to Honduras in the nineteenth century and now control most of the national economy. Although the term *turco* is indicative of their continued othering, their power and wealth ensures their position at the helm of Honduran society. Most Garifuna I spoke with did not distinguish between mestizos and *turcos*.

14. Notably, ODECO (Organization and Ethnic and Communitarian Development), then under the mandate of Celeo Álvarez, embraced the term *Afro-descendant*.

15. "Garífunas hondureños piden no llamarlos 'afro,'" *El Heraldo*, April 7, 2014.

16. For an overview of this history, see Jorge Amaya Banegas's *Los árabes y palestinos en Honduras (1900–1950)* and "Los árabes de Honduras: Entre la inmigración, la acumulación y la política" (Euraque 2009).

17. Garifuna claims to Indigeneity are undermined by the state precisely because they are Black and because their territorial pretensions too directly challenge the racial logics that position mestizos as the rightful owners of land and capital.

18. IACHR Judgment, October 8, 2015, para. 101.

19. Similar arguments have been deployed by state institutions to deny rights to Indigenous peoples who no longer reside within recognized Indigenous territories or who do not sustain "traditional" cultural practices. Lourdes Nájera and Korinta Maldonado (2017) have published work on this topic, highlighting the challenges of fastening Indigenous identity to culturally distinct geographies, which is of particular import given the growing incidence of migration among Indigenous populations both within Latin America and from Latin America to the United States.

20. IACHR Judgment, October 8, 2015, para. 97.

21. IACHR Judgment, October 8, 2015, para. 97. "El Estado alegó también que dentro del área que reclama la Comunidad como área tradicional se encuentran zonas de playa y mar, lo cual 'conforme a la Teoría de los Bienes de Uso Público recogida por la legislación nacional civil de la mayoría de los países . . . no es posible la apropiación de tales zonas, ni es posible emitir un título de dominio sobre los mismos, y están fuera de comercio de los hombres, sino que son de uso de la nación entera', y que el artículo 617 del Código Civil de Honduras inter alia dispone que 'el mar adyacente y sus playas, se llamas bienes nacionales de uso público o bienes públicos.'"

22. See chapters 3 and 4 for a more extensive discussion of these forms of refusal.

Conclusion

1. Eventually, after intense pressure from the international community, the Honduran National Criminal Court tried and convicted seven men for her murder who had been hired by DESA executives to carry out the hit. COPINH maintains that the intellectual authors responsible for her murder are being shielded by the government.

2. A fifth person, Junior Rafael Juárez Mejía, was also kidnapped, but he was not from the community.

3. Robert Nichols has produced a brilliant critique of dispossession and its use within critical social theory. To dispossess, he argues, assumes a violation of existing property rights, thereby reinforcing modes of social relationality that are predicated on ownership and which are often out of alignment with Indigenous cosmologies. In his reformulation, dispossession names "not only the forcible transfer of property, but the transformation into property" (Nichols 2018, 3).

4. In their critique of neoliberal "responsibilization," Judith Butler and Athena Athanasiou argue against the moral subject imagined by the neoliberal state, one that is capable of absorbing and deflecting the political economic crisis. Rather, in dialogue with Michel Foucault, they see and ethics a potentially transformative opening to restructure social relations: "the ethical relation is a way of rethinking and remaking society itself" (Butler and Athanasiou 2013, 103). I find this formulation informative for my own engagement with Garifuna modes of relationality and care, which transcend the liberal individuation.

REFERENCES

Abrams, Philip. (1977) 2006. "Notes on the Difficulty of Studying the State." In *Anthropology of the State*, edited by Aradhana Sharma and Akhil Gupta, 112–30. Oxford, UK: Blackwell.

Acosta, Alberto. 2013. "Extractivism and Neoextractism: Two Sides of the Same Curse." In *Beyond Development: Alternative Visions from Latin America*, edited by Miriam Lang and Dunia Mokrani, 61–86. Amsterdam: Transnational Institute.

Alexander, M. Jacqui. 2005. *Pedagogies of Crossing: Meditations on Feminism, Sexual Politics, Memory, and the Sacred*. Durham, NC: Duke University Press.

Alford-Jones, Kelsey. 2017. "Should the Inter-American Development Bank Fund Honduras to Implement Controversial Special Economic Zones." The Center for International Environmental Law (CIEL). https://www.ciel.org/wp-content/uploads/2017/12/ZEDEanalysis.pdf.

Allen, Jafari Sinclaire, and Ryan Cecil Jobson. 2016. "The Decolonizing Generation: (Race and) Theory in Anthropology since the Eighties." *Current Anthropology* 57 (2): 129–48.

Alonso-Fradejas, Alberto, Juan Liu, Tania Salerno, and Yunan Xu. 2016. "Inquiring into the Political Economy of Oil Palm as a Global Flex Crop." *Journal of Peasant Studies* 43 (1): 141–65.

Amaya, Jorge Alberto. 2004."Reimaginando la nación en Honduras: De la 'nación homogénea' a la 'nación pluriétnica': Los negros garifunas de Cristales y Trujillo." PhD diss., Universidad Complutense de Madrid.

Amaya Banegas, Jorge Alberto. 1997. *Los árabes y palestinos en Honduras, 1900–1950*. Tegucigalpa: Editorial Guaymuras.

Amnesty International. 2016. "'We Are Defending the Land with Our Blood': Defenders of the Land, Territory and Environment in Honduras and Guatemala." London: Amnesty International. https://www.amnestyusa.org/files/hondurasguatemalahrd-reporteng.compressed.pdf.

Anderson, Mark. 1997. "The Significance of Blackness: Representations of Garifuna in St. Vincent and Central America, 1700–1900." *Transforming Anthropology* 6 (1–2): 22–35.

———. 2000. "Garifuna Kids: Blackness, Modernity, and Tradition in Honduras." PhD diss., University of Texas at Austin.

———. 2007. "When Afro Becomes (Like) Indigenous: Garifuna and Afro-Indigenous Politics in Honduras." *Journal of Latin American and Caribbean Anthropology* 12 (2): 384–413.

———. 2009. *Black and Indigenous: Garifuna Activism and Consumer Culture in Honduras*. Minneapolis: University of Minnesota Press.

Appadurai, Arjun. 2006. *Fear of Small Numbers: An Essay on the Geography of Anger*. Durham, NC: Duke University Press.

Aretxaga, Begoña. 1997. *Shattering Silence: Women, Nationalism, and Political Subjectivity in Northern Ireland*. Princeton, NJ: Princeton University Press.

Asher, Kiran. 2009. *Black and Green: Afro-Colombians, Development, and Nature in the Pacific Lowlands*. Durham, NC: Duke University Press.

Barahona, Marvin. 1991. *Evolución histórica de la identidad nacional*. Tegucigalpa: Editorial Guaymuras.

———. 1998. "Imagen y percepción de los pueblos indígenas en Honduras." In *Rompiendo el espejo: Visiones sobre los pueblos indígenas y negros en Honduras*, edited by Marvin Barahona and Ramon Rivas. Tegucigalpa: Servicio Holandés de Cooperación al Desarrollo Editorial Guaymuras.

Bebbington, Anthony, Abdul-Gafaru Abdulai, Denise Humphreys Bebbington, Marja Hinfelaar, and Cynthia Sanborn. 2018. *Governing Extractive Industries: Politics, Histories, Ideas*. Oxford: Oxford University Press.

Berlant, Lauren. 2011. *Cruel Optimism*. Durham, NC: Duke University Press.

Berry, Maya J., Claudia Chávez Argüelles, Shanya Cordis, Sarah Ihmoud, and Elizabeth Velásquez Estrada. 2017. "Toward a Fugitive Anthropology: Gender, Race, and Violence in the Field." *Cultural Anthropology* 32 (4): 537–65.

Bhandar, Brenna. 2018. *Colonial Lives of Property: Law, Land, and Racial Regimes of Ownership*. Durham, NC: Duke University Press.

Bonilla, Yarimar. 2015. *Non-Sovereign Futures: French Caribbean Politics in the Wake of Disenchantment*. Chicago: University of Chicago Press.

Bourgois, Philippe I. 1989. *Ethnicity at Work: Divided Labor on a Central American Banana Plantation*. Baltimore: Johns Hopkins University Press.

Braudel, Fernand, and Immanuel Wallerstein. 2009. "History and the Social Sciences: The Longue Durée." *Review (Fernand Braudel Center)* 32 (2): 171–203.

Brockington, Dan, Rosaleen Duffy, and Jim Igoe. 2008. *Nature Unbound: Conservation, Capitalism and the Future of Protected Areas*. London: Earthscan.

Brondo, Keri. 2007. "Land Loss and Garifuna Women's Activism on Honduras' North

Coast." *Journal of International Women's Studies* 9 (1): 99–116.

———. 2010. "When Mestizo Becomes (Like) Indio . . . or Is It Garifuna? Multicultural Rights and 'Making Place' on Honduras' North Coast.'" *Journal of Latin American and Caribbean Anthropology* 15 (1): 170–94.

———. 2013. *Land Grab: Green Neoliberalism, Gender, and Garifuna Resistance in Honduras*. Tucson: University of Arizona Press.

Brondo, Keri, and Laura Woods. 2007. "Garifuna Land Rights and Ecotourism as Economic Development in Honduras' Cayos Cochinos Marine Protected Area." *Ecological and Environmental Anthropology* 3 (1).

Butler, Judith, and Athena Athanasiou. 2013. *Dispossession: The Performative in the Political*. Malden, MA: Polity.

Canales, Amparo. 2009. "Estudio sobre turismo rural en Honduras: Concepto, institucionalidad, legislación, actores, experiencias." Tegucigalpa: Instituto Interamericano para la Cooperación en Agricultura. http://orton.catie.ac.cr/repdoc/A4525e/A4525e.pdf.

Canelas Díaz, Antonio. 2001. *El estrangulamiento económico de La Ceiba 1903–1965*. La Ceiba, Honduras: Ed. ProCultura.

Castellanos, Bianet M. 2017. "Introduction: Settler Colonialism in Latin America." *American Quarterly* 69 (4): 777–81.

———. 2021. *Indigenous Dispossession: Housing and Mayan Indebtedness in Mexico*. Stanford, CA: Stanford University Press.

Césaire, Aimé. 2000. *Discourse on Colonialism*. New York: NYU Press, Monthly Review Press.

Chakravartty, Paula, and Denise Ferreira da Silva. 2012. "Accumulation, Dispossession, and Debt: The Racial Logic of Global Capitalism—An Introduction." *American Quarterly* 64 (3): 361–85.

Chambers, Glenn A. 2010. *Race, Nation, and West Indian Migration to Honduras*. Baton Rouge: Louisiana State University Press.

Colby, Jason. 2011. *The Business of Empire: United Fruit, Race and US Expansion in Central America*. Ithaca, NY: Cornell University Press.

Collins, Patricia Hill. 2000. *Black Feminist Thought: Knowledge, Consciousness, and the Politics of Empowerment*. 2nd ed. New York: Routledge.

Collins, John. 2015. *Revolt of the Saints: Memory and Redemption in the Twilight of Brazilian Racial Democracy*. Durham, NC: Duke University Press.

Córdoba Azcárate, Matilde. 2020. *Stuck with Tourism: Space, Power, and Labor in Contemporary Yucatán*. Berkeley: University of California Press.

Coronil, Fernando. 2000. "Towards a Critique of Globalcentrism: Speculations on Capitalism's Nature." *Public Culture* 12 (2): 351–74.

Coulthard, Glen S. 2007. "Subjects of Empire: Indigenous Peoples and the 'Politics of Recognition' in Canada." *Contemporary Political Theory* 6 (4): 437–60.

Cross, Jamie. 2010. "Neoliberalism as Unexceptional: Economic Zones and the Everyday Precariousness of Working Life in South India." *Critique of Anthropology* 30 (4): 355–73.

Dave, Naisargi N. 2012. *Queer Activism in India: A Story in the Anthropology of Ethics*.

Durham, NC: Duke University Press.

Davidov, Veronica, and Bram Büscher. 2014. Introduction to *The Ecotourism-Extraction Nexus: Political economies and rural realities of (un)comfortable bedfellows*, by Bram Büscher and Veronica Davidov. New York: Routledge.

de la Cadena, Marisol. 2010. "Indigenous Cosmopolitics in the Andes: Conceptual Reflections beyond 'Politics.'" *Cultural Anthropology* 25 (2): 334–70.

Díaz Arias, David. 2007. "Entre la guerra de castas y la ladinización: La imagen del indígena en la Centroamérica liberal, 1870–1944." *Revista de Estudios Sociales*, no. 26 (April): 58–72.

Edelman, Marc, and Andrés León. 2013. "Cycles of Land Grabbing in Central America: An Argument for History and a Case Study in the Bajo Aguán, Honduras." *Third World Quarterly* 34 (9): 1697–1722.

England, Sarah. 2006. *Afro Central Americans in New York City: Garifuna Tales of Transnational Movements in Racialized Space*. Gainesville: University Press of Florida.

Enloe, Cynthia. 2014. *Bananas, Bases and Beaches. Making Feminist Sense of International Politics*. London: Pandora.

ERIC (Equipo de Reflexión, Investigación y Comunicación). 2016. *Socioenvionmental Impact of Mining in the Northwestern Region of Honduras Seen through Three Case Studies*. Tegucigalpa: Editorial Guaymuras.

Escallón, María Fernanda. 2019. "Rights Inequality, and Afro-Descendant Heritage in Brazil." *Cultural Anthropology* 34 (3): 359–87.

Escobar, Arturo. 2018. *Designs for the Pluriverse: Radical Interdependence, Autonomy, and the Making of Worlds*. Durham, NC: Duke University Press.

———. 2020. *Pluriversal Politics: The Real and the Possible*. Durham, NC: Duke University Press.

Estes, Nick. 2019. *Our History Is the Future: Standing Rock versus the Dakota Access Pipeline, and the Long Tradition of Indigenous Resistance*. London: Verso.

Euraque, Dario. 1996. *Reinterpreting the Banana Republic: Region and State in Honduras, 1870–1972*. Chapel Hill: University of North Carolina Press.

———. 1998. "The Banana Enclave, Nationalism, and Mestizaje in Honduras, 1910s–1930s." In *Identity and Struggle at the Margins of the Nation-State: The Laboring Peoples of Central America and the Hispanic Caribbean*, edited by Aviva Chomsky and Aldo Laura-Santiago, 151–68. Durham, NC: Duke University Press.

———. 2003. "The Threat of Blackness to the Mestizo Nation: Race and Ethnicity in the Honduran Banana Economy, 1920s and 1930s." In *Banana Wars Power, Production, and History in the Americas*, edited by Steve Striffler and Mark Moberg, 229–49. Durham, NC: Duke University Press.

———. 2009. "Los árabes de Honduras: Entre la inmigración, la acumulación y la política." In *Contribuciones árabes a las identidades iberoamericanas*, 233–84. Madrid: Casa Árabe.

———. 2019. "The Historical Trajectory of Honduras's Elites before the Coup d'Etat of 2009." *Anuario de Estudios Centroamericanos* 45 (December): 19–48.

Fanon, Frantz. 2008. *Black Skin, White Masks*. Translated by Richard Philcox. Berkeley, CA: Grove Press.

Faubion, James D. 2010. "From the Ethical to the Thematical (and Back): Groundwork for an Anthropology of Ethics." In *Ordinary Ethics: Anthropology, Language, and Action, edited by Michael Lambek*, 84–101. New York: Fordham University Press.

Ferguson, James. 1994. *The Anti-Politics Machine: "Development," Depoliticization, and Bureaucratic Power in Lesotho*. Minneapolis: University of Minnesota Press.

———. 2006. *Global Shadows: Africa in the Neoliberal World Order*. Durham, NC: Duke University Press.

FoodFirst Information and Action Network. 2000. *Agrarian Reform in Honduras Fact Sheet*. Heidelberg: FoodFirst Information and Action Network. https://www.fian .org/fileadmin/media/publications_2015/Agrarian-Reform-in-Honduras-2000. pdf.

Freeman, Carla. 2014. *Entrepreneurial Selves: Neoliberal Respectability and the Making of a Caribbean Middle Class*. Durham, NC: Duke University Press.

Freitag, Tilman G. 1994. "Enclave Tourism Development for Whom the Benefits Roll?" *Annals of Tourism Research* 21 (3): 538–54.

Galeana, Fernando. 2020. "Legitimating the State and the Social Movement: Clientelism, Brokerage, and Collective Land Rights in Honduras." *Journal of Latin American Geography* 19 (4): 11–42.

García, Víctor Virgilio López. 2006. *Tornabé ante el proyecto turístico*. N.p.: V. V. López García.

Gilmore, Ruth Wilson. 2002. "Fatal Couplings of Power and Race: Notes on Racism and Geography" *Professional Geographer* 54 (1):15–24.

———. 2008. "Forgotten Places and the Seeds of Grassroots Planning" in *Engaging Contradictions: Theories, Politics, and Methods of Activist Research*, edited by Charles R. Hale, 31–61. Berkeley: University of California Press.

Glenn, Evelyn Nakano, Grace Chang, and Linda Rennie Forcey. 2016. *Mothering: Ideology, Experience, and Agency*. New York: Routledge.

Global Witness. 2017. "Honduras: The Deadliest Place to Defend the Planet." https:// www.globalwitness.org/en/campaigns/environmental-activists/honduras -deadliest-country-world-environmental-activism/.

Goett, Jennifer. 2017. *Black Autonomy: Race, Gender, and Afro-Nicaraguan Activism*. Stanford, CA: Stanford University Press.

Gomez, Ana. 2012. *Honduras: Biofuels Annual*. Global Agricultural Information Network, USDA Foreign Agricultural Service. https://apps.fas.usda.gov/newgainapi/ api/report/downloadreportbyfilename?filename=Biofuels%20Annual_ Tegucigalpa_Honduras_7-3-2012.pdf.

Gómez-Barris, Macarena. 2017. *The Extractive Zone: Social Ecologies and Decolonial Perspectives*. Durham, NC: Duke University Press.

González, Nancie L. Solien. 1988. *Sojourners of the Caribbean: Ethnogenesis and Ethnohistory of the Garifuna*. Urbana: University of Illinois Press.

Gordon, Edmund T. 1998. *Disparate Diaspora: Identity and Politics in an African Nicaraguan Community*. Austin: University of Texas Press.

Gregory, Steven. 2007. *The Devil behind the Mirror: Globalization and Politics in the Dominican Republic*. Berkeley: University of California Press.

Grosfoguel, Ramón. 2004. "Race and Ethnicity or Racialized Ethnicities? Identities within Global Coloniality." *Ethnicities* 4 (3): 315–36.

Gudmundson, Lowell, and Justin Wolfe. 2010. *Blacks and Blackness in Central America: Between Race and Place*. Durham, NC: Duke University Press.

Gudynas, Eduardo. 2009. "Diez tesis urgentes sobre el nuevo extractivismo: Contextos y demandas bajo el progresismo sudamericano actual." In *Extractivismo, política y sociedad*, edited by Mariela Buonomo, 187–225. Quito: Centro Andino de Acción Popular and Centro Latinoamericano de Ecología Social.

Hale, Charles. 2002. "Does Multiculturalism Menace? Governance, Cultural Rights, and the Politics of Identity in Guatemala." *Journal of Latin American Studies* 34: 485–524.

———. 2004. "Rethinking Indigenous Politics in the Era of the 'Indio Permitido.'" *NACLA Report on the Americas* 38 (2): 16–21.

———. 2006. "Indigenous Land Rights and the Contradictions of Politically Engaged Anthropology." *Cultural Anthropology* 21 (1): 96–120.

Hall, Derek. 2013. *Land*. Cambridge, UK: Polity Press.

Hall, Stuart. (1980) 2019. "Race, Articulation, and Societies Structured in Dominance." In *Foundations of Cultural Studies*, edited by David Morley, 1:172–221. Durham, NC: Duke University Press.

Hamilton, Jennifer A. 2008. *Indigeneity in the Courtroom: Law, Culture, and the Production of Difference in North American Courts*. New York: Routledge.

Han, Clara. 2012. *Life in Debt: Times of Care and Violence in Neoliberal Chile*. Berkeley: University of California Press.

Harris, Cheryl I. 1993. "Whiteness as Property." *Harvard Law Review* 106 (8): 1707–91.

Harrison, Faye. 1991. *Decolonizing Anthropology: Moving Further toward an Anthropology for Liberation*. Arlington, VA: Association of Black Anthropologists.

Hartman, Sadiya. 1997. *Scenes of Subjection: Terror, Slavery, and Self-Making in Nineteenth Century America*. New York: Oxford University Press.

———. 2019. *Wayward Lives, Beautiful Experiments: Intimate Histories of Social Upheaval*. New York: W. W. Norton & Co.

Harvey, David. 2009. "Is This Really the End of Neoliberalism?" *Counterpunch.Org* (blog). March 15, 2009. http://tomweston.net/EndNeoLib.pdf.

———. 2018. *Marx, Capital and the Madness of Economic Reason*. New York: Oxford University Press.

Helg, Aline. 2004. *Liberty & Equality in Caribbean Colombia, 1770–1835*. Chapel Hill: University of North Carolina Press.

Henry, O. 1905. *Cabbages and Kings*. New York: McClure, Phillips & Co.

Hernández-Castillo, Aída. 2010. "The Emergence of Indigenous Feminisms in Latin America. *Signs* 35 (3): 539–545

Hill Collins, Patricia. 2000. *Black Feminist Thought: Knowledge, Consciousness, and the Politics of Empowerment*. New York: Routledge.

Holland, Lynn. 2015. *The Dangerous Path toward Mining Law Reform in Honduras.* Washington DC: Council on Hemispheric Affairs. https://www.coha.org/wp-con tent/uploads/2015/12/The-Dangerous-Path-Toward-Mining-Law-Reform-in-Hon duras.pdf.

Honey, Martha. 2008. *Ecotourism and Sustainable Development: Who Owns Paradise?* 2nd ed. Washington, DC: Island Press.

Hooker, Juliet. 2005. "Indigenous Inclusion/Black Exclusion: Race, Ethnicity and Multicultural Citizenship in Latin America." *Journal of Latin American Studies* 37 (2): 285–310.

———. 2017. *Theorizing Race in the Americas: Douglass, Sarmiento, Du Bois, and Vasconcelos.* Oxford: Oxford University Press.

———, ed. 2020. *Black and Indigenous Resistance in the Americas: From Multiculturalism to Racist Backlash.* Lanham, MD: Lexington Books.

hooks, bell. 1992. "Eating the Other: Desire and Resistance." In *Black Looks: Race and Representation*, 21–40. Boston: South End Press.

Igoe, Jim, and Dan Brockington. 2007. "Neoliberal Conservation: A Brief Introduction." *Conservation and Society* 5 (4): 432–49.

Ihmoud, Sarah. 2019. "Murabata: The Politics of Staying in Place." *Feminist Studies* 45 (2–3): 512–40.

Inter-American Court of Human Rights (IACHR). Judgment of October 8, 2015. *Garifuna Community Triunfo de la Cruz and Its Members v. Honduras—Merits, Reparations and Costs.* http://www.corteidh.or.cr/docs/casos/articulos/seriec_305_esp .pdf.

Jansen, Kees, and Esther Roquas. 1998. "Modernizing Insecurity: The Land Titling Project in Honduras." *Development and Change* 29: 81–106.

Jeffrey, Paul. 2002. "Una mirada introspectiva: La respuesta al Huracán Mitch en el valle del Bajo Aguán." In *Descifrando a Honduras: Cuatro puntos de vista sobre la realidad política tras el Huracán Mitch*, edited by Jack Spence, 44–55. Cambridge, MA: Hemisphere Initiatives.

Jobson, Ryan Cecil. 2020. "The Case for Letting Anthropology Burn: Sociocultural Anthropology in 2019." *American Anthropologist* 122 (2): 259–71.

Karuka, Manu. 2019. *Empire's Tracks: Indigenous Nations, Chinese Workers, and the Transcontinental Railroad.* Oakland: University of California Press.

Kelley, Robin D. G. 2002. *Freedom Dreams: The Black Radical Imagination.* Boston: Beacon Press.

Kempadoo, Kamala. 2004. *Sexing the Caribbean: Gender, Race, and Sexual Labor.* New York: Routledge.

Kerns, Virginia. 1997. *Women and the Ancestors: Black Carib Kinship and Ritual.* Urbana: University of Illinois Press.

King, Tiffany Lethabo. 2019. *The Black Shoals: Offshore Formations of Black and Native Studies.* Durham, NC: Duke University Press.

Kirsch, Stuart. 2018. *Engaged Anthropology: Politics beyond the Text.* Oakland: University of California Press.

Kirtsoglou, Elisabeth, and Dimitrios Theodossopoulos. 2004. "'They Are Taking Our Culture Away': Tourism and Culture Commodification in the Garifuna Community of Roatan." *Critique of Anthropology* 24 (2): 135–57.

Klein, Naomi. 2005. "The Rise of Disaster Capitalism." *The Nation*, April 14, 2005.

León, Andres. 2015. "Rebellion under the Palm Trees: Memory, Agrarian Reform and Labor in the Aguán, Honduras." PhD diss., Graduate Center, City University of New York.

Li, Tania Murray. 2007. *The Will to Improve: Governmentality, Development, and the Practice of Politics.* Durham, NC: Duke University Press.

Loperena, Christopher A. 2016a. "Conservation by Racialized Dispossession: The Making of an Eco-Destination on Honduras's North Coast." *Geoforum* 69 (February): 184–93.

———. 2016b. "A Divided Community: The Ethics and Politics of Activist Research." *Current Anthropology* 57 (3): 332–46.

———.2016c. "Radicalize Multiculturalism: Garifuna Activism and the Double-Bind of Participation in Postcoup Honduras" *Journal of Latin American and Caribbean Anthropology* 21(3): 517–38.

———. 2017a. "Honduras Is Open for Business: Extractivist Tourism as Sustainable Development in the Wake of Disaster?" *Journal of Sustainable Tourism* 25 (5): 618–33.

———. 2017b. "Settler Violence? Race and Emergent Frontiers of Progress in Honduras." *American Quarterly* 69 (4): 801–7.

———. 2020. "Adjudicating Indigeneity: Anthropological Testimony in the Inter-American Court of Human Rights." *American Anthropologist* 122 (3): 595–605.

Loperena, Christopher, Rosalva Aída Hernández Castillo, and Mariana Mora. 2018. "Los retos del peritaje cultural. El antropólogo como perito en la defensa de los derechos indígenas." *Desacatos. Revista de Ciencias Sociales*, no. 57 (May): 8–19.

López Oro, Paul Joseph. 2016. "'Ni de aquí, ni de allá': Garifuna Subjectivities and the Politics of Diasporic Belonging." In *Afro-Latin@s in Movement: Critical Approaches to Blackness and Transnationalism in the Americas*, edited by Petra R. Rivera-Rideau, Jennifer A. Jones, and Tianna S. Paschel, 61–83. Afro-Latin@ Diasporas. New York: Palgrave Macmillan US.

———. 2021. "A Love Letter to Indigenous Blackness." *NACLA Report on the Americas* (53) 3: 211–14.

Lorde, Audre. 2007. "The Master's Tools Will Never Dismantle the Master's House." In *Sister Outsider: Essays and Speeches*, 110–14. Berkeley, CA: Crossing Press.

Lowe, Lisa. 2015. *The Intimacies of Four Continents.* Durham, NC: Duke University Press.

Lund, Christian. 2011. "Fragmented Sovereignty: Land Reform and Dispossession in Laos." *Journal of Peasant Studies* 38 (4): 885–905.

Martin, Joanne. 1990. "Motherhood and Power: The Production of a Women's Culture of Politics in a Mexican Community." *American Ethnologist* 17 (3): 470–90.

Marx, Karl. [1867] 1990. *Capital: A Critique of Political Economy*. Vol. 1. London: Penguin Books.

Mbaiwa, Joseph E. 2003. "The Socio-Economic and Environmental Impacts of Tourism Development on the Okavango Delta, North-Western Botswana." *Journal of Arid Environments* 54 (2): 447–67.

McGranahan, Carole. 2016. "Theorizing Refusal: An Introduction." *Cultural Anthropology* 31 (3): 319–25.

McKittrick, Katherine. 2006. *Demonic Grounds: Black Women and the Cartographies of Struggle*. Minneapolis: University of Minnesota Press.

———. 2016. "Rebellion/Invention/Groove." *Small Axe: A Caribbean Journal of Criticism* 20 1 (49): 79–91.

Melamed, Jodi. 2015. "Racial Capitalism." *Critical Ethnic Studies* 1 (1): 76–85.

Meza, Victor. 2010. "Política, partidos y dependencia externa." In *Golpe de Estado: Partido, instituciones y cultura política*, edited by Ramon Romero, Lucila Funes, Manuel Gamero, Leticia Salomón, and Antonio Murga, 1–22. Tegucigalpa: Centro de Documentación de Honduras.

Miranda, Miriam. 2011. "Presencia africana en Centro America, de rebeliones a avasallamientos." *America Latina en Movimiento (ALAI)* (2nd *época*): 30–33.

Mollett, Sharlene. 2006. "Race and Natural Resource Conflicts in Honduras: The Miskito and Garifuna Struggle for Lasa Pulan." *Latin American Research Review* 41 (1): 76–101.

———. 2011. "Racial Narratives: Miskito and Colono Land Struggles in the Honduran Mosquitia." *Cultural Geographies* 18 (1): 43–62.

———. 2014. "A Modern Paradise: Garifuna Land, Labor, and Displacement-in-Place." *Latin American Perspectives* 41 (6): 27–45.

———. 2016. "The Power to Plunder: Rethinking Land Grabbing in Latin America." *Antipode* 48 (2): 412–32.

———. 2018. "The Río Plátano Biosphere Reserve: A Postcolonial Feminist Political Ecological Reading of Violence and Territorial Struggles in Honduras." In *Land Rights, Biodiversity Conservation and Justice*, edited by Sharlene Mollet and Thembela Kepe, 184–205. London: Routledge.

Moore, Donald S. 2005. *Suffering for Territory: Race, Place, and Power in Zimbabwe*. Durham, NC: Duke University Press.

Moore, Jennifer. 2012. "Canada's Subsidies to the Mining Industry Don't Stop at Aid: Political Support Betrays Government Claims of Corporate Social Responsibility." *Mining Watch Canada*, https://miningwatch.ca/blog/2012/6/15/canada-s-subsidies-mining-industry-don-t-stop-aid-political-support-betrays.

Mora, Mariana. 2017. *Kuxlejal Politics: Indigenous Autonomy, Race, and Decolonizing Research in Zapatista Communities*. Austin: University of Texas Press.

Morris, Courtney Desiree. 2016. "Toward a Geography of Solidarity: Afro-Nicaraguan Women's Land Activism and Autonomy in the South Caribbean Coast Autonomous Region." *Bulletin of Latin American Research* 35 (3): 355–69.

Mosse, David. 2005. *Cultivating Development: An Ethnography of Aid Policy and Practice*. New York: Pluto Press.

Murray Li, Tania. 2014. *Land's End: Capitalist Relations on an Indigenous Frontier*. Durham, NC: Duke University Press.

Nájera, Lourdes Gutiérrez, and Korinta Maldonado. 2017. "Transnational Settler Colonial Formations and Global Capital: A Consideration of Indigenous Mexican Migrants." *American Quarterly* 69 (4): 809–21.

Nelson, Richard T. 2003. "Honduras Country Brief: Property Rights and Land Markets." Land Tenure Center. https://rmportal.net/framelib/ltpr/052709/hondurasbrief.pdf.

Nichols, Robert. 2018. "Theft Is Property! The Recursive Logic of Dispossession." *Political Theory* 46 (1): 3–28.

Ortner, Sherry B. 1972. "Is Female to Male as Nature Is to Culture?" *Feminist Studies* 1 (2): 5–31. https://doi.org/10.2307/3177638.

Pandian, Anan. 2008. "Devoted to Development: Moral Progress, Ethical Work, and Divine Favor in South India." *Anthropological Theory* 8 (2): 159–79.

Paschel, Tianna S. 2010. "The Right to Difference: Explaining Colombia's Shift from Color Blindness to the Law of Black Communities." *American Journal of Sociology* 116 (3): 729–69.

———. 2016. *Becoming Black Political Subjects: Movements and Ethno-Racial Rights in Colombia and Brazil*. Princeton, NJ: Princeton University Press.

Perez, Orlando J., and Jose René Argueta. 2011. *Political Culture of Democracy in Honduras, 2010: Democratic Consolidation in the Americas in Hard Times*. Nashville, TN: Vanderbilt University, USAID. https://www.vanderbilt.edu/lapop/honduras/2010-Honduras-Political-Culture.pdf.

Perez-Brignoli, Hector. 1989. *A Brief History of Central America*. Los Angeles: University of California Press.

Perry, Keisha-Khan Y. 2013. *Black Women against the Land Grab: The Fight for Racial Justice in Brazil*. Minneapolis: University of Minnesota Press.

Plan de Gobierno 2010–2014. 2010. República de Honduras [Government of Honduras]. Tegucigalpa, Honduras.

Plan Maestro de la Reconstrucción y Transformación Nacional (PMRTN). 1999. República de Honduras [Government of Honduras]. Tegucigalpa, Honduras.

Portillo, Suyapa. 2021. *Roots of Resistance: A Story of Gender, Race, and Labor on the North Coast of Honduras*. Austin: University of Texas Press.

Posas, Mario. 2019. "Movimientos sociales en Honduras." In *Antología del pensamiento hondureño contemporáneo*, edited by Ramón Romero, 259–92. Buenos Aires: CLACSO.

Povinelli, Elizabeth A. 2002. *The Cunning of Recognition: Indigenous Alterities and the Making of Australian Multiculturalism*. Durham, NC: Duke University Press.

———. 2011. "Routes/Worlds." *E-Flux* 27 (September). https://www.e-flux.com/journal/27/67991/routes-worlds/.

Preston, Jen. 2017. "Racial Extractivism and White Settler Colonialism: An Examination of the Canadian Tar Sands Mega-Projects." *Cultural Studies* 31 (2–3): 352–75.

Putnam, Lara. 2002. *The Company They Kept: Migrants and the Politics of Gender in Caribbean Costa Rica, 1870–1960*. Chapel Hill: University of North Carolina Press.

Reese, Ashanté M. 2019. *Black Food Geographies: Race, Self-Reliance, and Food Access in Washington, DC*. Chapel Hill: University of North Carolina Press.

Ritchie, Lyell H., William Fothergill, Robert Oliver, and Madison Wulfing. 1965. "A Regional Study of Tourist Development in Central America: A Study." Washington, DC: Porter International Company and Banco Centro Americano de Integración Económica.

Robinson, Cedric J. 2000. *Black Marxism: The Making of the Black Radical Tradition*. Chapel Hill: University of North Carolina Press.

Robinson, William I. 2003. *Transnational Conflicts: Central America, Social Change and Globalization*. New York: Verso.

Rodgers, Dennis, and Bruce O'Neill. 2012. "Infrastructural Violence: Introduction to the Special Issue." *Ethnography* 13 (4): 401–12.

Rosa, Jonathan. 2019. *Looking Like a Language, Sounding Like a Race: Raciolinguistic Ideologies and the Learning of Latinidad*. New York: Oxford University Press.

Ruiz Marrero, Carmelo. 2011. "The New Latin American 'Progresismo' and the Extractivism of the 21st Century." *The Americas Program*, February 17, 2011. https://www.americas.org/the-new-latin-american-progresismo-and-the-extractivism-of-the-21st-century/.

Saldaña-Portillo, María Josefina. 2016. *Indian Given: Racial Geographies across Mexico and the United States*. Durham, NC: Duke University Press.

Segato, Rita Laura. 2014. "Las nuevas formas de la guerra y el cuerpo de las mujeres." *Sociedade e Estado* 29 (2): 341–71.

Shange, Savannah. 2019. *Progressive Dystopia: Abolition, Anthropology, and Race in the New San Francisco*. Durham, NC: Duke University Press.

Sheller, Mimi. 2003. *Consuming the Caribbean: From Arawaks to Zombies*. International Library of Sociology. London: Routledge.

Sieder, Rachel. 1995. "Honduras: The Politics of Exception and Military Reformism (1972–1978)*." *Journal of Latin American Studies* 27 (1): 99–127.

Sieder, Rachel, L. Schjolden, and A. Angell, eds. 2005. *The Judicialization of Politics in Latin America*. London: Palgrave Macmillan US.

Simpson, Audra. 2014. *Mohawk Interruptus: Political Life across the Borders of Settler States*. Durham, NC: Duke University Press.

Smith, Christen A. 2016a. *Afro-Paradise: Blackness, Violence, and Performance in Brazil*. Urbana: University of Illinois Press.

———. 2016b. "Facing the Dragon: Black Mothering, Sequelae, and Gendered Necropolitics in the Americas." *Transforming Anthropology* 24 (1): 31–48.

Smith, Linda Tuhiwai. 2012. *Decolonizing Methodologies: Research and Indigenous Peoples*. London: Zed Books.

Solís, Daniel Villafuerte. 2018. "Entre La Pasión y el Bajo Aguán: El rostro violento del extractivismo palmero en Centroamérica." *Anuario de Estudios Centroamericanos* 44 (December): 315–40.

Soluri, John. 2005. *Banana Cultures: Agriculture, Consumption, and Environmental Change in Honduras and the United States.* Austin: University of Texas Press.

Soto, Hernando de. 2000. *The Mystery of Capital: Why Capitalism Triumphs in the West and Fails Everywhere Else.* New York: Basic Books.

———. 2002. *The Other Path: The Economic Answer to Terrorism.* New York: Basic Books.

Speed, Shannon. 2006. "At the Crossroads of Human Rights and Anthropology: Toward a Critically Engaged Activist Research." *American Anthropologist* 108 (1): 66–76.

———. 2017. "Structures of Settler Capitalism in Abya Yala." *American Quarterly* 69 (4): 783–90.

Stephen, Lynn. 1995. "Women's Rights Are Human Rights: The Merging of Feminine and Feminist Interests among El Salvador's Mothers of the Disappeared (CO-MADRES)." *American Ethnologist* 122 (4): 807–27.

———. 2002. *Zapata Lives! Histories and Cultural Politics in Southern Mexico.* Berkeley: University of California Press.

Stonich, Susan. 2000. *The Other Side of Paradise: Tourism, Conservation and Development in the Bay Islands.* New York: Cognizant Communication Corporation.

———. 2008. "International Tourism and Disaster Capitalism: The Case of Hurricane Mitch in Honduras." In *Capitalizing on Catastrophe: Neoliberal Strategies in Disaster Reconstruction*, edited by Nandini Gunewardena and Mark Schuller, 47–68. Lanham, MD: AltaMira Press.

Suazo, Salvador. 1997. *Los deportados de San Vicente.* Tegucigalpa: Editorial Guaymuras.

Sutton, Barbara. 2007. "*Poner el cuerpo*: Women's Embodiment and Political Resistance in Argentina." *Latin American Politics and Society* 49 (3): 129–62.

Svampa, Maristella. 2015. "Commodities Consensus: Neoextractivism and Enclosure of the Commons in Latin America." *South Atlantic Quarterly* 114 (1): 65–82.

Taussig, Michael T. 2010. *The Devil and Commodity Fetishism in South America.* Chapel Hill: University of North Carolina Press.

Taylor, Keeanga-Yamahtta. 2019. *Race for Profit: How Banks and the Real Estate Industry Undermined Black Homeownership.* Chapel Hill: University of North Carolina Press.

Thomas, Deborah A. 2019. *Political Life in the Wake of the Plantation: Sovereignty, Witnessing, Repair.* Durham, NC: Duke University Press.

Thorpe, Andy. 1992. "Las políticas de reforma agraria y la necesidad de planificación agrícola." In *Honduras: El ajuste estructural y la reforma agraria*, edited by Noé Pino and Andy Thorpe. Tegucigalpa: Centro de Documentación de Honduras.

Trouillot, Michel-Rolph. 2001. "The Anthropology of the State in the Age of Globalization: Close Encounters of the Deceptive Kind." *Current Anthropology* 42 (1): 125–38.

Trubek, David M., and Alvaro Santos. 2006. *The New Law and Economic Development: A Critical Appraisal*. Cambridge: Cambridge University Press.

Van Cott, Donna Lee. 2000. *The Friendly Liquidation of the Past: The Politics of Diversity in Latin America*. Pittsburgh, PA: University of Pittsburgh Press.

Vargas, João Helion Costa. 2018. *The Denial of Antiblackness: Multiracial Redemption and Black Suffering*. Minneapolis: University of Minnesota Press.

Verdery, Katherine. 2003. *The Vanishing Hectare: Property and Value in Postsocialist Transylvania*. Ithaca, NY: Cornell University Press.

Visweswaran, Kamala. 1997. "Histories of Feminist Ethnography." *Annual Review of Anthropology* 26 (1): 591–621.

Wade, Peter. 2010. *Race and Ethnicity in Latin America*. 2nd ed. London: Pluto Press.

Williams, Erica Loraine. 2013. *Sex Tourism in Bahia: Ambiguous Entanglements*. Urbana: University of Illinois Press.

Wolfe, Patrick. 1999. *Settler Colonialism and the Transformation of Anthropology: The Politics and Poetics of an Ethnographic Event*. New York: Cassell.

Woods, Clyde A. 2017. *Development Drowned and Reborn: The Blues and Bourbon Restorations in Post-Katrina New Orleans*. Athens: University of Georgia Press.

Wynter, Sylvia. 2003. "Unsettling the Coloniality of Being/Power/Truth/Freedom: Towards the Human, after Man, Its Overrepresentation—An Argument." *CR: The New Centennial Review* 3 (3): 257–337.

Yashar, Deborah J. 1999. "Democracy, Indigenous Movements, and the Postliberal Challenge in Latin America." *World Politics* 52 (1): 76–104.

Ybarra, Megan. 2018. *Green Wars: Conservation and Decolonization in the Maya Forest*. Berkeley: University of California Press.

Yusoff, Kathryn. 2018. *A Billion Black Anthropocenes or None*. Minneapolis: University of Minnesota Press.

Zigon, Jarrett. 2007. "Moral Breakdown and the Ethical Demand: A Theoretical Framework for an Anthropology of Moralities." *Anthropological Theory* 7 (2): 131–50.

INDEX

The authorized representative in the EU for product safety and compliance is:
Mare Nostrum Group
B.V Doelen 72
4831 GR Breda
The Netherlands

www.ingramcontent.com/pod-product-compliance
Lightning Source LLC
Chambersburg PA
CBHW030817270326
41928CB00007B/778